PROPERTIES AND PROPOSITIONS

This book articulates and defends Fregean realism, a theory of properties based on Frege's insight that properties are not objects, but rather the satisfaction conditions of predicates. Robert Trueman argues that this approach is the key not only to dissolving a host of longstanding metaphysical puzzles, such as Bradley's Regress and the Problem of Universals, but also to understanding the relationship between states of affairs, propositions, and the truth conditions of sentences. Fregean realism, Trueman suggests, ultimately leads to a version of the identity theory of truth, the theory that true propositions are identical to obtaining states of affairs. In other words, the identity theory collapses the gap between mind and world. This book will be of interest to anyone working in logic, metaphysics, the philosophy of language or the philosophy of mind.

ROBERT TRUEMAN is Lecturer in Philosophy at the University of York. He is the author of numerous articles on philosophical logic and metaphysics in journals including *Philosophical Studies, Australasian Journal of Philosophy* and *Mind*.

T0381623

PROPERTIES AND PROPOSITIONS

The Metaphysics of Higher-Order Logic

ROBERT TRUEMAN

University of York

CAMBRIDGE
UNIVERSITY PRESS

University Printing House, Cambridge CB2 8BS, United Kingdom

One Liberty Plaza, 20th Floor, New York, NY 10006, USA

477 Williamstown Road, Port Melbourne, VIC 3207, Australia

314-321, 3rd Floor, Plot 3, Splendor Forum, Jasola District Centre, New Delhi - 110025, India

103 Penang Road, #05-06/07, Visioncrest Commercial, Singapore 238467

Cambridge University Press is part of the University of Cambridge.

It furthers the University's mission by disseminating knowledge in the pursuit of education, learning and research at the highest international levels of excellence.

www.cambridge.org
Information on this title: www.cambridge.org/9781108814102
DOI: 10.1017/9781108886123

First published 2021
First paperback edition 2022

A catalogue record for this publication is available from the British Library

ISBN 978-1-108-84047-7 Hardback
ISBN 978-1-108-81410-2 Paperback

Cambridge University Press has no responsibility for the persistence or accuracy of URLs for external or third-party internet websites referred to in this publication, and does not guarantee that any content on such websites is, or will remain, accurate or appropriate.

For Michael Trueman, who never would have read this book anyway.

Contents

Acknowledgements

There are a lot of people that I want to thank for their help with this book. I'm not sure I have talked to anyone over the last ten years without at some point talking to them about the concept *horse* paradox. I am grateful for everyone's patience, but I would in particular like to thank all those who read parts of the manuscript: Arif Ahmed, Keith Allen, Dan Brigham, Tim Button, Ellie Byrne, Rob Davies, Ariel Gonzalez, Richard Gaskin, Owen Griffiths, Johan Gustafsson, Jen Hornsby, Owen Hulatt, Luca Incurvati, Dave Ingram, Chris Jay, Nick Jones, Brian King, Barry Lee, Mary Leng, Steven Methven, Daniel Morgan, Paul Noordhof, Michael Potter, Louise Richardson, Michael Rieppel, Lukas Skiba, Tom Stoneham, Peter Sullivan, Nathan Wildman, Crispin Wright, and Wes Wrigley.

I would like to thank the three reviewers who read the manuscript for Cambridge University Press; they all offered many insightful comments. Thanks also to Hilary Gaskin for supporting this project.

Next, I would like to offer special thanks to Brian King and James Williams. While writing this book, I was commuting back and forth to York, and Brian and James generously put me up in their house. They were good company, and they remain great friends.

Thanks to my parents, Margaret and Michael Trueman. My father sadly passed away shortly before I began writing this book, but he always supported my work in philosophy, even if he didn't always understand what I was doing or why anyone would want to do it. My mother continues to support me, and I am very grateful to her.

Finally, I would like to thank my wife, Sharon Trueman. I owe her more than I know how to express in words. Trying to articulate my gratitude to Sharon would be as futile as trying to say of a property what can be said of an object. (That is a great joke, which should become funny in about seven chapters' time.)

I have adapted material from four articles for this book. Two were published under a creative commons licence:[1] 'The Prenective View of propositional content' (*Synthese*, 2018a); and 'Substitution in a sense' (*Philosophical Studies*, 2018b). The publishers have kindly permitted me to repurpose material from the other two articles: 'Neutralism within the semantic tradition' (*Thought*, 2013a); and 'Idealism and the identity theory of truth' (*Mind*, in press).

---

[1]   https://creativecommons.org/licenses/by/4.0/

Introduction

Properties exist, but then again they don't. That is the fundamental thought of this book. Properties do not exist in the same way as ordinary objects, like knives and forks and tables and chairs. They don't even exist in the same way as unusual objects, like the number 9 or our galaxy's centre of mass. They exist in a way all of their own.

It is easy to see why a view like this would be attractive: it promises all the benefits of believing in properties, without any of the drawbacks of actually believing in them. It is also easy to see why it might seem like cheating. In fact, after Quine (1948), it became orthodoxy to insist that there is only *one* kind of existence, and it is expressed by the first-order existential quantifier, $\exists x \ldots x \ldots$. More recently, however, this orthodoxy has been on the decline. Some philosophers (e.g., Hirsch 2011) have insisted that existential quantifiers in different languages can express different notions of existence, and no one of those notions is privileged over the rest. Other philosophers (e.g., Sider 2011, §9.3) have claimed that in most of its uses, $\exists x \ldots x \ldots$ does not express existence at all; it only does that when it is used in a special language designed for discussing metaphysics, so-called Ontologese.

I want to be clear right from the start that I am not planning on challenging the Quinean orthodoxy in either of these ways. I am happy to grant that the first-order existential quantifier is univocal and expresses existence in all of its uses. What I want to challenge is the idea that the notion of existence expressed by $\exists x \ldots x \ldots$ is the *only* notion of existence. Let me explain.

I.1 Properties as Second-Order Existents

Earlier I distinguished between properties and objects. What does this distinction amount to? Throughout this book, I will use 'object' as a catch-all for anything which can be referred to with a singular term, and 'property' as a catch-all for anything which can be referred to with a predicate. Another way of putting the main thesis of this book is: properties are not objects.[1] If we assume for the moment that properties do exist, then it is easy to show that this thesis is equivalent to my original claim that they exist in a different way from objects.

First, we need to draw a distinction between different kinds of quantifier. *First-order* quantifiers bind first-order variables – i.e., variables in term-position. For example, the quantifier in '∃x x is a philosopher' binds the variable x, which is in the position of a singular term, like 'Socrates' or 'Plato'. Other kinds of quantifier bind variables in different kinds of position. Most important for our purposes, *second-order* quantifiers bind variables in predicate-position. For example, the quantifier in '∃X X(Socrates)' binds the variable X, which is in the position of a predicate, like '( ) was a philosopher' or '( ) drank hemlock'; very roughly, '∃X X(Socrates)' says that Socrates has some property.

The kind of existence which suits objects is the kind that is expressed by first-order existential quantification, ∃x . . . x . . . . An object exists just in case it falls within the domain of some first-order quantifier. That is a Quinean doctrine which I have no desire to dispute. But if properties are not objects, then they cannot fall within the domain of a first-order quantifier. An object is anything which can be referred to with a singular term, and everything in the domain of a first-order quantifier can be referred to with a singular term. This is an immediate consequence of the fact that first-order quantifiers bind variables in term-position. When we assign a value to a variable in term-position, we in effect transform that variable into a term referring to that value. For example, when we assign Socrates to the variable x in 'x is a philosopher', that *variable* comes to behave essentially as a *term* referring to Socrates. So if properties are not objects, then they cannot appear in the domain of a first-order quantifier.

But this does not mean that we cannot quantify over properties at all: we just need to use *second-order* quantifiers. Second-order quantifiers bind variables in predicate-position, and properties are the things that predicates can refer to. So just as the members of a first-order domain are all objects, the members of a second-order domain are all properties. The kind of existence which suits properties is thus the kind that is expressed by second-order existential quantification, ∃X . . . X . . . . A property exists just in case it falls

---

[1] As we will see in Chapter 4, this is not quite an accurate formulation of my view. What I really want to say is that it is *nonsense* to suppose that a property might be an object, but we won't get anywhere if we let ourselves get hung up on that now.

within the domain of some second-order quantifier. And crucially, the kind of existence expressed by $\exists X \ldots X \ldots$ is completely distinct from the kind expressed by $\exists x \ldots x \ldots$. In fact, if properties are not objects, then the domains of these two quantifiers cannot even overlap.

So if we assume that properties exist, then the claim that properties are not objects entails that properties and objects exist in two different ways: objects exist in the *first-order* way, and properties exist in a distinct *second-order* way.[2] And clearly, the reverse entailment holds too: if properties and objects exist in different ways, then no property is an object.

Of course, we do not yet actually have an argument that properties are not objects. Nor do we have an argument for the background assumption that properties exist. Why should we think of predicates as referring expressions in the first place? I will give my arguments in Chapters 1–7. In short, I will argue that the semantic roles of terms and predicates are so different that it just does not make any sense to suppose that they might co-refer (Chapters 1–5); and once we appreciate all that this entails, we will see that there is really nothing to object to in the claim that predicates refer to properties (Chapters 6–7).

I.2 The Concept *Horse* Paradox

Everything I have so far said was taken more or less straight from Frege. It was Frege who suggested that we conceive of objects and properties as the referents of terms and predicates, and Frege who insisted that in this sense, no property is an object. (The only difference is that Frege used the word 'concept' – or 'Begriff' in the original German – instead of 'property'; however, 'concept' comes with some unwanted cognitive connotations, which is why I prefer 'property'.) Indeed, I have taken so much from Frege that I will call my position, according to which properties exist but only in their own second-order sense, *Fregean realism*.[3]

So according to Fregean realism, no property is an object. However, as Frege himself recognised (1892a), this doctrine has a rather unsettling

---

[2] There is a point of contact here with the *ontological pluralism* of McDaniel (2009b, 2017) and Turner (2010, 2012) here. According to ontological pluralism, different kinds of existence are expressed by different kinds of existential quantifier. But crucially, McDaniel and Turner are dealing with different kinds of *first-order* quantifier. In other words, they are concerned with the kinds of existence that objects can enjoy. By contrast, I want to deny that properties are any kind of object at all.

[3] To be absolutely clear, the view that I will present in this book is not intended to be an accurate reconstruction of what Frege himself thought about properties. It is just a view that is fundamentally Fregean in the way described here.

consequence. If properties are not objects, then singular terms cannot refer to them, not even terms that look custom built for the job, like 'the property *horse*'. In accordance with Frege's own terminology, this has become known as the concept *horse* paradox.

At least in his published writings, Frege was rather unfazed by this paradox. He simply dug in his heels, declared that the property *horse* is not a property, and insisted that, properly understood, there is nothing paradoxical about that. In the end, I think that Frege was right that there is no real paradox here. But a lot more needs to be said to dissolve the *sense* of paradox. Much of what I have to say in Chapters 6 and 7 will be said with an eye to doing just that, although I will save the full discussion of the paradox for Chapter 9. For now, I will just give a quick sketch of what I will go on to say.

The reason that the concept *horse* paradox feels paradoxical is not just because 'the property *horse*' really looks like it should refer to a property. That is explained away easily enough: we wanted a term that referred to a property, so we built a term to do it; but we then discovered that terms cannot refer to properties, and thus that 'the property *horse*' cannot do what we built it to do. The really troubling problem is that a number of claims that we want to make about properties appear to require us to refer to them with singular terms. Frege himself was well aware of this awkwardness, but, again, in his published work, he was fairly dismissive of the problem:

> By a kind of necessity of language, my expressions, taken literally, sometimes miss my thought; I mention an object, when what I intend is a concept. I fully realise that in such cases I was relying upon a reader who would be ready to meet me halfway – who does not begrudge a pinch of salt. (Frege 1892a, 192)

There is a sense in which asking your reader to grant you a pinch of salt is completely unobjectionable. It is really nothing more than asking your reader to be charitable and accept that in order to keep things brief and readable, you had no choice but to speak a bit loosely. (I would certainly like to ask the readers of this book to add that much salt.) But this only remains reasonable so long as you *can* speak strictly and clearly state what your views amount to. What the concept *horse* paradox demands, then, is that we find a way of saying everything that we need to say about properties without ever trying to refer to them with singular terms. Frege made some progress on this front in an unpublished paper (1891–5), and in this book, I will try to go further.

I.3 Properties as Satisfaction Conditions

The most important thing we need to say about properties is that predicates refer to them. All we mean by 'property' is something that a predicate can refer to! But our ordinary way of talking about reference demands that we specify the referent of a given expression with a singular term. We cannot say,

> # '( ) is a horse' refers to is a horse,

because that is ungrammatical. To restore grammaticality, we have to say something like this:

> '( ) is a horse' refers to the property *horse*.

But that is exactly what a Fregean realist refuses to say. '( ) is a horse' is meant to refer to a property, but if 'the property *horse*' refers to anything, then it refers to an object.

To get out of this trouble, Fregean realists need to invent a whole new way of talking about predicate-reference, one which allows us to specify the referent of a predicate *with a predicate*. In Chapter 6, I will argue that we should use,

> (S) $\forall y(y \text{ satisfies } x \leftrightarrow Yy)$,

to express predicate-reference. If we do, then this is how we will specify what '( ) is a horse' refers to:

> $\forall y(y \text{ satisfies '( ) is a horse'} \leftrightarrow y \text{ is a horse})$.

On this conception, what it is for a predicate to refer to a property is just for it to have a satisfaction condition. And really, properties just are the satisfaction conditions of predicates.

This is clearly a very deflationary conception of properties. It is hard to imagine anyone denying that predicates refer to properties in *this* sense. There is really no room for a substantial debate between nominalists and Fregean realists over the existence of properties (see Chapter 7). And this is not the only debate that Fregean realism would put to bed. Although I think we can say everything that we *need* to say about properties without referring to them with singular terms, there are definitely things that philosophers have *wanted* to say about properties that cannot be re-expressed in this way. But these are all things that we are better off not being able to say. They are the roots of a number of stubborn puzzles in the metaphysics of properties. There will be a reward, then, for finding a way to live with the concept *horse* paradox: it will allow us to dismiss these metaphysical puzzles as mere pseudo-problems, which come up only because we mistakenly speak as if properties were a species of object. Or at least, that is what I will argue in Chapter 10.

I will go even further in Chapters 11–13 and argue that we can extend this conception of properties to cover propositions and states of affairs as well. We can think of states of affairs as zero-place properties, and so as the referents of zero-place predicates – i.e., sentences.[4] Now, since we have already signed up to the general idea that properties are satisfaction conditions, that makes states of affairs the satisfaction conditions of sentences, otherwise known as *truth conditions*. A *fact* can then be defined as a truth condition which happens to be satisfied. All of this will be discussed in more detail in Chapter 11.

Things are less straightforward when it comes to propositions, but I will argue that they are also best thought of as zero-place properties (Chapters 12–13). This will lead us to a version of the *identity theory of truth* (Chapter 14): true propositions do not merely correspond to facts; true propositions *are* facts. From this perspective, we will see no need to offer any account of how it is that propositions manage to represent the world, no gap between propositions and the world which needs to be filled by a bit of philosophy.

I.4   Williamson on Absolute Generality

I hope that I have said enough to justify my project on its own terms. However, I would also like to take a moment to talk about how it relates to the wider world of philosophical logic. For a long time, philosophers were deeply suspicious of second-order logic. The chief antagonist was, of course, Quine (1970, 66–8), who famously declared that second-order logic was set-theory in sheep's clothing: the inference from 'Socrates is wise' to '$\exists X\ X$(Socrates)' might look like an innocent existential generalisation, but really it introduces a commitment to sets that was not already latent in the original sentence.

These days, however, philosophers look more kindly on second-order logic. The tide was first turned by Boolos (1975, 1984, 1985), but much of the recent interest in second-order logic is due to Williamson's (2003) influential work on absolute generality.[5] It turns out that if we want to

---

[4] Throughout this book, I will mean *declarative sentence* by 'sentence', unless I clearly indicate otherwise.
[5] Williamson's (2013) work on higher-order modal logic has also been very influenital.

interpret our first-order quantifiers as ranging over absolutely every object, then we cannot think of interpretations themselves as a kind of object, on pain of Russell's Paradox. If interpretations are objects then there should be an interpretation, $\mathcal{I}$, which assigns the following satisfaction condition to some predicate '$F(\ )$':

$$\forall x(x \text{ satisfies } `F(\ )\text{' on } \mathcal{I} \leftrightarrow \neg x \text{ satisfies } `F(\ )\text{' on } x).$$

But now, if the quantifier $\forall x \dots x \dots$ ranges over absolutely all objects, including interpretation $\mathcal{I}$, then we can infer the following contradiction:

$$\mathcal{I} \text{ satisfies } `F(\ )\text{' on } \mathcal{I} \leftrightarrow \neg \mathcal{I} \text{ satisfies } `F(\ )\text{' on } \mathcal{I}.$$

Williamson's solution to this problem is simple: he denies that interpretations are objects. Interpretations are not the sorts of things that you quantify over with *first-order* quantifiers. If you want to quantify over interpretations, then you have to use a *second-order* quantifier.

As Williamson is well aware, this solution presupposes that Frege was broadly right about second-order quantification: second-order quantification must not be first-order quantification in disguise; second-order quantification has to be its own thing, a way of quantifying over properties, not objects. This could, I think, be made into a good argument for Fregean realism. But it is not the argument that I will give. My argument will be much more direct: I will focus on the semantic roles of terms and predicates themselves without making any assumptions about absolute generality. But this convergence of ideas is noteworthy nonetheless. My hope is that those who side with Williamson on absolute generality might look on Chapters 1–9 as providing some of the philosophical underpinnings for their view. Then, in Chapters 10–13, we will see what else Fregean realism can do.

CHAPTER I

Substitution in a Sense

My aim in the next few chapters (1–4) is to argue that terms and predicates cannot co-refer. Given my Fregean definitions of 'object' and 'property' – an *object* is something that can be referred to with a singular term, and a *property* is something that can be referred to with a predicate – this will imply that no property is an object.[1]

My argument will start with the premise that terms and predicates are not intersubstitutable. Whenever we try to substitute a term for a predicate, or a predicate for a term, we end up with nonsense. Consider the following sentence:

>   Socrates was mortal.

This sentence is grammatical, meaningful, and even true. But now try to substitute the term 'mortality' for the predicate '( ) was mortal':

>   # Socrates mortality.

This is a meaningless, ungrammatical mess. I want to use this observation somehow to show that the term 'mortality' cannot co-refer with the predicate '( ) was mortal'. The easiest way of doing that would be by appealing to what Wright (1998, 73) calls the *Reference Principle*:

> (RP) Co-referring expressions are everywhere intersubstitutable *salva congruitate*.[2]

Or in plainer words: if two expressions co-refer, then we can never turn a grammatical sentence into an ungrammatical one just by substituting one of these expressions for the other. Since substituting 'mortality' for '( ) was

---

[1] As we will see in Chapter 4, this is a bit of an inaccurate statement of what I will actually end up arguing for, but we can deal with that when we come to it.
[2] In fact, this is just one half of Wright's Reference Principle, but it is the only half that we need. It is also worth mentioning that Hale and Wright use 'the Reference Principle' for something quite different in 2012 (93).

mortal' can transform a grammatical sentence into an ungrammatical one, (RP) straightforwardly entails that these expressions do not co-refer.

However, I do not want to rely on (RP) as a premise in this book. (RP) can seem little more than a truism on first inspection, but as soon as you spot that it entails that predicates cannot co-refer with terms – i.e., that properties are not objects – it loses a lot of its initial appeal. We might suspect that (RP) is really true only of some limited class of expressions, say singular terms, and that we mistake the fully general (RP) for a truism because we have an unfortunate tendency to focus on just this class. Or maybe (RP) does apply to expressions of all kinds, but it only applies to them one kind at a time: co-referring *terms* must be intersubstitutable, and so must be co-referring *predicates*, but there is no requirement that a term and a predicate be intersubstitutable, even if they co-refer; we can always account for these substitution failures just by emphasising that terms and predicates are different kinds of expression, and so do different work with the things that they refer to.[3]

To be clear, I think that these reactions to (RP) are misguided. I believe a fully general version of the principle. But these reactions are certainly not *obviously* wrong, and that is enough to show that we cannot just rely on (RP) as an unargued-for premise. I will, then, argue that terms and predicates cannot co-refer without at any point appealing to (RP). My argument will still start with the premise that terms and predicates are not intersubstitutable (see Chapters 2 and 3). But rather than relying on (RP), I will get from this premise to my conclusion by appealing to the essential relationship between reference and disquotation (see Chapter 4). Importantly, however, this is not the end for (RP). If my argument works for terms and predicates, then it can be developed into a general proof of (RP) (see Chapter 5).[4]

That, then, is the plan. The first step is to look more closely at what we should mean by 'substitution'. It turns out that when we understand substitution in the most obvious and straightforward way, there are a number of simple counterexamples to (RP). And although I will at no point rely on (RP) as a premise, these counterexamples still threaten to undermine my project: my argument that terms and predicates cannot co-refer generalises into an argument for (RP), so if the counterexamples to (RP)

---

3   Wright (1998), Hale (2010) and MacBride (2011a) all make suggestions along these lines. See Chapter 8 for discussion.

4   Again, I must now add the disclaimer that (RP) as it stands is not *quite* what I will argue for. My version of (RP) will say, roughly, that if two expressions are not everywhere intersubstitutable, then it is *nonsense* to say that they co-refer. But I will get to that in Chapter 5.

are allowed to stand, they will stand equally against my own argument. In this chapter, then, I will develop a more sophisticated conception of substitution and use it to defend (RP) from the putative counterexamples. I will then use this new conception of substitution throughout the rest of the book.

1.1   Some Counterexamples to the Reference Principle

The counterexamples that I am going to consider are all due to Oliver (2005).[5] Oliver offers a dizzying array of these counterexamples, but for now, it will suffice to consider just two. First, take the sentence,

(1a) Brilliant Bertrand solved a paradox.

'Bertrand' and 'the referent of "Bertrand"' co-refer,[6] but if we substitute 'the referent of "Bertrand"' for 'Bertrand' in (1a), we get an ungrammatical muddle:

(1b) # Brilliant the referent of 'Bertrand' solved a paradox.

Second, take the sentence,

(2a) I am Robert.

'I' and 'me' co-refer in any given context, but the result of substituting 'me' for 'I' in (2a) is at the very least not the Queen's English:

(2b) # Me am Robert.[7]

What are we to make of these counterexamples to (RP)? Well, they both rely on a particular conception of substitution, which I will call *simple-substitution*. According to this conception, we substitute one expression for another by (almost literally) cutting out the latter and pasting the former in its place. (This is the sort of substitution that you can perform with

---

[5] Similar examples are given by Schiffer (2003, 92–5).
[6] Or at least they do on the assumption that 'Bertrand' and 'the referent of "Bertrand"' are referring singular terms. As MacBride (2011a, 302–4) points out, we could try to stop this counterexample in its tracks by rejecting this assumption. In the case of 'the referent of "Bertrand"', MacBride suggests that we might be thoroughgoing Russellians and insist that, strictly speaking, definite descriptions are incomplete symbols. In the case of 'Bertrand', MacBride suggests that we might sign up to the modern view that grammatically proper names are really predicates true of the objects which have that name. I, however, am happy to concede to Oliver that 'Bertrand' and 'the referent of "Bertrand"' are referring singular terms.
[7] Rosefeldt's (2008, 309) supposedly fixed version of (RP) is not immune to this counterexample.

the find-and-replace function on a word processor.) Oliver has therefore presented counterexamples to the following precisified version of (RP):

(RP$_1$) Co-referring expressions are everywhere simple-intersubstitutable *salva congruitate*.

However, I do not think that this is really the best way to interpret (RP). While simple-substitution may be appropriate for well designed formal languages, it is surely *too* simple when it comes to messy natural languages. My aim in this chapter is to develop an alternative conception of substitution and then present a version of (RP) that is immune to Oliver's counterexamples.

1.2 Sense-Substitution

Consider the following argument:

    (i) Robert is hungry
    (ii) I am Robert
∴ (iii) I am hungry

This argument is obviously valid. Indeed, I would say that it is a natural language instance of the following valid argument form:

(SI) *Fa*; *b* = *a*; ∴ *Fb*.

However, the validity of (SI) crucially turns on our substituting '*b*' for '*a*' in '*Fa*'. So if (i)–(iii) is to be an instance of (SI), then (iii) must in some sense count as a result of substituting 'I' for 'Robert' in (i). And clearly, we do not have a case of simple-substitution here. As we move from (i) via (ii) to (iii), we do not unthinkingly write 'I' into the gap in '( ) is hungry'. Rather, we swap '( ) is hungry' for '( ) am hungry', and then write 'I' into that gap instead. Moreover, in making this swap, we in no way impugn the validity of the argument. As far as the argument is concerned, (iii) really is a result of substituting 'I' for 'Robert' in (i). What we must now ask, then, is: why should (iii) count as a result of this substitution?

I would like to propose the following answer: because '( ) am hungry' and '( ) is hungry' have the same *sense*, in something like Frege's sense of 'sense'. As Frege thought of it, the sense of a sentence (which I will also call a *proposition*) determines the logical properties of that sentence,[8] and the sense of a subsentential expression is that expression's contribution to the senses of the sentences in which it appears.[9] So the idea here is that the grammatical difference between '( ) am hungry' and '( ) is hungry' does not reflect a difference in the contributions that these expressions make to the senses of the sentences in which they appear. If that is right, then we can explain why (i)–(iii) should count as an instance of (SI): '( ) is hungry' and '( ) am hungry' make exactly the same contribution to the senses of (i) and (iii), and it is those senses that determine what those sentences entail.[10]

More certainly needs to be said about the notion of sense appealed to in this answer, and I will try to say more in §1.4. For now, though, I would like to ask the reader to go with my answer, if only to see where it leads: (iii) counts as a result of substituting 'I' for 'Robert' in (i) because '( ) am hungry' has the same sense as '( ) is hungry'. This suggests that there is a conception of substitution according to which the following is true:

$\Psi(\beta)$ is a result of substituting β for the displayed occurrence of α in $\Phi(\alpha)$ whenever $\Psi(\ ) \approx \Phi(\ )$,[11]

where '$\approx$' is shorthand for 'has the same sense as', and 'the displayed occurrence of α in $\Phi(\alpha)$' is shorthand for 'the occurrence of α in $\Phi(\alpha)$ that fills the gap in $\Phi(\ )$'. The 'displayed occurrence' clause is strictly necessary, since there may be other occurrences of α in $\Phi(\alpha)$, but for the sake of readability, I will often leave it implicit.

Now consider this argument:

(iv) Sharon helped Robert with a paper
(v) I am Robert
∴ (vi) Sharon helped me with a paper

---

[8]   In fact, Frege (e.g., 1906b, 318 and 332) made the stronger claim that logical relations hold primarily between propositions and only derivatively between sentences; for Frege (1918, 334–7), propositions are abstract objects, and it is these abstract objects that are the primary relata of logical relations. I, however, would like to distance myself from the whole idea that senses are a kind of object (see §1.4). For an incredibly helpful discussion of Frege's conception of logic, see Blanchette 2012.

[9]   See Frege 1893, §32. Here and elsewhere (e.g., 1923, 390), Frege uses a mereological metaphor: he says that the sense of a part of a sentence is a part of the sense of that sentence. I do not find that metaphor very helpful, not least because it encourages us to think of senses as objects.

[10] I am by no means suggesting that this is the *only* possible answer (see the appendix to Trueman 2018b). Indeed, if we only had to deal with cases like (i)–(iii), my answer would probably be overkill. However, these kinds of case help to ease us into my new conception of substitution, and the real worth of this new conception will become clearer as the chapters go on.

[11] These Greek letters are metalinguistic variables that range over linguistic expressions. If we were being fastidious, we would put Quine-quotes around '$\Psi(\beta)$' and '$\Phi(\alpha)$'. However, Quine-quotes tend to make things harder to understand, and so I will only use them when I really have to.

Again, this argument is obviously valid, and, again, I would say that it is a natural language instance of (SI). But as we move from (iv) via (v) to (vi), we do not unthinkingly write 'I' into the gap in 'Sharon helped ( ) with a paper'. This time, we swap 'I' for 'me' and write that into the gap instead. Moreover, in making this swap, we in no way impugn the validity of the argument. As far as the argument is concerned, (vi) really is a result of substituting 'I' for 'Robert' in (iv). And now, of course, what we must ask is: why should (vi) count as a result of this substitution?

I would like to propose the following answer: because 'I' and 'me' have the same sense (in any given context, at least).[12] Again, the idea is that the grammatical difference between 'I' and 'me' does not reflect a difference in the contributions that these expressions make to the senses of the sentences in which they appear.[13] If that is right, then we can explain why (iv)–(vi) should count as an instance of (SI): 'I' and 'me' make exactly the same contribution to the senses of the sentences in which they appear, and so for logical purposes, we are free to swap between them as grammar demands. This suggests that there is a conception of substitution according to which the following is true:

$\Phi(\gamma)$ is a result of substituting β for the displayed occurrence of α in $\Phi(\alpha)$ whenever $\gamma \approx \beta$.

Putting these answers together, I would like to introduce the following conception of substitution, which I will call *sense-substitution*:

To sense-substitute β for the displayed occurrence of α in a meaningful sentence $\Phi(\alpha)$ is to construct a meaningful sentence $\Psi(\gamma)$ such that:

(a) $\Psi(\ ) \approx \Phi(\ )$
and (b) $\gamma \approx \beta$.

We will work through some examples of sense-substitution in the next section, but for now, I can explain the guiding idea like this.

---

[12] From now on, I will leave the 'in any given context' qualification tacit.

[13] Of course, this does not mean that differences in case are pointless grammatical flourishes. Like word order, case helps to determine which terms fill which argument places in a given predicate. I will discuss this further in §8.3.1, but there is one quick point that I would like to make now. Throughout this book, I will follow the standard practice of representing predicates by simply deleting a term from a sentence and leaving a gap in its place. This is usually adequate for largely uninflected languages like English, but it would be inadequate for highly inflected languages like Latin. If we want to represent Latin predicates unambiguously, then we also need to mark the cases of their gaps: if the gap in 'Caesar in ( ) currit' is marked for the ablative then it translates as 'Caesar runs in ( )', but if its gap is marked for the accusative then it translates as 'Caesar runs into ( )'. Even more complex systems may be required to represent the predicates of other languages.

Simple-substitution is appropriate when we are interested in the straight-forward substitution of expressions thought of as ink marks on a page (or lights on a computer screen, or whatever). But sense-substitution is the conception to use when we are interested in the substitution of *senses*, not ink marks. Of course, we cannot directly substitute one sense for another; all we can really do is substitute one expression for another. But when we are interested only in the senses of these expressions, we can wholly disregard what the expressions look like. Whether $\Psi(\gamma)$ counts as a result of sense-substituting β for α in $\Phi(\alpha)$ has nothing to do with orthography. $\Psi(\ )$ and $\Phi(\ )$ do not need to share any orthographic similarity, and neither do γ and β. All that matters is that $\Psi(\ )$ have the same sense as $\Phi(\ )$, and γ have the same sense as β.

1.3   A New Reference Principle

We can use the notion of sense-substitution to give a new precisification of (RP):

(RP$_2$) Co-referring expressions are everywhere sense-intersubstitutable.

Conspicuously, I have not included a *salva congruitate* clause in (RP$_2$). This is because sense-substitution is defined only over meaningful sentences: in the definition of sense-substitution, I stipulated that $\Phi(\alpha)$ and $\Psi(\gamma)$ be *meaningful* sentences. I made this stipulation because sense-substitution is meant to give us a way of substituting one sense in a proposition for another, and only meaningful sentences express propositions. (RP$_2$) should there-fore be understood as follows: if α and β co-refer, then there is no occur-rence of α in a *meaningful* sentence such that it is impossible to construct another *meaningful* sentence that counts as a result of sense-substituting β for that occurrence of α. In short, we do not need to include an explicit *salva congruitate* clause because sense-substitution always preserves mean-ingfulness.[14]

(RP$_2$) can be defended from Oliver's counterexamples. Let us again start with:

(1a) Brilliant Bertrand solved a paradox.

---

[14]   But to be clear, sense-substitution does not always preserve meaning. Suppose we sense-substitute β for α in $\Phi(\alpha)$. This will yield a sentence $\Psi(\gamma)$, such that $\Psi(\ )$ has the same sense as $\Phi(\ )$ and γ has the same sense as β. But unless β (and thus γ) happens to have the same sense as α, $\Psi(\gamma)$ will have a different sense from $\Phi(\alpha)$.

'Bertrand' co-refers with 'the referent of "Bertrand" ', and so (RP_2) entails that the latter can be sense-substituted for the former in (1a). My suggestion is that the following counts as a result of this sense-substitution:

(1c) The referent of 'Bertrand' is brilliant and solved a paradox.

(1c) is a result of this sense-substitution if:

(a) '( ) is brilliant and solved a paradox' ≈ 'Brilliant ( ) solved a paradox'

and (b) 'the referent of "Bertrand" ' ≈ 'the referent of "Bertrand" '.

(a) strikes me as plausible,[15] and we can take (b) for granted: all that (b) tells us is that 'the referent of "Bertrand" ' has the same sense as itself.[16] However, it is worth noting that I am suggesting only that (1c) is *a*, not *the*, result of this sense-substitution. Unlike simple-substitution, more than one sentence can count as a result of sense-substituting one expression for another. Take the following sentence, for example:

(1d) The thing to which 'Bertrand' refers is brilliant and solved a paradox.

Presumably, 'the thing to which "Bertrand" refers' has the same sense as 'the referent of "Bertrand" '. If so, then (1c) is a result of sense-substituting 'the referent of "Bertrand" ' for 'Bertrand' in (1a) if and only if (1d) is as well.

We turn now to:

(2a) I am Robert.

'I' co-refers with 'me', and so (RP_2) entails that the latter can be sense-substituted for the former in (2a). I would like to suggest that (2a) is *itself* a result of sense-substituting 'me' for 'I' in (2a). (2a) counts as a result of this sense-substitution if:

(a) '( ) am Robert' ≈ '( ) am Robert'

and (b) 'I' ≈ 'me'.

---

[15] On one way of reading (1a). Alternatively, we might read (1a) as saying of brilliant Bertrand that he solved a paradox. On this alternative reading, (1a) is equivalent to 'The thing that is brilliant and identical to Bertrand solved a paradox'. If we read (1a) in this way, then we should obviously give the following instead of (1c): the thing that is brilliant and identical to the referent of 'Bertrand' solved a paradox. That is more than a little ugly, but given that 'Bertrand' can refer to at most one thing, it is equivalent to: the brilliant referent of 'Bertrand' solved a paradox. For more readings of (1a), see Dolby 2009.

[16] This is an instance of Reflexivity: $\alpha \approx \alpha$. See §5.2 for discussion of an apparent counterexample to this principle.

In this case, it is (a) that can be taken for granted and (b) that is plausible. So, it seems, (2a) is a result of sense-substituting 'me' for 'I' in (2a). In other words, substituting 'me' for 'I' is a limiting case of sense-substitution, like substituting 'I' for 'I' or 'Bertrand' for 'Bertrand'.[17] Again, I am claiming only that (2a) is *a* result of sense-substituting 'me' for 'I' in (2a). In fact, there is no reason to limit our attention to English sentences when looking for results of this sense-substitution. Consider the French sentence,

(2c) Je suis Robert.

This sentence is a result of sense-substituting 'me' for 'I' in (2a) if:

(a) '( ) suis Robert' ≈ '( ) am Robert'
and (b) 'je' ≈ 'me'.

(a) looks like a safe assumption; certainly, '( ) suis Robert' is the French translation of '( ) am Robert', and while translation may not always pre-serve sense, it is hard to see what the difference could be in this case. As for (b), 'je' is the French translation of 'I', and again it seems reasonable to say that, in this case, translation preserves sense; if we add to this the earlier assumption that 'I' and 'me' also have the same sense, we can infer (b).[18] In short, then, (2a) is a result of sense-substituting 'me' for 'I' in (2a) if and only if (2c) is as well.

This brings us to an important point. When we ask whether one expres-sion can be sense-substituted for another, the modality we have in mind should be a very permissive one. We should be asking whether it is *in prin-ciple possible* for there to be a sentence which counts as a result of this sense-substitution. After all, sense-substitution is meant to give us a way of sub-stituting senses in propositions. So, saying that β can be sense-substituted for α in $\Phi(\alpha)$ is meant to capture the idea that we can substitute the sense of β for the sense of α in the proposition expressed by $\Phi(\alpha)$. It should not matter, then, if the proposition that results from this substitution of senses cannot be expressed in the same language as $\Phi(\alpha)$. It should not even matter if it cannot be expressed in any of the languages that anyone has ever actually spoken. All that matters is that it is *in principle possible* to construct a sentence that expresses the proposition, even if doing so involves inventing a whole new language. Of course, there is a good question about how exactly to characterise this permissive modality, but I hope that I have

---

[17]   I first got the idea that substituting 'me' for 'I' might be a limiting case of substitution from Dolby 2009, 291.

[18]   This is an instance of Transitivity: if $\alpha \approx \beta$ and $\beta \approx \gamma$, then $\alpha \approx \gamma$. See §5.2 for further discussion.

said enough for present purposes. In what follows, then, I will understand the modality involved in 'sense-intersubstitutable' in this permissive sort of way.

This point is related to a counterexample to (RP_1) that we have not yet considered. 'Frege' co-refers with 'Der Autor der *Grundlagen der Arithmetik*', and so (RP_1) entails that they are everywhere simple-intersubstitutable *salva congruitate*. However, whereas,

(3a) Frege was a philosopher,

is a grammatical English sentence,

(3b) # Der Autor der *Grundlagen der Arithmetik* was a philosopher,

is not a grammatical sentence in English or German. This is another of Oliver's (2005, 186) counterexamples, but he does not put too much weight on it. As he concedes, it can be disarmed by restricting (RP_1) so that it applies to only one language at a time; what the counterexample shows is just that (RP_1) should not be taken to imply that co-referring expressions *taken from different languages* are everywhere intersubstitutable *salva congruitate*. However, this clash of languages does nothing to stop us *sense*-substituting 'Der Autor der *Grundlagen der Arithmetik*' for 'Frege' in (3a). 'The author of *The Foundations of Arithmetic*' presumably has the same sense as 'Der Autor der *Grundlagen der Arithmetik*', and so one result of the sense-substitution will be:

(3c) The author of *The Foundations of Arithmetic* was a philosopher.

And assuming that the German predicate '( ) war Philosoph' has the same sense as the English predicate '( ) was a philosopher', another result will be:

(3d) Der Autor der *Grundlagen der Arithmetik* war Philosoph.

And, of course, there will be plenty of other results of this substitution, not just in German and English, but in innumerable other languages too. (RP_2) need not, then, be restricted to one language at time. More than that, it should not be: again, to say that β can be sense-substituted for α in $\Phi(\alpha)$ is meant to capture the idea that we can substitute the sense of β for the sense of α in the proposition expressed by $\Phi(\alpha)$, and so it really should not matter whether α and β belong to the same language. I will, then, take (RP_2) to apply simultaneously to *all* languages, including merely possible ones.

In summary, (RP_2) is not vulnerable to any of the counterexamples we have considered – or at least not *obviously* vulnerable. It is impossible to miss the slightly hesitant tone running throughout the discussion so far. I have made lots of 'safe assumptions' and 'plausible suggestions' about whether one expression has the same sense as another. And really, I cannot be more definitive than that. It is notoriously difficult to show once and for all that two expressions have exactly the same sense. The difficulties here are partly philosophical – just how finely grained should our concept of sense be? – but also partly empirical: demonstrating that two expressions share a sense will certainly require a close examination of how those expressions are actually used. It is not my aim in this chapter to announce once and for all that (1c) is a result of sense-substituting 'the referent of "Bertrand"' for 'Bertrand' in (1a), or that (2a) is itself a result of sense-substituting 'me' for 'I' in (2a), and so on through the other examples. All I want to do is undermine Oliver's counterexamples, taken as counterexamples to (RP$_2$) rather than (RP$_1$). And we surely have enough here to do that: as of yet, we have been given no reason to suspect that there might be co-referring expressions that are not everywhere sense-intersubstitutable.

Still, it would be nice not to leave things on such an uncertain note. It would be great if we could give a *general* argument for (RP$_2$), one which did not rely on any controversial assumptions about which pairs of expressions have the same sense and which do not. I will eventually present such an argument for a slightly tweaked version of (RP$_2$), but not until Chapter 5.

1.4   The Sense in Sense-Substitution

In this section, I will take a closer look at the sense in sense-substitution. To be clear, I do not hope to give a comprehensive theory of sense. That is far, far beyond the scope of this book. Really, all I want to to do is make clear what I am, and what I am *not*, assuming about sense in my account of sense-substitution.

In §1.2, I said that I was working with a broadly Fregean notion of sense. Now I would like to emphasise the word *broadly*. In fact, I have only made two substantial assumptions about sense: first, that the sense of a sentence determines the the logical properties of that sentence; second, that the sense of a subsentential expression is that expression's contribution to the senses of the sentences in which it appears. And while it is true that I took both of these assumptions from Frege, they are hardly peculiarly Fregean. Accepting them certainly does not force us to accept any of Frege's more controversial claims about sense. This point is well illustrated by the following example. One of Frege's most famous doctrines is that (even simple) singular terms can co-refer and yet have different senses (1892b, 151–2). Now, I am inclined to agree with Frege on this issue, but for all I will say in this book, it may be that co-referring (simple) singular terms automatically share a sense – i.e., automatically make the same contribution to the senses of the sentences in which they appear.

Here is another illustration of the same point. Frege (1892b, 154; 1918, 334–7) thought that senses were *objects*; that is, Frege thought that senses could be referred to with singular terms. However, some philosophers (e.g., McDowell 1977) think that it is a mistake to reify senses in this way. This is not to deny that one expression can have the same sense as another. It is just to deny that what it is for α to have the same sense as β is for α and β to stand in the *having* relation to the same special object, which we call their 'sense'. Instead, to say that α has the same sense as β is just a way of saying that, for all logical purposes, α is synonymous with β. This is clearly a very minimal conception of sense. Indeed, it would be very hard to deny that expressions have this minimal kind of sense: all that claim amounts to is that some expressions are (logically) synonymous with others, and so to deny it, you would have to reject the very idea of (logical) synonymy. Of course, some philosophers have managed to deny this, most notably Quine (1951b), but his is certainly a minority view. It is important to observe, then, that my definition of sense-substitution does not treat senses as if they were objects: sense is only mentioned in the course of saying that one expression *has the same sense as* another.[19]

At this point, it might be objected that while my definition of sense-substitution does not treat senses as objects, my less formal remarks about sense do. In fact, my two assumptions about sense are cases in point: I assumed that *the sense* of a sentence determines the logical properties of that sentence, and that *the sense* of a subsentential expression is that expression's contribution to *the senses* of the sentences in which it appears. However, it is my belief that we can offer explanations – or, more accurately, *explications* – of everything I say about sense that do not treat senses as objects. Again, take my two assumptions about sense as examples. It is easy to offer an explication of the claim that the sense of a sentence determines the logical properties of that sentence: if two sentences have the same sense, then they have the same logical properties. (We might then add that two sentences have the same logical properties iff they have the same logical entailments.) It is a little harder to offer an explication of the claim that the sense of a

---

[19] The one point in the definition at which this is not *absolutely* explicit is when I stipulate that $\Phi(\alpha)$ and $\Psi(\gamma)$ are *meaningful* sentences; however, we can understand the claim that a sentence is meaningful as the claim that it has the same sense as itself.

subsentential expression is its contribution to the senses of the sentences in which it appears, but here is a start: subsentential expressions α and β have the same sense if and only if substituting β for α in a sentence can never change the sense of that sentence, and *vice versa*.[20]

But if it really is possible for me to say everything I want to say without appearing to reify senses, then why don't I? Why do I insist on speaking as if we could refer to senses with singular terms? There are two answers to this question, one shallower and one deeper. The shallower answer is this: if I steadfastly refused to speak as if we could refer to senses with terms, this book would become so unwieldy and complex that it would be impossible to understand. Even including all of the necessary explications in parentheses or footnotes would prove impractical, and so, for the most part, I will leave it to the reader to come up with them as needed. The deeper answer is this: part of the point of this chapter is to explicate some of our talk that apparently reifies senses. On the face of it, we can only talk about substituting senses if propositions are complex objects made up of senses; however, we can use my definition of sense-substitution to explicate this sort of talk without treating senses as objects. Crucially, though, I could not offer this explication unless I *started* by talking in the ordinary, unexplicated way about substituting senses. It is only by first displaying this unexplicated way of speaking that we can consider ways of explicating it.

1.5   A Circularity Objection

In the last section, I offered an explanation of what it is for two subsentential expressions to have the same sense, and that explanation was framed in terms of substitution: subsentential expressions α and β have the same sense iff substituting β for α in a sentence never changes the sense of that sentence, and *vice versa*. But how should substitution be understood in this explanation? Not as simple-substitution. 'I' and 'me' may well have the same sense, but when we simple-substituted 'me' for 'I' in (2a), we ended up with

---

[20] Do 'I' and 'me' pass this test for sameness of sense? On the face of it, sense-substituting 'I' for 'me' *can* sometimes change the sense of a sentence – for example: (i) 'Sharon likes Simon more than me', and (ii) 'Sharon likes Simon more than I'. However, this case is misleading. The predicate 'Sharon likes Simon more than ( )' is syntactically ambiguous, and can be disambiguated either as 'Sharon likes Simon more than Sharon likes ( )' or as 'Sharon likes Simon more than ( ) likes Simon'. The accusative case of 'me' forces us to disambiguate this predicate in the first way, and the nominative case of 'I' forces us to disambiguate it in the second way. So 'Simon likes Sharon more than ( )' has different senses in (i) and (ii), and thus (ii) is *not* a result of sense-substituting 'I' for 'me' in (i).

(2b), which was ungrammatical and hence did not have any sense at all. So we must be using a more sophisticated conception of substitution. And it seems as though only one conception will do: sense-substitution! But now, doesn't my definition of sense-substitution run in a circle? I defined sense-substitution in terms of subsentential expressions' having the same sense, and then I explained what it is for subsentential expressions to have the same sense in terms of sense-substitution.[21]

It might be possible to avoid this circularity, but the prospects on this front seem dim. There are only two strategies to try. First, we could try to offer a new explanation of what it is for two subsentential expressions to share a sense that does not proceed in terms of substitution. However, I simply have no idea of how to develop such an explanation, at least so long as we refuse to reify senses. Second, we could grant that any explanation of what it is for subsentential expressions to have the same sense will involve substitution, but deny that this needs to be understood as sense-substitution. But if not sense-substitution, then what? What conception of substitution will fit the bill? Again, I just do not know of any other kind of substitution which could do the job.[22]

It seems that I have no choice, then, but to live with the circularity in my definition of sense-substitution. Fortunately, however, that is something I think I can do. There are two points that I want to make in this connection. First, what this circularity shows us is that we can neither explain sense-substitution to someone who has no inkling of what it is for subsentential expressions to share a sense, nor explain what it is for subsentential expressions to share a sense to someone who has no inkling of sense-substitution. The proper response to this predicament is not to withdraw the definition of sense-substitution but to reconsider the spirit in which we lay it down. We cannot hope to explain the notions of sense and sense-substitution to someone who has come to them cold; instead, all we can do is map the pre-existing relations that hold between these two notions. Taken in this spirit, my definition of sense-substitution is not an attempt to invent an all-new notion of substitution, but to articulate a notion of substitution that was already, if only tacitly, essential to our notion of sense.

Second, the circularity in my definition of sense-substitution is starkest when we are speaking in a very general way about what it takes for two arbitrary expressions to have the same sense. But when we are discussing two particular expressions, we can sometimes mitigate this circularity by

[21] Thanks to Peter Sullivan for pushing this objection.
[22] I discuss one proposal in the appendix to Trueman 2018b, but as I explain there, I do not think that it works.

bringing to bear special assumptions about the senses of the expressions we are dealing with. This is a point that I will exploit throughout the next chapter.

1.6   The Differences between Reference Principles

I want to end this chapter by briefly discussing the differences between (RP_1) and (RP_2). The most obvious difference is that applying (RP_2) is a lot harder than applying (RP_1). Simple-substitution is a mechanical procedure that yields unique results. If we want to argue that β cannot be simple-substituted *salva congruitate* for α in $\Phi(\alpha)$, then all we really need to do is write out $\Phi(\beta)$; after that, anyone fluent in the relevant language can see whether we are right. Sense-substitution, on the other hand, is not mechanical and does not yield unique results. If we want to argue that β cannot be sense-substituted for α in $\Phi(\alpha)$, then we need somehow to show that *no possible* sentence could count as a result of this sense-substitution.

It is, then, pretty difficult to apply (RP_2). But that is not to say that it is impossible: in the next chapter, I will argue that terms and predicates are nowhere sense-intersubstitutable. If that is right, then (RP_2) will entail that terms and predicates cannot co-refer. Of course, that result is not all that exciting, since we have not yet been given any argument for (RP_2). But as I promised earlier, we can use the fact that terms and predicates are nowhere sense-intersubstitutable as the basis for an argument that they cannot co-refer (see Chapter 4); and we can generalise that argument into an argument for something very much like (RP_2) (see Chapter 5). We can do all this because, unlike simple-substitution, sense-substitution is a *philosophically significant* conception of substitution. Simple-substitution operates on the surface of language, which is why it is so easy to use. But sense-substitution operates on a much deeper level than that. To decide whether two expressions are sense-intersubstitutable, we must reflect on the kinds of contribution these expressions make to the senses of the sentences in which they appear. Here I can do no better than to borrow a line from Ramsey:

> Let us remind ourselves that the task on which we are engaged is not merely one of English grammar; we are not school children analysing sentences into subject, extension of the subject, complement and so on, but are interested not so much in sentences themselves, as in what they mean, from which we hope to discover the logical nature of reality. (Ramsey 1925, 117)

CHAPTER 2

The Term/Predicate Distinction

In this chapter, I am going to argue that terms and predicates are nowhere intersubstitutable. As I made clear in the last chapter, the notion of sub- stitution in play here is *sense-substitution* (although, for ease of expression, I will often drop the 'sense-' bit), and I hope that it immediately strikes you as plausible that terms and predicates are not *sense*-intersubstitutable. Terms and predicates have very different kinds of sense, and it is hard to see how we could substitute one of these kinds of sense for the other. The aim of this chapter is just to work through this line of thought in more detail.

2.1 The Senses of Terms and the Senses of Predicates

The first thing we need to do is get clearer on the different kinds of sense that terms and predicates have. As an initial rough gloss, the difference comes to this: terms pick out objects,[1] and predicates say things of objects; for example, in 'Socrates is wise', 'Socrates' picks out Socrates, and '( ) is wise' says of him that he is wise. Now, that really is a rough gloss, and the details could be filled out in a number of different ways. For example, it would be consistent with this gloss to say that two terms have the same sense whenever they pick out the same object; but it would equally be consistent to follow Frege (1892b) and say that if two terms have the same sense, then they must not only pick out the same object but must pick it out in the same way. Fortunately, however, we do not need to fill any details in right now; this initial rough gloss is enough to get us started.

I intend this distinction between different kinds of sense to be *exclusive*: no expression can simultaneously have the sense of a term and the sense of

---

[1] It would be better to say that terms *purport* to pick out objects; however, to avoid the risk of getting distracted, I will largely disregard empty terms in this book.

a predicate.[2] However, it is important that I explain *why* this distinction is meant to be exclusive. As I have already made clear, I do not think that predicates refer to objects. Predicates refer to properties and, I want to insist, properties are not a kind of object. But I am certainly not in a position to insist upon that now. This chapter is meant to serve as a preliminary to Chapter 4, in which I will try to *argue* that properties are not objects. My argument would, then, be blatantly circular if I just assumed now that predicates do not refer to objects. In fact, I have to admit, the idea that predicates refer to objects is fairly natural. Applied to the sentence 'Socrates is wise', the idea would go like this: '( ) is wise' refers to the property of being wise, which is thought of as a special kind of object, and attributes that property to Socrates, the referent of 'Socrates'. To repeat, I think that this picture of predication is all wrong, but I cannot just assume that now.

I am not, then, assuming from the outset that terms do something that predicates do not, namely referring to objects. What I want to assume is that predicates do something which terms do not, namely saying things of objects. The job of a term is to pick out an object, not to say something of an object. This is equally true of definite descriptions, if they are treated as real singular terms and not analysed away in Russellian fashion. '( ) is a teacher of Plato' says of an object that it is a teacher of Plato, but 'the teacher of Plato' does not; its job is to pick out the unique object which satisfies '( ) is a teacher of Plato'. This point can be obscured by the fact that we talk about objects 'satisfying' definite descriptions as well as predicates, but 'satisfaction' means very different things in these two cases. When an object satisfies '( ) is a teacher of Plato', '( ) is a teacher of Plato' is *true of* that object. (Or, a little more verbosely: '( ) is a teacher of Plato' *says something true of* that object.) When an object uniquely satisfies 'the teacher of Plato', 'the teacher of Plato' *refers to* that object.

So terms pick out objects, and predicates say things of them. It is this difference which makes it so natural (following Frege) to call terms 'complete' and predicates 'incomplete'. The semantic role of a predicate is defined in relation to the semantic role of a term: the job of a predicate is to say something of a given object, and in the most basic cases, that object is given by a term. The semantic role of a term, on the other hand, stands by itself: it is simply to pick out an object. Of course, this is not to say that a term can play that role all on its own, without being embedded in a sentence. Terms and predicates are made to work together. The point is

---

[2] Of course, this does not rule out the possibility that there might be some sense of 'meaning' in which some term and predicate share a meaning. See §2.5 for further discussion.

just that the role played by terms is involved in the *very characterisation* of the role played by predicates in a way that the role played by predicates is not similarly involved in the characterisation of the role played by terms.[3]

In the last chapter, I said that the sense of a subsentential expression is its contribution to the senses of the sentences in which it appears. (The sense of a whole sentence then determines the logical properties of that sentence.) So the preceding characterisation of the senses of terms and predicates comes to the following: terms make their contributions to the senses of sentences by picking out particular objects (allowing that the way in which a term picks out an object may somehow affect the contribution it makes); predicates, on the other hand, make their contributions to the senses of sentences by saying things of objects. Indeed, I would like to treat these two claims as definitions of what it is to be a term and what it is to be a predicate: terms and predicates *just are* expressions which make their contributions to the senses of sentences in these two different but complementary ways.

There is, I have to admit, a certain circularity to my definitions: I just defined *terms* as those expressions which contribute to the senses of sentences by picking out objects, and earlier I defined *objects* as those things which terms can refer to. We could, if we liked, try to eliminate this circularity by offering a new definition of either 'object' or 'term'.[4] That would be fine by me, so long as the following two things remain true: first, that the sense of a term consists in its picking out an object, not in its saying anything of anything; second, that objects are whatever terms can refer to. However, I myself do not hold out great hopes for the possibility of giving any such definitions. I am inclined to think that the notions of *object* and *singular term* are coeval,[5] and that the circularity involved in their definitions is unavoidable. But still, that does not mean that my definitions are vacuous. They tell us that a singular term is an expression which contributes to the senses of sentences by picking out *something*, which we have called an 'object'; and, just as important, singular terms do not *say anything* of anything.

3 Sullivan (2010, 100–2) provides a very clear explanation of this point.
4 Most obviously, you might try to give a *syntactic* characterisation of terms, along the lines of Hale (1994; 1996).
5 Rumfitt (2003, esp. 200–1) recommends this view, as opposed to the idea that singular terms can be characterised in syntactic terms.

2.2 Substituting Predicates for Predicates

In Chapter 1, I only considered examples of sense-substituting one *singular term* for another. But we can also sense-substitute one *predicate* for another. Let's start by looking at some examples of this kind of substitution.

The first thing we need to do is introduce some more terminology and notation. *First-level* predicates are predicates that have gaps for singular terms. Everything I have so far said about predicates has really been about first-level predicates,[6] and in general, I will mean first-level predicates by 'predicate' unless I make clear otherwise. But there are other kinds of predicates too. *Second-level* predicates are predicates that have gaps for first-level predicates.[7] Since it can be useful to visually differentiate first-level predicates from second-level ones, I will use lowercase sans-serif letters to mark gaps for singular terms, and uppercase sans-serif letters to mark gaps for first-level predicates. So, for example, the gap marked x in 'x is a horse' is a gap for a singular term, and the gap marked X in '$\exists x X x$' is a gap for a first-level predicate. To be absolutely clear: these sans-serif letters are not variables or schematic letters; they merely mark the gaps in predicates.[8]

With this terminology in hand, we can now look at some examples of substituting one predicate for another. Consider the sentence,

(1a) I am tired,

and imagine that we wanted to substitute 'x is hungry' for 'x am tired'. If we were dealing with simple-substitution, we would end up with something ungrammatical:

(1b) # I is hungry.

But, as I emphasised in Chapter 1, sense-substitution is a far more flexible tool than simple-substitution. Here is one result of sense-substituting 'x is hungry' for 'x am tired' in (1a):

(1c) I am hungry.

---

[6] In fact, it has really only been about *monadic* first-level predicates, but everything I will say can easily be extended to cover polyadic cases.

[7] Predicates which contain gaps for singular terms *and* first-level predicates are of *mixed-level*. More generally, a predicate is of mixed-level if it contains a gap for a term and a gap for a predicate or if it contains gaps for different levels of predicate. To keep things simple, I will set mixed-level predicates to one side for the time being.

[8] Frege used Greek letters like ξ and ζ rather than these sans-serif letters. I was tempted to follow Frege's notation, but in the end, I preferred to use Greek letters as metalinguistic variables ranging over expressions. And anyway, using the same letters in different fonts as gap markers and as variables has the added benefit of allowing us to move smoothly between the two.

(1c) is a result of this sense-substitution if:

(a) '$X(I)$' $\approx$ '$X(I)$'

and (b) 'x am hungry' $\approx$ 'x is hungry'.

We can take (a) for granted: '$X(I)$' is the second-level predicate you get by removing 'x am tired' from 'I am tired', and (a) simply says that this second-level predicate has the same sense as itself.[9] (b), on the other hand, seems overwhelmingly plausible: the *grammatical* difference between 'x am hungry' and 'x is hungry' surely does not reflect any difference in the *senses* of these expressions – i.e., in the contributions that these expressions make to the senses of the sentences in which they appear.

Here is another example. Suppose that we wanted to substitute the English predicate 'x is crowded' for the French predicate 'x est jolie' in:

(2a) Londres est jolie.

If we were dealing with simple-substitution, we would end up with a mismatch of languages:

(2b) # Londres is crowded.

But things change when we move over to sense-substitution. Here is one result of this sense-substitution:

(2c) Londres est bondée.

This will count as a result of the sense-substitution we are after if:

(a) '$X(\text{Londres})$' $\approx$ '$X(\text{Londres})$'

and (b) 'x est bondée' $\approx$ 'x is crowded'.

Again, we can take (a) for granted – it merely tells us that the French second-level predicate '$X(\text{Londres})$' has the same sense as itself – and (b) is just a matter of translating 'x is crowded' into French. Of course, (2c) is not the only result of sense-substituting 'x is crowded' for 'x est jolie' in (2a). Here is another one:

(2d) London is crowded.

This will count as a result of this sense-substitution if:

(a) '$X(\text{London})$' $\approx$ '$X(\text{Londres})$'

and (b) 'x is crowded' $\approx$ 'x is crowded'.

---

9 I have not yet said anything about what kind of sense a second-level predicate has. I will touch on this briefly in §§2.3–2.4 and then return to related issues in §3.3.

This time, it is (b) which can be taken for granted and (a) which is a matter of translation.

Just as I said when I first introduced sense-substitution in §1.2, the guiding image through all of these examples should be that of substituting the sense of one predicate for the sense of another. Of course, as I then emphasised in §1.4, we should not take that picture too seriously: I want to steadfastly avoid reifying senses in this book. But the picture is useful, because it helps to make vivid that sense-substitution has absolutely nothing to do with the particular signs we use to express particular senses. If we have to turn 'x is hungry' into 'x am hungry' in the process of some sense-substitution, then no matter, so long as 'x am hungry' has the same sense as 'x is hungry'.

2.3   Substituting Predicates for Terms

We can, then, sense-substitute one predicate for another. But what we cannot do is sense-substitute a predicate for a singular term. Imagine that we wanted to substitute 'x is wise' for 'Socrates' in:

(3a) Philosophers love Socrates.

Clearly, a simple-substitution would give us something completely ungrammatical:

(3b) # Philosophers love is wise.

But this time, using sense-substitution will not help us. Suppose, for example, that we made (3b) grammatical by tweaking it as follows:

(3c) Philosophers love wisdom.

There is nothing wrong with this sentence in and of itself, but it is not a result of sense-substituting 'x is wise' for 'Socrates' in (3a). It would count as a result of that substitution only if:

(a) 'Philosophers love x' $\approx$ 'Philosophers love x'
and (b) 'wisdom' $\approx$ 'x is wise'.

But while we may take (a) for granted, (b) simply is not true. There is clearly a close link between 'wisdom' and 'x is wise',[10] but they do not have

---

[10]   You might think that 'wisdom' is what you get when you apply some kind of type-shifting operation to 'x is wise'. See §2.5 for discussion of these kinds of operation.

the same sense. They cannot have the same sense because 'x is wise' is a predicate, and 'wisdom' is a singular term. The job of 'x is wise' is to say of an object that it is wise; the job of 'wisdom', on the other hand, is simply to refer to wisdom, not to say something of anything.[11]

Of course, this is not really enough to show that it is absolutely impossible to sense-substitute 'x is wise' for 'Socrates' in (3a). It just shows that (3c) is not a result of that substitution. However, we can present a more abstract, general argument to show that this substitution cannot be performed. To perform this substitution, we would need to construct a meaningful sentence $\Psi(\gamma)$ such that:

(a) $\Psi(\ )$ ≈ 'Philosophers love x'
and (b) γ ≈ 'x is wise'.

(a) and (b) tell us that $\Psi(\ )$ and γ both have the senses of first-level predicates. But we cannot construct a meaningful sentence by writing an expression with the sense of a first-level predicate into the gap in an expression that *also* has the sense of a first-level predicate. The senses of first-level predicates are designed to combine with the senses of singular terms: in (3a), 'Socrates' picks out an object – Socrates – and 'Philosophers love x' says something of that object – that philosophers love it. But obviously, we cannot make the senses of two first-level predicates work together in anything like this way. In $\Psi(\gamma)$, γ is trying to say something of an object, but it has no object to say anything of. That is why I have not marked the type of gap in $\Psi(\ )$: (a) tells us that $\Psi(\ )$ is a first-level predicate, $\Psi(x)$, but (b) tells us that it cannot be.[12]

It is worth pre-empting two possible misunderstandings here. First, you might suspect that I have secretly assumed that predicates do not refer to objects, despite my promise not to. Otherwise, I would have seen no obstacle to constructing a meaningful sentence by writing a first-level predicate into the gap of another first-level predicate: in the sentence $\Psi(\gamma)$, γ picks out the property of being wise, and $\Psi(\ )$ says of that property that philosophers love it.[13] But I made no such assumption. The problem with $\Psi(\gamma)$

---

[11] Or at least, this is the standard view of how 'wisdom' functions. Hofweber (2016b, ch. 8) has recently proposed an alternative, according to which 'wisdom' has the syntactic form but *not* the semantic function of a term. However, even if Hofweber is right, the general argument that I am about to give will show that (3c) is still not a result of sense-substituting 'x is wise' for 'Socrates' in (3a).

[12] Frege offers a similar argument in volume 1 of his *Grundgesetze* (1893, §21). Whitehead and Russell also present a similar argument, using their own distinctive terminology, in the introduction to the first edition of *Principia* (1927, ch. II §4).

[13] It seems to me that this line of thought is present in Magidor (2009, 6–7).

was that since γ has the sense of a predicate, at least part of its job is to say something of an object, and that is something it cannot do in $\Psi(\gamma)$. It cannot because *terms* do not say anything of objects, and $\Psi(\ )$ has a sense which is designed to combine with the senses of terms. All of this still holds even if predicates also refer to objects of their own. Indeed, the proposed way of understanding $\Psi(\gamma)$ illustrates that fact: clearly, γ does not there serve to say something of anything; instead of acting like the predicate 'x is wise', it acts like the term 'wisdom'.

Second, the preceding remarks are not meant to suggest that the *only* way to construct a meaningful sentence with a first-level predicate is to fill its gap with a singular term. Obviously, we can also use a first-level predicate to fill the gap in a second-level predicate. But, crucially, this is possible only because second-level predicates have a different kind of sense from first-level predicates: first-level predicates say things of objects; second-level predicates say things of things said of objects. The paradigmatic examples of second-level predicate are the first-order quantifiers, '$\forall x X x$' and '$\exists x X x$': '$\exists x X x$' says something true of what 'Fx' says of an object iff 'Fx' says something true of some object; '$\exists x X x$' says something false of what 'Fx' says of an object iff 'Fx' says something false of every object. The same goes for other, non-paradigmatic examples of second-level predicates. For example, 'X(Socrates)', which is a limiting case of a second-level predicate, says something true(/false) of what 'Fx' says of an object iff 'Fx' says something true(/false) of Socrates. Put generally, the senses of second-level predicates are designed to work with the senses of first-level predicates, just as the senses of first-level predicates are designed to work with the senses of terms.

2.4 Substituting Terms for Predicates

It is also impossible to sense-substitute a term for a predicate. This time, start with,

(4a) Socrates is wise,

and try to substitute the term 'wisdom' for 'x is wise'. Again, a simple substitution would give us something ungrammatical:

(4b) # Socrates wisdom.

And again, moving over to sense-substitution will not help us. Suppose we made (4b) grammatical by tweaking it as follows:

(4c) Socrates instantiates wisdom.

There is nothing wrong with this sentence in and of itself, but it is not a result of sense-substituting 'wisdom' for 'x is wise' in (4a). It would count as a result of that substitution only if:

(a) 'X(Socrates)' ≈ 'X(Socrates)'

and (b) 'x instantiates wisdom' ≈ 'wisdom'.

But, while we may take (a) for granted, (b) simply is not true. 'Wisdom' and 'x instantiates wisdom' cannot have the same sense because the former is a term and the latter is a predicate. The job of 'wisdom' is to refer to wisdom, whereas the job of 'x instantiates wisdom' is to say of an object that it instantiates wisdom.

As before, this only really shows that (4c) is not a result of sense-substituting 'wisdom' for 'x is wise' in (4a), but we can give a more abstract argument to show that this substitution is impossible. To perform this substitution, we would need to construct a meaningful sentence $\Psi(\gamma)$ such that:

(a) $\Psi(\ )$ ≈ 'X(Socrates)'

and (b) γ ≈ 'wisdom'.

(a) tells us that $\Psi(\ )$ has the sense of a second-level predicate and (b) tells us that γ has the sense of a singular term. But we cannot meaningfully combine the senses of a second-level predicate and a term in this way. As I explained earlier, the senses of second-level predicates are designed to work with the senses of first-level predicates. An instance of 'F(Socrates)' is true(/false) iff 'Fx' says something true(/false) of Socrates. But singular terms do not say *anything* of objects. So if we tried to substitute a term into the gap in 'X(Socrates)', we could not get anything truth-evaluable. In general, second-level predicates need to be completed by expressions which say things of objects. Terms do not say anything of objects, so they cannot be used to complete second-level predicates.[14]

Linnebo and Rayo (2012) have recently proposed a cumulative type theory, in which terms can be substituted for predicates. (See also Williamson 2013, 237–8.) The argument I have just given shows that the kind of substitution involved in a cumulative type theory cannot be sense-substitution. In other words, the substitutions must be trading on some kind of pun: if α has the sense of a term and β has the sense of a predicate, then $\Phi(\alpha)$ and

---

[14] Again, Whitehead and Russell present a similar argument in the introduction to the first edition of *Principia* (1927, ch. II §4).

$\Phi(\beta)$ cannot both be meaningful unless $\Phi(\ )$ has different senses in these two sentences.[15]

2.5 Type-Shifting Principles

I have just argued that there is an important sense in which terms and predicates are nowhere intersubstitutable. But at this point, some readers may worry that this conclusion fits poorly with contemporary linguistics. Many linguists these days think that it is a mistake to assign an expression a fixed, inflexible type. Instead, they posit a range of *type-shifting principles*, which allow an expression to change its type from one circumstance to another. Take the word 'red', for example. In some contexts, 'red' behaves like a predicate, as in:

(5a) My car is red.[16]

Other times, 'red' behaves like a term:

(5b) Red is a warm colour.

We could account for what is going on here by positing a type-shifting principle along the following lines: although 'red' is fundamentally a first-level predicate, when it is concatenated with another first-level predicate, it shifts its type to *term*.[17] On the face of it, this sort of type-shifting will allow us to substitute predicates for terms after all.

Importantly, nothing I have said is meant to suggest that there is anything wrong with this use of type-shifting principles. I can of course allow that there is some sense in which terms and predicates may be intersubstitutable. My claim is merely that they are nowhere *sense*-intersubstitutable. When we shift the type of 'red' from *predicate* to *term*, we change its sense.[18] 'Red' makes very different contributions to the senses of (5a) and (5b): the job of

[15] See §5.5 for related discussion.
[16] For the sake of this example, I am assuming that the copula, 'is', is semantically vacuous. In other words, 'red' as it appears in (5a) is semantically equivalent to 'x is red'. Some philosophers reject this assumption, see §8.4.
[17] I have simplified things considerably here, and used philosophers' jargon instead of linguists'. (Rather than talking about terms and predicates, linguists are more likely to talk about expressions of type e and type $\langle e, t \rangle$.) Type-shifting principles were introduced by Partee and Rooth (1983). Partee discusses the type-shifting operation illustrated by (5a) and (5b), which she calls *nom*, in her 1986 work (esp. §§3–4).
[18] On the face of it, this seems to be a counterexample to the reflexivity of *has the same sense as*: 'red' – as it appears in (5a) – does not have the same sense as 'red' – as it appears in (5b). However, as I will explain in §5.2, I do not think that this is a genuine counterexample to Reflexivity, properly understood.

'red' in (5a) is to say of my car that it is red; its job in (5b) is just to refer to the colour red. There is clearly a close relationship between these two senses, which is surely why we can think of the one as being reached by applying a type-shifting operation to the other, but they are two different senses nonetheless.

Why does it matter so much that 'red' changes its sense when it shifts its type? Well, *sense* is the conception of meaning which is most directly relevant to logical and philosophical inquiries. The sense of a subsentential expression is its contribution to the senses of whole sentences, and it is the senses of whole sentences which determine their logical properties. (It also seems to be the notion of meaning which matters most to many linguists, who often describe type-shifting principles as changing the meaning of an expression.[19]) That is not to deny that there might be some other conception of meaning, according to which 'red' means the same thing in both (5a) and (5b). Someone might suggest, for example, that speakers are not fully competent in the use of 'red' until they know how to use it as a term as well as a predicate, and that might make them say that it means the same thing in both uses. (I am not actually endorsing this suggestion, just presenting it as something that someone might sensibly think.[20]) But that is not a conception of meaning which matters for my purposes. I care only about the logical contributions that expressions make.

2.6   An Assumed Distinction

I hope that I have said enough to convince you that terms and predicates are nowhere sense-intersubstitutable, and to reassure you that there is no tension between this conclusion and contemporary linguistics. Now I want to address a different kind of worry. I am working with a particular conception of terms and predicates: a term is an expression which picks out an object, and a (first-level) predicate is an expression which says something of an object. Why should we assume that there actually are any terms and predicates in this sense?

Well, the first thing that I should emphasise is just how minimal this assumption is. I am not making any assumptions about which expressions are terms and which are predicates. It comes naturally to say that 'Socrates' is the term in 'Socrates is wise', and that 'x is wise' is the predicate. But

---

[19]   See Partee and Rooth 1983, §4; Partee 1986, 358–9; Groenendijk and Stokhof 1989, 429; Geurts 2006, §2; Winter 2007, 172; Gray 2017, 437–8.
[20]   For something like this model of meaning, see Langacker 2002, 266–8.

maybe we could read it in other ways. One natural suggestion: 'Socrates' and 'wise' are both terms, and 'x is y' is the predicate. Or a less natural one: 'wise' is the term, and 'Socrates is x' is the predicate. For my purposes, the details do not matter, so long as we *somehow* break sentences down into terms and predicates.[21] In fact, it does not even matter if there are some sentences which resist being broken down in this kind of way. It is sometimes suggested that there are languages which lack the term/predicate distinction altogether.[22] If so, then so be it. All that matters for my purposes is that at least some sentences in at least some languages can be broken down in this way.

As I said, that seems to be a fairly minimal assumption. Indeed, it is an assumption which pretty much every contemporary analytic philosopher makes.[23] That is obvious enough when it comes to philosophers of language. The vast majority of these philosophers just silently take it for granted that at least some simple sentences can be broken down into expressions which pick out objects (terms) and expressions which say things of objects (predicates). That much forms the unchallenged backdrop for their subsequent disagreements.[24]

But the term/predicate distinction also runs deeper than that. It is not just that we reach for it when we are theorising *about* language. More than that, the distinction informs the way that we (contemporary analytic philosophers) *understand* our language. We automatically read our sentences as picking out objects and saying things of them.[25] This quickly becomes clear when we want to lay out an argument with care. Then, without hesitation, we explicitly distinguish between terms and predicates, and a sentence like 'Socrates is wise' is transformed into 'Wise(Socrates)'. The term/predicate distinction has become an entrenched part of our conceptual scheme.

---

21 Having said that, I will, of course, continue to speak as if 'Socrates', 'Plato', etc., are the terms, and 'is wise', 'is a philosopher', etc., are the predicates. I will return to the idea that 'x is a horse' is a complex predicate, made of 'x is a y' and 'horse', in §8.4.

22 Whorf was famous for claiming that the subject/predicate distinction is absent from some non-Indo-European languages. For a collection of essays on this theme, see Whorf 1956.

23 It is also a widely held assumption among linguists. As Klein and Sternefeld (2017, 65) put it: 'As has become standard practice, linguists translate a fragment of English into an intensional extension of classical predicate logic'.

24 Of course, there is the Quinean tradition of denying that there are any *constant* singular terms. According to this tradition, apparent constants like 'Frege' should be analysed into definite descriptions, and then those descriptions should be eliminated in the Russellian style. But even the philosophers in this tradition agree that there are singular variables, and once we assign a value to one of these variables, they act like terms picking out that value.

25 More accurately, we read our simplest sentences like that.

Of course, this is not to say that we are obliged to work with this distinction. Maybe we could give it up. However, it would take a thoroughgoing repudiation of the term/predicate distinction to stop my argument in its tracks. It would not just be a matter of tweaking things around the edges. We would need a radically new way of understanding our language. I will try to give a sense of what would be required in the next chapter, where we will look at Ramsey's famous attack on the term/predicate distinction.

CHAPTER 3

Ramsey's Challenge

Ramsey's stated aim in his celebrated paper 'Universals' (1925, 112) was to challenge the thesis that 'there is a fundamental division of objects into two classes, particulars and universals'. However, early in the paper, Ramsey tells us that he will challenge this thesis by attacking an assumption which underlies it: that there is

> a fundamental antithesis between subject and predicate, that if a proposition consists of two terms copulated, these two terms must be functioning in different ways, one as subject, the other as predicate. (Ramsey 1925, 116)

Now, put like this, it does not quite sound like Ramsey is targeting the Fregean term/predicate distinction. It sounds much more like he has the traditional grammatical distinction between subjects and predicates in mind. And the notion of *predicate* appealed to in the traditional distinction is not the same as the Fregean notion we are working with. On the Fregean analysis, 'Socrates is wise' breaks down into the term 'Socrates' and the (Fregean) predicate 'x is wise'; on the traditional analysis, it breaks down into 'Socrates', the copula 'is', and the traditional (non-Fregean) predicate 'wise'. Equally, the Fregean notion of a *term* is not quite the same as the traditional notion of a *subject*: 'Plato' is a term, but not a subject, in 'Socrates taught Plato'. However, it quickly becomes clear that Ramsey *does* intend his attack to undermine the Fregean distinction between terms and predicates,[1] and that is how I will understand him in what follows.

My aim in this chapter is to examine Ramsey's challenge to the term/predicate distinction and, more importantly, to consider the alternatives that he suggests. It is not really my ambition to show that there is anything wrong with these alternatives. What I want to do is give a sense

---

[1] Not that he would have thought of it as the *Fregean* distinction. To the best of my knowledge, Ramsey did not engage directly with Frege's logic in any of his writings.

of how far we can move away from the term/predicate distinction without upsetting the structure of the argument I have planned for Fregean realism.[2]

3.1   Socrates and Wisdom

Ramsey's first attack on the term/predicate distinction is probably the best known passage from 'Universals':

> in 'Socrates is wise', Socrates is the subject, wisdom the predicate. But suppose we turn the proposition round and say, 'wisdom is a characteristic of Socrates', then wisdom formerly the predicate is now the subject. Now it seems to me as clear as anything can be in philosophy, that the two sentences 'Socrates is wise', 'wisdom is a characteristic of Socrates' assert the same fact and express the same proposition. They are not, of course, the same sentence, but they have the same meaning, just as two sentences in two different languages can have the same meaning. Which sentence we use is a matter either of literary style, or of the point of view from which we approach the fact. If the centre of our interest is Socrates we say 'Socrates is wise', if we are discussing wisdom we may say 'wisdom is a characteristic of Socrates'; but whichever we say we mean the same thing. Now of one of these sentences 'Socrates' is the subject, of the other 'wisdom'; and so which of the two is subject, which predicate, depends upon what particular sentence we use to express our proposition, and has nothing to do with the logical nature of Socrates or wisdom, but is a matter entirely for grammarians. In the same way, with a sufficiently elastic language any proposition can be so expressed that any of its terms is the subject. Hence there is no essential distinction between the subject of a proposition and its predicate, and no fundamental classification of objects can be based upon such a distinction. (Ramsey 1925, 116)

How forceful is this first attack? Well, at first glance, it appears to miss its target completely. Ramsey claims that the predicate from,

(1) Socrates is wise,

is the subject in,

(2) Wisdom is a characteristic of Socrates.

But that is not quite right. The predicate in (1) is 'x is wise', and the subject in (2) is 'wisdom'. Now, clearly, there is a very close relationship between 'x is wise' and 'wisdom': 'wisdom' is a term derived from the predicate 'x is wise',

---

[2]   I laid out my plan at the start of Chapter 1.

often called a *nominalisation* of that predicate. But still, there is nothing in this example which immediately puts any pressure on the term/predicate distinction.

If this example is so inept, then why did Ramsey include it? Well, here it is important to bear in mind that although Ramsey was attacking the term/predicate distinction, his *real* target was the particular/universal distinction. And while the preceding example may not undermine the term/predicate distinction in and of itself, there is no denying that it casts serious doubt over the idea that we could read off a metaphysical division between particulars and universals from the linguistic division between terms and predicates.[3] It is very tempting to agree with Ramsey that (1) and (2) do say the same thing, and thus that whether we use the predicate 'x is wise' or the term 'wisdom' is just a matter of style.

Nonetheless, I *do* think that we can read off a metaphysical distinction from the term/predicate distinction: in the next chapter, I will argue that terms and predicates cannot co-refer, and thus that properties are not objects. What, then, do I want to say about (1) and (2)? Following Simons (1991, 151–2), we can distinguish between two readings of (2). On the first, we deny that 'wisdom' occurs as a term. This is not to deny that 'wisdom' is the subject of (2) in a superficial grammatical sense.[4] Rather, it is to deny that 'wisdom' plays the role of a term, namely the role of picking out an object. Instead, 'Wisdom is a characteristic of x' is a single, indivisible predicate, synonymous with 'x is wise'. On this reading, it is obviously true that (1) and (2) say the same thing, but it is also utterly trivial. It goes no way towards suggesting that a term and a predicate might co-refer.[5]

On the second reading of (2), 'wisdom' does occur as a term. But now I simply want to deny that (1) and (2) say the same thing: 'wisdom' refers to an object in (2) that is not referred to by anything in (1). Nonetheless, I can still grant that (1) and (2) are equivalent in some sense: for example, it may yet be that they have the same truth-value at every world. (That will all depend on whether expressions like 'wisdom' refer to anything. I will return to that question in §10.1.) Of course, I have not yet explained *why* I want to deny that properties are objects. But for now my point is merely that the existence of pairs like (1) and (2) does not put any pressure on us to identify properties with objects.[6]

---

[3] This point is emphasised by MacBride (2005b; 2018, 209–10).
[4] This is not meant to suggest that *any* grammatical sense would be superficial, but only that the sense in which 'wisdom' is automatically the subject of (2) is a superficial one.
[5] For a more systematic development of this line of thought, see Hofweber 2007; 2016a, ch. 2.
[6] Some philosophers might think that Ramsey was making a very different point. They might take Ramsey to be pointing out that we are not *compelled* to treat 'Socrates' as a term and 'x is wise' as a

3.2 Complex Predicates

Ramsey (1925, 117) is very clear that his first attack on the term/predicate distinction was not meant to decide the matter, and in the remainder of the paper, he presents the argument he really wants to lean on. His argument follows a two-step strategy. First he argues that if we are going to draw a metaphysically significant term/predicate distinction, then we will have to draw it at the level of *atomic* sentences, not complex ones. He then attempts to show that there are no grounds for drawing this distinction at the atomic level. In this section, I will discuss the first of these steps, and in the next section, I will discuss the second.

Ramsey tries to convince us to set aside complex sentences and focus on atomic ones as follows. Consider the sentence 'Either Socrates is wise, or Plato is foolish'. From this sentence, we can extract three different complex predicates: 'Either x is wise, or y is foolish', 'Either x is wise, or Plato is foolish', and 'Either Socrates is wise or x is foolish'. But Ramsey insists that it would be absurd to imagine that these predicates are referring expressions:

> In order to make things clearer let us take a simpler case, a proposition of the form '*aRb*'; then this theory will hold that there are three closely related propositions; one asserts that the relation *R* holds between the terms *a* and *b*, the second asserts the possession by *a* of the complex property of 'having *R* to *b*', while the third asserts that *b* has the complex property that *a* has *R* to it. These must be three different propositions because they have different sets of constituents, and yet they are not three propositions, but one proposition, for they all say the same thing, namely that *a* has *R* to *b*. So the theory of complex universals is responsible for an incomprehensible trinity, as senseless as that of theology. (Ramsey 1925, 118)

Whether you will find this argument convincing will largely depend on whether you accept Ramsey's rule of thumb: different constituents, different propositions. Much later (Chapters 11–14), I will present theories of propositions and states of affairs which obviously invalidate that rule.[7] However, even if we are unconvinced by Ramsey's argument, I do not think that we can refuse Ramsey's request to focus on atomic sentences. It would be very odd to insist that there is a semantically significant class of

---

predicate in (1). We could instead treat 'wise' as the term, and 'Socrates is x' as the predicate; on this reading, (1) could be perspicuously rewritten as (2). (See Gaskin 2008, §51.) However, as I explained in §2.6, nothing in my argument really turns on our treating 'Socrates' as the term and 'x is wise' as the predicate. All that matters is that we *somehow* break down a range of sentences into terms and predicates.

7 For philosophers who reject this argument on similar grounds, see Anscombe 1959, 95; Geach 1975; Dummett 1981b, 264–6. For a defence of Ramsey's argument, see MacBride 2005b, 88–94; 2018, 210–20.

predicates, but it includes no simple examples. After all, the simple expressions are the basic inputs of our semantic theories; as Sullivan (2010, 107–8) puts it, the simple expressions 'define the expressive resources of a language'. Now, to be clear, I do not doubt at all that there are meaningful, complex predicates. It's just that complex predicates seem to be something of a secondary matter. The battle for the term/predicate distinction must surely be won or lost on the simple cases.

3.3   Ramsey's Alternative Scheme

Can we draw the term/predicate distinction at the level of atomic sentences? Well, answering this question is tricky, because we first need to decide which sentences count as atomic. Most of us today would probably be willing to say that 'Socrates is wise' is atomic, if only in the very dull sense that it contains no logical constants. But for Ramsey, who at the time of 'Universals' was a card-carrying Tractarian, 'Socrates is wise' could not possibly count as atomic: atomic propositions picture atomic facts, which are composed of simple entities, and Socrates is complex, not simple. But let's not worry about that now, treat sentences like 'Socrates is wise' as if they were atomic, purely for the sake of having some examples.[8]

   So can we draw the term/predicate distinction in the case of 'Socrates is wise'? On the face of it, nothing would be simpler: the term is 'Socrates', and the predicate is 'x is wise'. However, dividing these expressions up in this way involves thinking of them as playing two different roles: 'Socrates' picks an object out – Socrates – and 'x is wise' says something of that object – that it is wise. And ultimately, Ramsey does not think that there is any reason to distribute the subsentential labour in this way.

   According to Ramsey (1925, 123–5), the reason we think that 'Socrates' and 'x is wise' play these different roles comes down to this. If we consider all of the sentences in which 'wise' occurs, we can distinguish a privileged subclass that are all of the form 'x is wise'; 'Socrates is wise' and 'Plato is wise' both belong to this privileged subclass, but 'Neither Plato nor Socrates is wise' and 'Socrates is wise only if Plato is foolish' do not. By contrast, there does not seem to be any similarly privileged subclass of sentences in which 'Socrates' occurs.

---

[8]   This seems to be the attitude that Ramsey (1925, 126–7) wants us to take to 'Socrates is wise', although he goes on to explain how to apply his discussion to that sentence even if it is not atomic.

As Simons (1991, 155–6) points out, we can connect this observation with the Fregean practice of arranging predicates into levels: the first way of making a sentence out of 'x is wise' is by filling its argument place with a term; the second way is by using 'x is wise' to fill the argument place in a second-level predicate, like 'X(Socrates) only if Plato is foolish'. The privileged subclass of sentences containing 'wise' comprises just those sentences which can be made in the first of these ways. There is no similarly privileged subclass of sentences containing 'Socrates', because 'Socrates' does not come with an argument place to be filled. The only thing we can do with 'Socrates' is plug it into the argument place of a first-level predicate.

However, Ramsey goes on to insist that despite appearances to the contrary, it *is* possible to distinguish a privileged subclass of sentences containing 'Socrates':

> Suppose we can distinguish among the properties of Socrates a certain subset which we can call qualities; the idea being roughly that only a simple property is a quality. Then we could form in connexion with 'Socrates' two sets of propositions just as we can in connexion with 'wise'. There would be the wide set of propositions, in which 'Socrates' occurs at all, which we say assert properties of Socrates, but also there would be the narrower set which assert qualities of Socrates. Thus supposing justice and wisdom to be qualities, 'Socrates is wise', 'Socrates is just' would belong to the narrower set and be values of a function 'Socrates is q'. But 'Socrates is neither wise nor just' would not assert a quality of Socrates but only a compound characteristic or property, and would only be a value of the function 'ϕ(Socrates)', not of 'Socrates is q'. (Ramsey 1925, 125)

It is very tempting here to describe Ramsey as identifying the term 'Socrates' with the second-level predicate 'X(Socrates)'. This is, for example, how Dummett (1981a, 61–7) describes Ramsey. But while there is surely something right about this, we need to tread carefully. The concept of a *second-level predicate* is Fregean: second-level predicates are expressions which occupy a certain position in Frege's hierarchy of expressions, and they occupy a different position in that hierarchy from terms. It is not an option, then, to identify a term with a second-level predicate. To make such an identification would be to collapse the very structure which defines what we mean by a 'second-level predicate'.[9]

---

[9] Sullivan (2010, 101–2) gives a very clear explanation of this point. Although we cannot identify a term with a second-level predicate, we *can*, of course, deny that 'Socrates' functions as a term, and insist instead that it really functions as a second-level predicate (see Montague 1973). As I emphasised in §2.6, none of my arguments in this book rely on the assumption that grammatically proper names are singular terms.

Rather than literally identifying a term with a second-level predicate, Ramsey is presenting an alternative way of thinking about 'Socrates is wise', which leaves no space for the Fregean distinction between the term 'Socrates' and the second-level predicate 'X(Socrates)'. Filling in some details which Ramsey did not bother with, the picture seems to be this. There are two types of expressions: type A – which includes 'Socrates', 'Plato' and so on – and type B – which includes 'wise', 'mortal' and so on. A-expressions refer to things, and so do B-expressions: A-expressions refer to entities like Socrates and Plato, and B-expressions refer to entities like wisdom and mortality. B-expressions say things of entities, and so do A-expressions: 'wise' says of an entity that it instantiates wisdom, and 'Socrates' says of an entity that it is instantiated by Socrates.

A-expressions are clearly a lot like our terms, but they are also importantly different: terms do not say anything of anything, but A-expressions do. There is no sense, then, in which a B-expression is any more incomplete than an A-expression: in 'Socrates is wise', an A-expression and a B-expression mutually complete each other (Ramsey 1925, 121–2). On this picture, 'wise' and 'Socrates' *both* come with gaps – '( ) is wise' and 'Socrates is [   ]' – and we could perspicuously rewrite 'Socrates is wise' as '(Socrates) is [wise]'.

If Ramsey's scheme can be fully worked out, then it will be an attractive alternative to the term/predicate distinction. Now, it is not entirely clear that it can be *fully* worked out. Nothing has been said yet about how to deal with cases more complex than 'Socrates is wise', like 'Socrates taught Plato' or 'Someone is a philosopher', and it is not easy to see what should be said. But never mind that. For the sake of argument, let's just grant that Ramsey's scheme could be developed into a fully satisfying alternative to the term/predicate distinction.

Fortunately, we can grant that without doing any real damage to my project. Although there is a great deal of symmetry between A-expressions and B-expressions, it is still not the case that you can sense-substitute a B-expression for an A-expression (or *vice versa*). Suppose that we wanted to sense-substitute '( ) is wise' for 'Socrates is [ ]' in:

(3) (Socrates) is [virtuous].

We might have thought that the following sentence would count as a result of this substitution:

(4) (Wisdom) is [virtuous].

But that would be a mistake. If (4) is to count as a result of sense-substituting '( ) is wise' for 'Socrates is [ ]' in (3), then 'wisdom is [ ]' and '( ) is wise' must have the same sense. But they do not. That is not because 'wise' has been swapped for 'wisdom'. The difference between these words could be dismissed as merely grammatical, like the difference between 'I' and 'me'. The problem is that we have changed the kind of gap that goes with 'wise': we have gone from '( ) is wise' to 'wisdom is [ ]'. '( ) is wise' is a B-expression. In sentence (1),

(1) (Socrates) is [wise],

'( ) is wise' says of Socrates that he instantiates wisdom. By contrast, 'wisdom is [ ]' is an A-expression. In sentence (4), 'wisdom is [ ]' says of virtue that wisdom instantiates it. '( ) is wise' and 'wisdom is [ ]' thus make very different contributions to the senses of (1) and (4).

Of course, this is not really enough to show that it is absolutely impossible to sense-substitute '( ) is wise' for 'Socrates is [ ]' in (3). It just shows that (4) is not a result of that substitution. However, we can present a more general, abstract argument to show that this substitution is impossible. To perform this substitution, we would need to construct a meaningful sentence $(\alpha)(\beta)$ such that:

(a) $\alpha(\ ) \approx$ '( ) is wise'
and (b) $(\ )\beta \approx$ '( ) is virtuous'.[10]

But we cannot construct such a sentence: if $\alpha(\ )$ and $(\ )\beta$ both have the senses of B-expressions, then we cannot make a meaningful sentence by putting them together. In (1), '( ) is wise' says of Socrates that he instantiates wisdom, and 'Socrates is [ ]' says of wisdom that Socrates instantiates it. It is easy to see how these two can come together to make a meaningful sentence: whichever way you slice it, (1) says that Socrates instantiates wisdom. But in $(\alpha)(\beta)$, $(\ )\beta$ would say of wisdom that it instantiates virtue, and $\alpha(\ )$ would say of virtue that it instantiates wisdom. These are two completely different things, wisdom's being virtuous and virtue's being wise. What, then, would $(\alpha)(\beta)$ as a whole say?

It might be tempting to suggest that $(\alpha)(\beta)$ says *two* things: it says that wisdom is virtuous, *and* it says that virtue is wise.[11] But it is important to realise just how strange that suggestion would be. We are not dealing

---

[10] I have here tweaked my definition of sense-substitution in §1.2 so that it applies more naturally to Ramsey's scheme.
[11] Thanks to Nick Jones for pushing this response.

with a case of ambiguity. It is not that $(\alpha)(\beta)$ says one thing on one interpretation, and another thing on another. Rather, $(\alpha)(\beta)$ says two things
on *one* interpretation. What truth-value should this sentence have on this
interpretation? Well, it says that wisdom is virtuous, and (we will assume)
wisdom is indeed virtuous.[12] A sentence is true iff things are as it says they
are. So $(\alpha)(\beta)$ is true. But $(\alpha)(\beta)$ also says that virtue is wise, and virtue
is not the sort of thing that can be wise (or foolish, for that matter). A
sentence is false iff things are not as it says they are. So $(\alpha)(\beta)$ is also false.

We have just derived a contradiction from the assumption that $(\alpha)(\beta)$
says both that wisdom is virtuous and that virtue is wise. However, this
derivation relied on the following two principles:

(T_1) s says that $P \rightarrow (s$ is true $\leftrightarrow P)$
(F_1) s says that $P \rightarrow (s$ is false $\leftrightarrow \neg P)$.

(T_1) and (F_1) look obviously right when we assume that sentences only say
one thing at a time. But if we want to be open to sentences saying more than
one thing at once, then perhaps we should revise them. It is helpful here
to draw an analogy between sentences that say many things and theories.
Theories are made up of many sentences, and so in that sense, they also
say many things. To be true, a theory must be completely true; a theory is
true iff every sentence in the theory is true. By analogy, we could say that
a sentence is true iff things are *all* the ways it says they are. To be false, a
theory just needs to get one detail wrong; a theory is false iff it contains a
false sentence. By analogy, we could say that a sentence is false iff it says that
things are *some* way they are not. We can formalise these new principles as
follows:

(T_2) s is true $\leftrightarrow \forall P((s$ says that $P) \rightarrow P)$
(F_2) s is false $\leftrightarrow \exists P((s$ says that $P) \wedge \neg P).$[13]

These formalisations involve quantification into sentence-position, which
I will discuss at length in Chapters 11–14. But for now, we can work with

---

[12]   If you are not happy with this assumption, you can just change the example. All you need is a pair
of properties, such that one instantiates the other but not *vice versa*.
[13]   It is important to note that it would be a mistake to replace (F_2) with:

(F_3) s is false $\leftrightarrow \forall P((s$ says that $P) \rightarrow \neg P)$.

Someone might try to motivate (F_3) by drawing an analogy with supervaluationism: 'Simon is bald'
is supertrue iff it is true on every precisification, and superfalse iff it is false on every precisification.
But that would be a faulty analogy. 'Simon is bald' does not express all of its precisifications. 'Simon
is bald' simply says that Simon is bald. The supervaluation is only used to determine what truth-
value a sentence which says that Simon is bald should receive. The better analogy is with theories,
and that analogy motivates (F_2).

the intuitive explanations of (T_2) and (F_2) that I just gave. And by these principles, $(\alpha)(\beta)$ is just plain false: it says that virtue is wise, which it is not.

The contradiction we derived earlier has now been blocked, but a similar contradiction quickly appears when we consider $\neg(\alpha)(\beta)$. Here are two principles concerning negation:

(N_1) s is false $\rightarrow$ $\ulcorner \neg s \urcorner$ is true
(N_2) s says that $P \rightarrow \ulcorner \neg s \urcorner$ says that $\neg P$.

(N_1) seems close to analytic, and (N_2) is highly plausible account of the meanings of negated sentence.[14] $(\alpha)(\beta)$ is false by (F_2), and so (N_1) implies that $\neg(\alpha)(\beta)$ is true. But (T_2) and (N_2) together imply that $\neg(\alpha)(\beta)$ is not true. By (N_2), $\neg(\alpha)(\beta)$ says that wisdom is not virtuous, and that virtue is not wise. So by (T_2), $\neg(\alpha)(\beta)$ is true iff wisdom is not virtuous and virtue is not wise. But wisdom is virtuous (we are assuming), and so $\neg(\alpha)(\beta)$ is not true. Contradiction.

What this shows is that, for all the symmetry between A-expressions and B-expressions, we still cannot intersubstitute them. And as we will see in Chapter 5, this is all that I need to show that they cannot co-refer. So although I am working with the scheme of terms and predicates in this book, I could write an alternative version of the book that worked with the Ramseyian scheme instead. More generally, so long as we grant that there are at least *two* types of expression, and that expressions from one type cannot be substituted for expressions from the other, then something like my arguments could still be made to run.

3.4 Subsentential Monism

At this point, it is worth noting that Ramsey (1925, 133) himself was willing to entertain the possibility that at the atomic level, subsentential expressions are all of the same type, and so intersubstitutable. Unfortunately, Ramsey offers us absolutely no explanation of how this *subsentential monism* might work. He felt no obligation to, because he subscribed to the Tractarian doctrine that we can know nothing whatsoever about the forms of

---

[14] Here it is important to note that it would be a mistake to replace (N_2) with:

(N_3) $\ulcorner \neg s \urcorner$ says that $\neg \forall P((s$ says that $P) \rightarrow P)$.

(N_3) would make negation inherently metalinguistic, which it is not. 'Socrates is not foolish' does not say anything about the sentence 'Socrates is foolish'; it just says that Socrates is not foolish.

atomic propositions.[15] Now, this may be a reasonable thing to say if you are concerned with atomic propositions in the rarefied Tractarian sense. But outside of the context of the *Tractatus*, it is a lot less satisfying.

What sort of explanation do we need? Well, we need an account of how a number of expressions all belonging to the same type – i.e., all playing exactly the same kind of semantic role – could work *together* to make a meaningful (atomic) sentence. It is not enough merely to show that we could map all of the sentences in our language onto sentences in a language which conforms to Ramsey's subsentential monism. No doubt we could do that (see Button 2017), but we still need more: we need a compositional story which explains *how* combining expressions of a single type yields meaningful sentences. Unfortunately, it is not at all clear how to give such an account.

Here is a tempting starting point. We could try imagining a language in which we keep terms but give up on predicates as follows: rather than expressing relations with relational predicates, we will use relations between *terms* to express relations between *objects*. So rather than saying 'Socrates taught Plato', we will put the terms 'Socrates' and 'Plato' into some relation to each other. For example, we could just write them next to each other: Socrates Plato.[16] Similarly, we will use properties of terms to express properties of objects. So rather than saying 'Socrates is wise', we will just write 'Socrates' in a particular way. For example, we could just put it in bold: **Socrates**. Wouldn't this be a language in which the atomic sentences were built out of a number of expressions all drawn from the same type?

Despite the appearances to the contrary, I believe that the answer is 'no'. As Long (1969) made clear in a remarkable paper, there is still a sense in which there are two types of expression (or 'symbol', in Long's terminology) in 'Socrates Plato'. On the one hand, we have the terms 'Socrates' and 'Plato', and on the other, we have the relation between them. Now, it might seem strange to call a relation an 'expression' (or a 'symbol'), but recall that it is the relation between 'Socrates' and 'Plato' which says of Socrates and Plato that the former taught the latter. But if that still feels too strange for you, then fine. The point is merely that the subsentential labour involved in 'Socrates Plato' is still divided along term/predicate lines: there are terms which refer to objects, 'Socrates' and 'Plato'; and there is another thing which says something of those objects, the relation between 'Socrates' and

---

[15]   Interestingly, Ramsey later (1926, 135) came to doubt this doctrine. For a discussion of this change of heart, see Methven 2018a.

[16]   Or an alternative implementation of the same idea: we can say that Socrates instantiates mortality just by writing 'Socrates Mortality'. Everything I will say applies equally to this implementation.

'Plato'. Moreover, it would be manifestly absurd to try to substitute the relation that says something of Socrates and Plato in 'Socrates Plato' for either 'Socrates' or 'Plato'. The same goes, mutatis mutandis, for '**Socrates**'.

Up until this point, I think that Long was absolutely right. But then he went further and insisted that relations between objects are *always* expressed by relations between names, even in languages like our own. For example, Long thought that the job of the word 'taught' in 'Socrates taught Plato' is just to set up a certain indirect relation between 'Socrates' and 'Plato'. In this sentence, 'Socrates' and 'Plato' bear the relation *being written on either side of the word 'taught'* to one another, and Long (1969, 93–5) insisted that it was this indirect relation between 'Socrates' and 'Plato' that expresses the *teaching* relation between Socrates and Plato.[17] This seems to me to be an overreaction. All Long has shown is that in the language described above, relations play something like the role that I have ascribed to predicates. That falls far short of showing that it is relations which play that role in *every* language. Nonetheless, it is enough to undermine the idea that this language does without something analogous to the term/predicate distinction, and that suffices for my purposes.[18]

There might be other ways of trying to fill out Ramsey's subsentential monism, but I really find it very hard to think of them. Still, this may just be a lack of imagination on my part. At this point, then, it is worth making the following observation. Even if we accept *subsentential* monism, we must surely acknowledge that subsentential expressions are of a different type from *sentences themselves*. Sentences express complete thoughts, and whatever it is that subsentential expressions do, it is not that.[19] And this difference is surely deep enough to guarantee that subsentential expressions will be nowhere sense-intersubstitutable with sentences. We will, then, be able to use the argument of Chapter 5 to show at least that no subsentential expression can co-refer with a sentence. What is more, this is no fringe or bizarre application of that argument: as we will see in Chapter 11, it gives us an account of states of affairs which is entirely analogous to the Fregean account I will give of properties.

---

[17] Long was here following the Wittgenstein of the *Tractatus*: 'We must not say, "The complex sign '*aRb*' says '*a* stands in relation *R* to *b*' "; but we must say, "That '*a*' stands in a certain relation to '*b*' says that *aRb*" ' (Wittgenstein 1922, 3.1432).

[18] See Parsons 1970 for some further criticisms of Long's conclusions. For a more general discussion of what sort of thing predicates are, see Oliver 2010.

[19] Frege himself (1893, §2) famously came to think that sentences were a kind of term. But pretty much everyone agrees that that was a backward step.

3.5   Back to the Term/Predicate Distinction

Perhaps Ramsey was right, and we do not have to divide any of our sentences into terms and predicates. So far I have tried to explain how much of my project could survive even if we abandoned this distinction. But I would now like to make a rather different point.

Even if we are not *obliged* to work with the term/predicate distinction, it is undeniable that we, contemporary analytic philosophers, *do* work with it. And, as I emphasised in §2.6, this does not just mean that we appeal to the distinction when we are theorising *about* language; this distinction informs the way that we *understand* our language. Giving up on the term/predicate distinction would, then, require us to revise the way that we have become accustomed to speaking and thinking when we do philosophy. The extent of the necessary revisions would, of course, depend on how far we had departed from the term/predicate distinction. I suspect that we would hardly need to change anything at all, including the arguments of this book, if we moved over to the Ramseyian scheme of A-expressions and B-expressions. But it seems all but impossible to imagine what our metaphysics would look like if we tried to understand our language in accordance with some version of subsentential monism. All we can safely say is that it would be very different from what we are doing now.

From now on, then, I will just take our term/predicate distinction for granted. In this sense, the arguments to come are conditional on the assumption that this distinction is in good standing. Now, as I have repeatedly stressed, that assumption is fairly minimal and seems to be a commonplace amongst contemporary philosophers, but there might still be some readers who have their doubts. However, I hope that any such reader will find something of interest in this book nonetheless. As we will see in later chapters, philosophers have run into all sorts of puzzles and problems while working within our scheme of terms and predicates. These puzzles concern the relations between objects, properties, facts and propositions. The primary aim of this book is to show how these puzzles can be dissolved *from within* our term/predicate scheme. My ambition is to show that these puzzles are really just misunderstandings of how that scheme works: once we understand it properly, we will see that those puzzles simply cannot come up.

CHAPTER 4

Two Types of Reference

Terms and predicates are nowhere intersubstitutable. That is the conclusion from the last few chapters which we need to take forward. Now I will use that conclusion to show that terms and predicates cannot co-refer. Or something like that, anyway. As those readers who enjoy footnotes will already know, I actually want to argue for something far more radical: *it does not even make sense* to suppose that a term and a predicate might co-refer. Or using 'object' and 'property' as our catch-alls for the things that terms and predicates can refer to: it is literally nonsense to say that a property is an object.[1]

Some readers may doubt that we really need to offer any arguments against the idea that predicates refer to objects. Back in §2.1, I characterised the term/predicate distinction as follows: terms refer to objects, and predicates say things of objects. So referring to an object just isn't in a predicate's job description! But that is much too hasty. Consider the sentence 'Socrates is wise'. The job of 'Socrates' is to refer to a particular object – Socrates – and the job of 'x is wise' is to say something of that object – that he is wise. However, we might still want to add that 'x is wise' refers to a special object of its own – wisdom. On this sort of picture, 'x is wise' says of Socrates that he is wise *precisely by* attributing wisdom to him. Or to put it a little inelegantly: wisdom is the *something* which 'x is wise' says of Socrates.[2]

Now, to repeat, I think that this picture of predication is all wrong. I want to argue that it does not make any sense at all to suppose that a predicate might refer to an object. But this *does* require an argument. It certainly isn't enough just to point out that I initially characterised predicates without explicitly saying that they refer to objects.

---

[1]   I will talk more about what it means to call something 'nonsense' in §9.2. Until then, I will take it that the meaning is clear enough.

[2]   See Chapter 8 for discussions of a number of theories of predication which work along these lines.

4.1   The Argument in Brief

In this section, I will sketch the shape of my argument. It begins with what I will call the *disquotation problem* for predicate-reference.[3]

4.1.1   The Disquotation Problem

We are all familiar with the thought that disquotation is somehow essential to reference. You can always specify the referents of the terms in your home language disquotationally. Here is an example:

(1) 'Socrates' refers to Socrates.

This sentence is obviously true. More generally, we always get a true sentence when we substitute an English referring term into the following disquotational scheme:

(D) '*a*' refers to *a*.[4]

Some philosophers, the *disquotationalists*, have gone so far as to say that the instances of (D) collectively tell us all that there is to know about reference. But even if you think that that is going too far (and, for the record, I do), we can all surely agree that the relationship between reference and disquotation is a particularly intimate one. Reference just wouldn't be reference without disquotation![5]

However, things do not go well if we try to substitute a predicate into (D). The best we can do is something totally ungrammatical, like:

(2) # 'x is wise' refers to is wise.

We now seem to have a simple argument against the idea that predicates are referring expressions: disquotation is essential to reference; we cannot disquote predicates; so predicates do not refer.

---

[3] The argument to follow is a descendent of the one I presented in Trueman (2015). My hope is that what I have here substantially improves upon what I had there. Amongst other things, the new argument is fairly obviously immune to Price's (2016) objection.

[4] There are some apparent counterexamples, such as ' "I" refers to I'. I will return to them in §4.4.

[5] When I first wrote this paragraph, I was sure that everyone would agree. But since then I have discovered that Rieppel (2018) denies (1), along with all other instances of disquotation. However, I suspect that Rieppel and I are simply talking past each other. Rieppel is working with a *non-intentional* conception of reference (or as he prefers to call it, 'denotation'), and as I explain in §4.2, my conception of reference is resolutely intentional.

4.1.2 *The Solution*

There is, I think, only one way to save the idea of predicate-reference from the disquotation problem. We need to draw a sharp distinction between two different kinds of reference: one for singular terms and one for predicates. We could then say that the problem with (2) is that 'x refers to y' expresses term-reference, not predicate-reference. 'x refers to y' simply has the wrong form for predicate-reference: the second gap in 'x refers to y' is a gap for terms, not predicates. If we want to express predicate-reference, then we need to use an expression of the form '$R(x, Y)$': the first gap, marked x, is a gap for a term referring to a predicate, and the second gap, marked Y, is a gap for a predicate.

There is a very good question about which expression of this form we should use to express predicate-reference, and we will come back to it in Chapter 6, but for the time being, I will just use 'x predicate-refers to Y' as a new primitive.[6] (And when it is helpful, I will also write 'x term-refers to y' instead of just 'x refers to y'.) We can now disquote 'x is wise' as follows:

(3) 'x is wise' predicate-refers to is wise.

Of course, on the face of it, (3) looks no more grammatical than (2). But 'x predicate-refers to Y' is just a temporary stand-in, to be replaced with something better in Chapter 6. In the meantime just remember that 'x predicate-refers to Y' is my new addition to English, and (3) is grammatical by design.

4.1.3 *A Consequence*

Suppose that everything I have said so far is right. Predicates do not refer in the same sense as singular terms; they refer in their own, bespoke sense. We can now draw the following important consequence: term-reference and predicate-reference are so different that it would be *nonsense* to say that a term and a predicate refer in their different ways to the same thing. If we wanted to say that 'wisdom' term-refers to the same thing that 'x is wise' predicate-refers to, we would need to bind both the free variables in,

(4) 'wisdom' term-refers to y ∧ 'x is wise' predicate-refers to Y,

---

[6] In fact, things get a little bit more complicated. 'x predicate-refers to Y' is only fit for *monadic first-level* predicates. We will need different kinds of reference for different types of predicate. However, for now, I will keep things simple by focussing on the monadic first-level case. I discuss the dyadic case in §10.4, and the o-adic case in Chapter 11.

with a single existential quantifier. But that is not something we can do. The little y and the big Y are different kinds of variable, one in term-position and one in predicate-position, and no one quantifier could bind both of those variables at once.[7]

4.1.4   The Plan from Here

That, in a nutshell, is my argument. Disquotation is essential to reference, and so the notion of reference appropriate for predicates must allow us to disquote predicates. But predicate-reference will then be so different from term-reference that it will become literally impossible to say that a term and a predicate might co-refer.

Presented like that, I think the argument is straightforward enough. But that is just a preliminary sketch. Now we have to fill in the details. I will start in §4.2, by explaining why disquotation is essential to term-reference. Then, in §4.3, I will present the disquotation problem in more detail; much of this section will be spent arguing that disquotation is essential to predicate-reference in just the same way that it is essential to term-reference. After that, I will briefly pause in §4.4 to discuss the notion of substitution involved in the disquotation problem. I will then draw my distinction between term-reference and predicate-reference in §4.5. Finally, in §4.6, I will argue that it is nonsensical to imagine that one thing might be referred to by both a term and a predicate.

4.2   Preliminaries: Disquotation and Singular Terms

I want to place a great deal of weight on the relationship between reference and disquotation, so the first thing we need to do is get clearer on what this relationship actually is. We will start with the case where all goes well: singular terms. My hope is that everything I say in this section will strike you as more or less platitudinous. The point of articulating these platitudes is to pave the way for the disquotation problem, by reminding you of why disquotation is essential to term-reference.

What is so special about (1)?

(1) 'Socrates' refers to Socrates.

---

[7]   I am here disregarding the possibility of a cumulative type theory, for the reason given in §2.4.

Well, it is not really anything to do with what (1) *says*. All that (1) says is that a particular person, Socrates, has a particular name, 'Socrates'. And there is no essential relationship between a person and their name: we could have used 'Socrates' as a name for Plato rather than Socrates. However, we can begin to see what *does* make (1) special by imagining that 'Socrates' did refer to Plato. In that case, (1) would no longer say that 'Socrates' refers to Socrates; it would say that 'Socrates' refers to Plato, and so it would still be true. More generally, (1) would remain true no matter what 'Socrates' referred to.

The important thing about (1) is not, then, what it says; the important thing is how it is put together. (1) acts as a bridge principle, connecting our metalanguage to our object-language. From the object-language, we have the term 'Socrates', and from the metalanguage, we have the predicate ' "Socrates" refers to y'. (1) is there to make sure that our use of the metalinguistic predicate does not float free from our use of the object-linguistic term.

We use the term 'Socrates' to refer to a particular person. This is an *intentional* relation, in the following sense: if a referring term is used in a sentence, then that sentence says something *about* the object referred to by that term.[8] So we use 'Socrates' to talk about the referent of 'Socrates'. We use ' "Socrates" refers to y', on the other hand, to say of an object that 'Socrates' refers to it. It is obviously essential that these uses hook up with each other in the right way. In particular, it is essential that ' "Socrates" refers to y' be true of the person that we talk about when we actually use 'Socrates'; otherwise, ' "Socrates" refers to y' would have the wrong extension. And this is just what the truth of (1) guarantees. (1) is what you get when you slot the term 'Socrates' into the predicate ' "Socrates" refers to y':

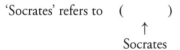

---

8   This sense of 'intentional' derives from Brentano (1874). (I am not making any claim about the relation between reference and our 'intentions' in the everyday sense.) Here is an example of what I have in mind: 'Socrates is wise' says about the referent of 'Socrates' that he is wise. It may be worth noting that the sense in which a sentence *says something about* an object is not quite the same as the sense in which a predicate *says something of* an object. Predicates do not express complete propositions; what 'x is wise' says of an object is not the sort of thing that you could *believe*, for example. By contrast, sentences do express complete propositions; you can believe what 'Socrates is wise' says about the referent of 'Socrates'. However, there is clearly an important relation to discern here: if α is a referring term and $\Phi(x)$ says of an object that it is F, then $\Phi(\alpha)$ says about the referent of α that it is F.

In general, if α is a referring term, then $\Phi(\alpha)$ is true iff $\Phi(\ )$ is true of the referent of α. So (1) is true iff ' "Socrates" refers to y' is true of the referent of 'Socrates'. In other words, (1) is true iff our use of ' "Socrates" refers to y' is tied to our use of 'Socrates' in just the way that it should be.[9]

Now compare (1) with (1′):

    (1) 'Socrates' refers to Socrates
    (1′) ' "Socrates" refers to y' is true of the referent of 'Socrates'.

These sentences have something in common: they are both true iff ' "Socrates" refers to y' is true of the referent of 'Socrates'. But there is also an important difference between them. (1′) *says that* ' "Socrates" refers to y' is true of the referent of 'Socrates'. (1), on the other hand, says no such thing. All that (1) says is that 'Socrates' refers to Socrates. Rather than *saying* that our uses of 'Socrates' and ' "Socrates" refers to y' are linked together in a certain way, the truth of (1) *actually links them together*: in (1), we *use*, rather than merely *mention*, both 'Socrates' and ' "Socrates" refers to y'.

This brings us to an observation that will prove important later: there is a sense in which the intended *meaning* of (1′) presupposes the *truth* of (1). Imagine that sentence (1) is not true, even though 'Socrates' is a successful referring term. In this scenario, ' "Socrates" refers to y' cannot be true of the referent of 'Socrates'. (Recall that if α is a referring term, then $\Phi(\alpha)$ is true iff $\Phi(\ )$ is true of the referent of α.) And in that case, ' "Socrates" refers to y' cannot say of an object that 'Socrates' refers to it: if it did, then it would have to be true of the referent of 'Socrates'![10] So we are imagining a scenario in which ' "Socrates" refers to y' does not mean what it actually means. But if ' "Socrates" refers to y' means something different, then (1′) as a whole must mean something different too. In (1′), we don't just mention ' "Socrates" refers to y' we also use it: it is embedded in 'the referent of "Socrates" ', which is shorthand for 'the thing that "Socrates" refers to'. So if ' "Socrates" refers to y' does not say of an object that 'Socrates' refers to it, then whatever (1′) says, it cannot be that ' "Socrates" refers to y' is true of the *referent of 'Socrates'*. Thus, if (1) were not true, then (1′) would not say what it is meant to say.[11]

---

9 I am greatly indebted here to Dummett's idea that the name/bearer relation is the prototype of reference. It is not easy to say exactly what Dummett had in mind, but it is clear that an important part of it was that reference is intentional, and that Dummett saw a connection between this intentionality and disquotation. See Dummett 1981a, 245–6 and 404–5; 1981b, 160–4.

10 This conclusion would not have followed if we had not stipulated that 'Socrates' is still a referring term in our imaginary scenario: if 'Socrates' did not refer, then there would be no referent of 'Socrates' for ' "Socrates" refers to y' to be true of.

11 When evaluating this conditional, it is essential that we continue to hold fixed the fact that 'Socrates' is a referring term (see fn. 10).

We can now see why disquotation is essential to term-reference. The truth of (1) acts as a bridge principle, linking our uses of 'Socrates' and ' "Socrates" refers to y': (1) is true iff ' "Socrates" refers to y' is true of the referent of 'Socrates'. What is more, (1) does not do this by *saying* that our uses of these expressions are linked together, like (1′) does. The truth of (1) *itself* links them together. As a result, (1) plays an indispensable role in our practice of using ' "Socrates" refers to y' to say of an object that 'Socrates' refers to it. If (1) were not true then the whole practice would fall apart, and sentences like (1′), which make use of ' "Socrates" refers to y', would not say what they are meant to.

4.3 The Disquotation Problem for Predicate-Reference

It is now time to start fleshing out the disquotation problem for predicate-reference. To get this problem going, we will make two new assumptions. First, we will assume that at least some predicates refer to properties. (I will use 'x is wise' as my example of a referring predicate, but you should feel free to swap it for any other predicate you like.) And second, we will assume that talk about predicate-reference takes the same form as talk about term-reference. More precisely, we will assume that 'x refers to y' expresses the reference relation for predicates as well as terms.[12]

With these assumptions in place, let's look again at our failed instance of disquotation for 'x is wise':

(2) # 'x is wise' refers to is wise.

Why should the fact that (2) is ungrammatical worry us? We saw in §4.2 that instances of disquotation act as indispensable bridge principles, connecting our metalanguage to our object-language. In this case, we are after a bridge between the object-linguistic predicate 'x is wise' and the metalinguistic predicate ' "x is wise" refers to y'. Predicate-reference is, I take it, every bit as intentional as term-reference: if a referring predicate is used in a sentence, then that sentence says something *about* the property referred to by that predicate. (You can think of this as a stipulation about what I mean by 'predicate-reference', if you like.[13]) So using 'x is wise' is a way

---

[12] Actually, that is a little bit more than we really need to assume. All that we require is that predicate-reference be expressed by a first-level predicate, '*Rxy*'. We will come back to this point in §8.1. But for now, it will helpful to keep things concrete by focussing on 'x refers to y'.

[13] Here is a rough example of what I have in mind: 'Socrates is wise' says about the referent of 'x is wise' that Socrates instantiates it. This is a *rough* example because it treats properties as if they were

of talking about the referent of 'x is wise'. And using ' "x is wise" refers to y' is meant to be a way of saying of an object that 'x is wise' refers to it. It is obviously essential that these uses be linked together in the right way: ' "x is wise" refers to y' must be true of the thing that we actually talk about when we use 'x is wise'. But if we try to supply this link with an instance of disquotation, then we end up with (2), which is not even grammatical.

At first, this problem may not seem too serious. Granted, we need a bridge principle that connects our use of ' "x is wise" refers to y' to our use of 'x is wise'. And clearly, (2) cannot be that bridge principle because it is ungrammatical. But maybe we can use some *other* principle as our bridge. The obvious suggestion would be:

(2′) ' "x is wise" refers to y' is true of the referent of 'x is wise'.

Unfortunately, however, (2′) cannot really provide the link that we require. We can see that (2′) falls short by reminding ourselves that we cannot replace (1), the disquotation sentence for 'Socrates', with (1′). When we assert (1′) we attempt to *say* that ' "Socrates" refers to y' is true of the referent of 'Socrates'. But as we saw, this attempt is successful only if (1) is true. Similarly, when we assert (2′), we attempt to *say* that ' "x is wise" refers to y' is true of the referent of 'x is wise'. But again, the success of this attempt depends on the truth of a further principle. This principle would not be an attempt to *say* that our uses of 'x is wise' and ' "x is wise" refers to y' are properly linked together. It would be a principle which directly linked our uses of those expressions together by *actually using them*: it would *use* 'x is wise' to pick out a property, and then *use* ' "x is wise" refers to y' to say of this property that 'x is wise' refers to it. But unfortunately, when we try to produce this principle, we end up with something like (2), which is ungrammatical.

This is the heart of the disquotation problem for predicate-reference. If we want to maintain that 'x is wise' is a referring predicate, and that ' "x is wise" refers to y' says of an object that 'x is wise' refers to it, then we must find some principle that can act as the crucial link between our uses of 'x is wise' and ' "x is wise" refers to y'. If (2) had been grammatical (a strange conditional, I know), then it would have been that principle. But it is not, and it seems that no other principle could possibly do the job.

objects, which is exactly what I am trying to argue against. However, we will not learn to speak without reifying properties until Chapter 6 (see also §10.3).

4.4 Disquotation and Sense-Substitution

Before we look at how we should respond to the disquotation problem, I would like to take a quick moment to deal with a potential line of objection. I have tried to argue that there is an absolutely essential relationship between reference and disquotation. But on the face of it, some terms seem to resist disquotation. Here is an example where disquoting a term seems to yield something ungrammatical:

(5a) # 'I' refers to I.

Fortunately, however, we have the means to deal with this case. The problem is that we *simple*-substituted 'I' into the gap in ' "I" refers to y', when we should have *sense*-substituted it.[14] If we assume that 'I' has the same sense as 'me', as I suggested back in §1.1, then the following will count as a result of this sense-substitution:

(5b) 'I' refers to me.

Moreover, even though we have been forced to swap 'I' for 'me' in (5b), we can still grant that (5b) provides the crucial disquotational link between our use of ' "I" refers to y' and our use of 'I'. To say that 'I' and 'me' have the same sense is to say that, from a logical point of view, these two terms are used in precisely the same way: they are both used to make exactly the same contribution to the senses of the sentences in which they appear.[15] So by linking our use of ' "I" refers to y' to our use of 'me', (5b) thereby links it to our use of 'I'.

Here is another example of failed disquotation:

(6a) # 'Londres' refers to Londres.

You might initially be tempted to dismiss this example. 'Londres' is a French term, and so it is hardly surprising that we cannot disquote it in English. However, we do still need a bridge principle which ensures that the English predicate ' "Londres" refers to y' is true of what the French term 'Londres' refers to. And at this point, it is useful again to think in terms of sense-substitution. Simple-substituting 'Londres' into the gap in ' "Londres" refers to y' might yield a mishmash of languages, but there is

---

[14] I am speaking slightly loosely here. As I emphasised in §1.3, sense-substitution is defined only in relation to meaningful whole sentences. This loose way of speaking is, however, harmless: to say that α can be sense-substituted into the gap in $\Phi(\ )$ is to say that α can be sense-substituted for β in any meaningful sentence $\Psi(\beta)$ where $\Psi(\ ) \approx \Phi(\ )$.

[15] Of course, in another, more grammatical sense, 'I' and 'me' are obviously *not* used in the same way. See §8.3.1 for related discussion.

no obstacle to sense-substituting it. Here are two possible results of this sense-substitution:

> (6b) 'Londres' refers to London
> (6c) 'Londres' se réfère à Londres.

(6b) will count as a result of this sense-substitution if 'London' has the same sense as 'Londres', and (6c) will if ' "Londres" se réfère à y' has the same sense as ' "London" refers to y'. But any result of sense-substituting 'Londres' into ' "Londres" refers to y' will provide the disquotational link that we are after.

Now let's return to our failed attempt to disquote a predicate:

> (2a) # 'x is wise' refers to is wise.

We can, of course, patch (2a) up and make it grammatical in various ways, such as:

> (2b) 'x is wise' refers to wisdom
> (2c) 'x is wise' refers to the property of being wise
> (2d) 'x is wise' refers to the property that an object has iff it is wise.

However, none of (2b–d) counts as a result of sense-substituting 'x is wise' into the gap in ' "x is wise" refers to y'.[16] Nothing can count as a result of this sense-substitution! The gap in ' "x is wise" refers to y' is a gap for singular terms, and as we saw in §2.3, predicates cannot be sense-substituted for singular terms. Of course, by exactly the same token, (2a) is not a result of this sense-substitution either. Rather, (2a) is just a handy illustration of the sort of nonsense we will come up with if we *try* to sense-substitute 'x is wise' into the gap in ' "x is wise" refers to y'.

4.5   A Different Type of Reference

The disquotation problem for predicate-reference relies on two assumptions: first, that at least some predicates refer to properties; second, that 'x refers to y' expresses the reference relation for predicates as well as terms. The problem forces us to reject one of these two assumptions. We could reject either one, but for the time being, I want to set aside the option of denying that predicates refer. I will return to this nominalistic option in

---

[16] To be clear, the only gap in ' "x is wise" refers to y' is the gap marked y; 'x' appears within quotation marks and so is merely mentioned.

Chapter 7, but before then, I want to get clearer on what is actually involved in thinking that predicates *do* refer.

If we do not want to give up on the idea that at least some predicates refer to properties, then we have no choice but to deny that 'x refers to y' expresses the reference relation for predicates as well as terms. How does that help with the disquotation problem? Well, the reason that we cannot use 'x refers to y' to disquote 'x is wise' is that the gap marked y is a gap for terms, not predicates. So to express predicate-reference, we need to use something of the form '$R(x, Y)$', where the Y marks a gap for predicates, not terms. We will look at what expression of this form we should use in Chapter 6, but for now, we will just use 'x predicate-refers to Y' as a placeholder. With it, we can disquote 'x is wise' as follows:

(3) 'x is wise' predicate-refers to is wise.

As it stands, (3) may not look grammatical, but that is just because we are using our placeholder, 'x predicate-refers to Y'. This problem will be dealt with when we find our real expression for predicate-reference in Chapter 6. In the meantime, the important point is this. If we use 'x predicate-refers to Y' to express predicate-reference, then we will use ' "x is wise" predicate-refers to Y' to say of a property that 'x is wise' refers to it. And (3) now provides the bridge that we need between our use of 'x is wise' and our use of ' "x is wise" predicate-refers to Y': in (3), we *use* 'x is wise' to refer to a property, and then *use* ' "x is wise" predicate-refers to Y' to say of this property that 'x is wise' refers to it.

4.6   No Co-reference between Terms and Predicates

I have just argued that if we want to keep hold of the idea that predicates refer to properties, then we must draw a fundamental distinction between term-reference and predicate-reference: term-reference is expressed by 'x term-refers to y', but predicate-reference is expressed by something of the form 'x predicate-refers to Y'.

However, as I briefly argued in §4.1, drawing this distinction has consequences. If we express term-reference and predicate-reference in these different ways, then it will become impossible to say that a term term-refers to the same thing that a predicate predicate-refers to. Saying that would be a matter of binding both of the variables in the following formula with a single existential quantifier:

(4) 'c' term-refers to y ∧ 'Fx' predicate-refers to Y.

But that is something we cannot do. Just imagine trying to form an instance of this generalisation. We would have to substitute one expression for both the variables in (4). Now, the notion of substitution people usually have in mind when they talk about forming an instance of a generalisation is simple-substitution, but in the current context, that seems wrongheaded. Better to use sense-substitution instead. So, we would need to sense-substitute one expression for both the variables in (4). But no *one* expression can be sense-substituted for *both* of these variables: we can sense-substitute a term but not a predicate for the y in ' "c" term-refers to y', and we can sense-substitute a predicate but not a term for the Y in ' "Fx" predicate-refers to Y'. It is not, therefore, possible to form an instance of the generalisation that would result from binding both the variables in (4) with a single existential quantifier,[17] and that surely just means that it is not possible to form that generalisation in the first place.

It is worth pre-empting a possible misunderstanding here. It is tempting to say that an existential generalisation is *true* only if we can produce a *true* instance of that generalisation. But whether or not that thought is right,[18] it was not the thought underwriting the preceding argument. Rather, my thought was that we cannot form a *meaningful* generalisation, true or false, unless we can produce a *meaningful* instance of that generalisation. And that is a thought that I cannot imagine gainsaying.[19]

4.7 Looking Ahead

That, then, is why I think it is nonsense to say that a term and a predicate co-refer. Of course, this is a slightly loose way of speaking. It is *not* nonsense to say that a term term-refers to the same thing that a predicate *term*-refers to. It is just false: predicates are not in the business of term-referring. And by exactly the same token, it is just false to say that a term *predicate*-refers to the same thing that a predicate predicate-refers to. What *is* absolutely nonsensical is saying that a term *term*-refers to the same thing that a predicate

---

[17] We will discuss quantifiers that bind variables for predicates, known as *second-order quantifiers*, in Chapter 7.
[18] It turns out that this thought is a little more problematic than it might seem. For discussion, see Levine 2013.
[19] We could use exactly the same kind of argument to show that it is nonsensical for predicates and *plural* terms to co-refer. This is worth noting because some philosophers (e.g., Mill 1843, ch. II §3) have suggested that predicates refer plurally to all the things they are true of.

predicate-refers to.[20] But that is a horribly long-winded thing to say, and so for ease, I will mostly speak loosely.

There is a sense in which everything I have said in this chapter is merely promissory. I have not yet said anything about what this new predicate-reference actually is; all I have so far given you is the utterly unilluminating 'x predicate-refers to Y' as a temporary means for expressing it. Until I say more, the conclusion of this chapter is merely schematic. I will take up the challenge of offering a positive story about predicate-reference in Chapter 6. But even that is not enough all by itself. After explaining what I think a Fregean realist should say predicate-reference is, I will still need to return to the nominalist thought that, really, predicates just are not referring expressions at all. I will eventually confront that thought, but not until Chapter 7.

Before any of that, though, I want to spend Chapter 5 explaining how to generalise the argument I have just given into an argument for a version of the Reference Principle.

---

[20]   Thanks to Price (2016, 2736–8) for pushing me to be clearer on this.

The Reference Principle

Back in Chapter 1, I introduced the *Reference Principle*:

(RP) Co-referring expressions are everywhere intersubstitutable *salva congruitate*.

I then suggested that we should read 'intersubstitutable' in (RP) as *sense-intersubstitutable*, which yields:

(RP$_2$) Co-referring expressions are everywhere sense-intersubstitutable.

After that, in Chapter 2, I argued that terms and predicates are nowhere sense-intersubstitutable. (RP$_2$) would therefore have us conclude that terms and predicates do not co-refer. But we actually reached a much more striking conclusion than that by the end of Chapter 4: it is *nonsense*, not false, to say that terms and predicates co-refer. This suggests that, rather than working with (RP$_2$), we should move over to another new version of (RP). But before we can formulate this new principle, we will need some new notation.

In this chapter, I will use 'x refers$_\alpha$ to ( )' to express the appropriate notion of reference for expressions of α's type; the first gap, marked x, is a gap for a term referring to α, and the second gap, whose type I have not marked, is a gap into which α can be sense-substituted.[1] The idea behind this notation is a generalisation of what I said about predicate-reference in Chapter 4. I argued that if we want to talk about predicate-reference, then we need to use a notion of reference that allows us to disquote predicates. And, of course, that is not something special about predicates: in general,

---

[1] I have just stretched my definition of sense-substitution a little bit. What does it mean to say that α can be sense-substituted into the second of the *two* open gaps in $\Phi( )_1( )_2$? This will do for now: α can be sense-substituted for γ in any possible meaningful sentence $\Psi(\beta)_1(\gamma)_2$ where $\Psi( )_1( )_2 \approx \Phi( )_1( )_2$.

if we want to talk about the reference of an expression α, then we must use a notion of reference that allows us to disquote α.[2]

I can now present my final version of (RP):

> (RP$_3$) If it makes sense to say that α refers$_\alpha$ to what β refers$_\beta$ to, then α and β are everywhere sense-intersubstitutable.[3]

It is worth emphasising how different this is from any other version of (RP) we have so far considered. Two expressions do not need to actually co-refer for (RP$_3$) to tell us that they are everywhere intersubstitutable. True or false, if it makes any sense at all to say that they co-refer, then they are everywhere intersubstitutable.

The aim of this chapter is to show how we can generalise the argument about terms and predicates into an argument for (RP$_3$).

5.1 Sense-Substitution

To begin with, it might be useful to briefly remind ourselves of the definition of *sense-substitution*:

> To sense-substitute β for the displayed occurrence of α in a meaningful sentence $\Phi(\alpha)$ is to construct a meaningful sentence $\Psi(\gamma)$ such that:
>
> (a) $\Psi(\ ) \approx \Phi(\ )$
> and (b) $\gamma \approx \beta$.

Recall that $\approx$ expresses the *has the same sense* relation. As I explained in §1.2, the intuitive picture behind this definition is that when we sense-substitute one expression for another in a given sentence, we are, in effect, substituting one *sense* for another in a given *proposition*.

With this definition fresh in our minds, I will now outline the premises of my argument.

---

[2] In case there is any confusion, I am not suggesting that every expression has its own unique notion of reference. If α and β are everywhere sense-intersubstitutable, then I see no reason to deny that 'x refers$_\alpha$ to ( )' and 'x refers$_\beta$ to ( )' both express the same notion of reference.

[3] Unlike (RP$_1$) and (RP$_2$), (RP$_3$) must be read as a schema rather than a universal generalisation. That is because 'α' and 'β' both play two roles in (RP$_3$): they appear in the positions of terms and in undetachable subscripts. In particular, (RP$_3$) is intended to be a schematic generalisation over possible *meaningful* expressions.

5.2   Premise 0

The first premise is a structural assumption about the *has the same sense as* relation:

(0) $\approx$ is an equivalence relation over meaningful expressions.

I have labelled this Premise 0 rather than 1 because all of my appeals to it will be tacit. If we paused to mention (0) every time we needed to chain together various uses of $\approx$, or reverse their order, or whatever, then the proof of (RP$_3$) would be totally unreadable.

(0) is a natural assumption to make. It is probably fair to say that we slip into it without ever really pausing to think about it. At the same time, however, (0) is not *entirely* unproblematic. A word has a sense only in a given language, as used by a particular speaker, in a particular context, etc. And, of course, one and the same word can have different senses on different occasions. Here is one example:

(a) My car is red.
(b) Red is a warm colour.

'Red' makes different contributions to the senses of (a) and (b): it makes the contribution of a predicate in (a)[4] and the contribution of a term in (b). As I explained in §2.5, I take this to show that 'red' has different senses in (a) and (b). (More on that in §5.5.) So here we seem to have a counterexample to the claim that *has the same sense as* is reflexive: 'red' – as it appears in (a) – does not have the same sense as 'red' – as it appears in (b).

Happily though, there is a straightforward way around this kind of problem. Rather than individuating expressions purely orthographically, we can incorporate a *sameness of sense* requirement into their criteria of identity:

$\alpha = \beta$ iff (i) α and β are orthographically equivalent, and (ii) $\alpha \approx \beta$.

If we individuate expressions in this way, 'red' no longer serves as a counterexample to the reflexivity of $\approx$. Instead, it just turns out that the 'red' in (a) is a distinct expression from the 'red' in (b); they are orthographically equivalent, but they have different senses. This obviously generalises: if we include (ii) in our criteria of identity for expressions, then there can be *no* counterexamples to the reflexivity of $\approx$. And, more generally, the assumption that $\approx$ is an equivalence relation seems unobjectionable.

---

[4] For the sake of this example, I am assuming that the copula is semantically vacuous. That is a controversial assumption (see §8.4), but for now, I will set any worries about it to one side.

5.3 Premise 1

Here is Premise 1:

(1) α can be sense-substituted into the second gap in 'x refers$_\alpha$ to ( )'.

This premise is just a record of what our new notation – 'x refers$_\alpha$ to ( )' – was designed to do: 'x refers$_\alpha$ to ( )' can express the appropriate notion of reference for α only if we can sense-substitute α into its second gap.

Mightn't there be a meaningful expression, α, for which there is no appropriate notion of reference? Maybe, but in that case, the relevant instances of (RP$_3$) will be vacuous. 'x refers$_\alpha$ to ( )' will be meaningless, and so the antecedent will be false: it will not make sense to say that α refers$_\alpha$ to what β refers$_\beta$ to. (I will have more to say about the meaning of sentences which begin 'It does not make sense to say that...' in §9.2.) In what follows, then, I will make the more interesting assumption that there are appropriate notions of reference for the expressions under discussion.

5.4 Premise 2

The next premise is a bit of a nightmare to look at, but really it is just an application of the idea that we can form a generalisation only if it is possible to form an instance of that generalisation:

(2) If it makes sense to say that α refers$_\alpha$ to what β refers$_\beta$ to, then it is possible to sense-substitute a single expression into the gaps in both $\ulcorner A$ refers$_\alpha$ to ( )$\urcorner$ and $\ulcorner B$ refers$_\beta$ to ( )$\urcorner$, where A is some term referring to α and B is some term referring to β.

The corner-quotes in this premise are Quine-quotes, which, unfortunately, we cannot get away with omitting. Since Quine-quotes can be a headache, it might be useful to give an example. Let α be 'Bertrand'. A needs to be a term referring to α, so let A be ' "Bertrand" '. And since 'Bertrand' is a term, let's assume that its reference-predicate is 'x term-refers to y'. With all this in place, $\ulcorner A$ refers$_\alpha$ to ( )$\urcorner$ is ' "Bertrand" term-refers to y', and $\ulcorner A$ refers$_\alpha$ to $\alpha\urcorner$ is ' "Bertrand" term-refers to Bertrand'.

5.5 Premise 3

A little more needs to be said about the final premise:

(3) If β can be sense-substituted for α in $\Phi(\alpha)$ but not for γ in $\Psi(\gamma)$, then $\alpha \not\approx \gamma$.

We need (3) to make sure that sense-substitution behaves as it should. Suppose that β is everywhere sense-substitutable for α and that α is everywhere sense-substitutable for δ. It should follow that β is everywhere sense-substitutable for δ. But without (3), it doesn't. Sense-substituting α for δ in $\Omega(\delta)$ produces another sentence, $\Psi(\gamma)$. γ must have the same sense as α, but it does not have to be the very same expression as α. As a result, the fact that β can always be sense-substituted for α does not automatically imply that it can be sense-substituted for γ. However, with the help of (3), we can complete the inference. Let $\Phi(\alpha)$ be any sentence featuring an occurrence of α.[5] By hypothesis, β can be sense-substituted for α in $\Phi(\alpha)$. And since α has the same sense as γ, it follows by (3) that β can be sense-substituted for γ in $\Psi(\gamma)$. The results of this substitution will count as results of sense-substituting β for δ in $\Omega(\delta)$.

Premise (3) also has an important corollary: if β can be sense-substituted for *some* occurrence of α, then β can be sense-substituted for *every* occurrence of α. To see this, just let γ in (3) be identical to α:

If β can be sense-substituted for α in $\Phi(\alpha)$ but not for α in $\Psi(\alpha)$, then $\alpha \not\approx \alpha$.

By (0), α must have the same sense as α. So if β can be sense-substituted for α in $\Phi(\alpha)$, then it can also be sense-substituted for α in $\Psi(\alpha)$.

That is what (3) does. But do we have any reason to think that (3) is actually true? Well, sense-substitution is a way of substituting one sense for another, and the sense of a subsentential expression is its contribution to the senses of the sentences in which it appears. So sense-substitution is a way of substituting these contributions. Now suppose that β can be sense-substituted for α in $\Phi(\alpha)$, but not for γ in $\Psi(\gamma)$. It surely follows that α and γ make different kinds of contribution to the senses of $\Phi(\alpha)$ and $\Psi(\gamma)$: the contribution of α can be replaced by the contribution of β, but the contribution of γ cannot. To repeat, differences in contribution are differences in sense. So α and γ have different senses.

I can think of only one way of trying to resist this argument. The sense of a subsentential expression is its contribution to the senses of the sentences in which it appears. That much is non-negotiable; it is just part of how I

---

[5]   I am assuming here that every (possible) meaningful subsentential expression appears in at least one (possible) meaningful sentence.

define 'sense'. However, there is space for disagreement about how to *apply* this definition. Let's return to an earlier example:

(a) My car is red.
(b) Red is a warm colour.

'Red' makes different contributions to the senses of (a) and (b), and I take this to show that 'red' has two different senses in (a) and (b). But you might instead say that all it really shows is that the sense of 'red' is *multifaceted*. That is, you might say that we should characterise the contribution that 'red' makes to the senses of whole sentences like this: 'red' makes the contribution of a predicate in some sentential contexts – e.g., (a) – and the contribution of a term in others – e.g., (b). If this is how we thought of the sense of 'red', then my argument for (3) would no longer go through: expressions which only ever functioned as predicates could be sense-substituted for 'red' in (a) but not in (b), even though 'red' has the same (multifaceted) sense in both sentences.[6]

We have here two broad models of sense. On my preferred model, sense is not multifaceted. Once you have identified the contribution that a sub-sentential expression makes to the sense of a single sentence, you know all there is to know about the sense of that expression.[7] On the alternative multifaceted model, you cannot always identify the sense of an expression just by identifying the contribution it makes to the sense of just one sentence; sometimes you need to identify the contributions it makes to the senses of a range of different sentences.

There is, I think, good reason to choose my preferred model. Sense is supposed to be the aspect of meaning that is relevant to logic. It would, then, be counterproductive to adopt a model of sense which allows two expressions to have the same sense even if they have different logical properties. 'Red' does have importantly different logical properties in (a) and (b); for example, 'red' can be negated in (a), but not in (b). So we should reject the model of sense as multifaceted, since it does allow 'red' to have the same sense in (a) and (b). We should instead stick with my preferred model, which tells us that α and γ have the same sense iff they make exactly the same contributions to the senses of $\Phi(\alpha)$ and $\Psi(\gamma)$. This model both implies that 'red' has different senses in (a) and (b), and validates my argument for (3).

---

[6] Thanks to Nick Jones for pushing this objection.
[7] Recall that I am individuating expressions partly by their sense, so I would say that the 'red' in (a) is a different expression from the 'red' in (b).

5.6   The Proof

Here are all of the premises listed together:[8]

(0) $\approx$ is an equivalence relation over meaningful expressions.

(1) α can be sense-substituted into the second gap in 'x refers$_\alpha$ to ( )'.

(2) If it makes sense to say that α refers$_\alpha$ to what β refers$_\beta$ to, then it is possible to sense-substitute a single expression into the gaps in both $\ulcorner A$ refers$_\alpha$ to ( )$\urcorner$ and $\ulcorner B$ refers$_\beta$ to ( )$\urcorner$, where A is some term referring to α and B is some term referring to β.

(3) If β can be sense-substituted for α in $\Phi(\alpha)$ but not for γ in $\Psi(\gamma)$, then $\alpha \not\approx \gamma$.

With these four premises, we can argue as follows:

Suppose that it makes sense to say that α refers$_\alpha$ to what β refers$_\beta$ to. It follows from (2) that we can sense-substitute one expression γ into the gaps in both $\ulcorner A$ refers$_\alpha$ to ( )$\urcorner$ and $\ulcorner B$ refers$_\beta$ to ( )$\urcorner$. Therefore, we can construct a sentence $\Phi(\phi)$ such that,

(a) $\Phi( ) \approx \ulcorner A$ refers$_\alpha$ to ( )$\urcorner$

and (b) $\phi \approx \gamma$,

and another sentence $\Psi(\psi)$ such that,

(a) $\Psi( ) \approx \ulcorner B$ refers$_\beta$ to ( )$\urcorner$

and (b) $\psi \approx \gamma$.

By (1) it is possible to sense-substitute α into the gap in $\ulcorner A$ refers$_\alpha$ to ( )$\urcorner$, and thus we can construct a sentence $\Sigma(\sigma)$ such that:

(a) $\Sigma( ) \approx \ulcorner A$ refers$_\alpha$ to ( )$\urcorner \approx \Phi( )$

and (b) $\sigma \approx \alpha$.

Similarly, by (1) it is possible to sense-substitute β into the gap in $\ulcorner B$ refers$_\beta$ to ( )$\urcorner$, and thus we can construct a sentence $\Delta(\delta)$ such that:

(a) $\Delta( ) \approx \ulcorner B$ refers$_\beta$ to ( )$\urcorner \approx \Psi( )$

and (b) $\delta \approx \beta$.

It is now trivial that we can sense-substitute α for ϕ in $\Phi(\phi)$: $\Sigma(\sigma)$ counts as a result of this sense-substitution. And since $\phi \approx \gamma \approx \psi$, it follows by (3) that we can sense-substitute α for ψ in $\Psi(\psi)$. So we can construct a sentence $\Lambda(\lambda)$ such that:

---

[8]   Like (RP$_3$), (1) and (2) must be read as schematic generalisations. And for the purposes of the following argument, (3) may as well be a schema too.

(a) $\Lambda(\ ) \approx \Psi(\ ) \approx \ulcorner \mathcal{B} \text{ refers}_\beta \text{ to } (\ ) \urcorner$
and (b) $\lambda \approx \alpha$.

Since $\Lambda(\ ) \approx \ulcorner \mathcal{B} \text{ refers}_\beta \text{ to } (\ ) \urcorner \approx \Delta(\ )$, $\Lambda(\lambda)$ also counts as a result of sense-substituting α for δ in $\Delta(\delta)$. And as $\delta \approx \beta$, it follows by (3) that α can be sense-substituted for every occurrence of β.

So, from the supposition that it makes sense to say that α refers$_\alpha$ to what β refers$_\beta$ to, we can infer that α can be sense-substituted for every occurrence of β; and, of course, exactly the same reasoning will also allow us to infer from this supposition that β can be sense-substituted for every occurrence of α. Thus we have (RP$_3$).

CHAPTER 6

Fregean Realism

For our purposes, a *realist* is anyone who thinks that at least some predicates refer to properties. In Chapter 4, I argued that realists need to draw a distinction between two kinds of reference: one for terms, expressed by 'x term-refers to y', and one for predicates, expressed by 'x predicate-refers to Y'. I will call any realist who draws this distinction a *Fregean realist*, since Frege (1892a) famously insisted that it was a mistake to say that terms and predicates could co-refer.

My aim in this chapter is to get clearer on what Fregean realism actually amounts to. To be clear, this is not a historical project. The aim is not to figure out what the real life historical Frege thought. Fregean realism is 'Fregean' only in the sense that it incorporates Frege's insight that it is a mistake to think of properties as a kind of object.[1] The real aim, then, is to figure out what a realist who is Fregean in this minimal sense should say about predicate-reference. 'x predicate-refers to Y' was only ever meant to serve as a temporary placeholder, and now we need to fill in some details about what predicate-reference actually is. I should also be clear now that I do not plan to offer any arguments *for* the realist assumption that predicates refer to properties in this chapter. For now, I will just take that for granted. What I want to know more about is the relation which is supposed to connect a predicate to the property it refers to. We will return to the deeper question of why we should think that predicates refer in the first place in Chapter 7.

But before we get going, I would like to acknowledge the debt that this whole chapter owes to Dummett's (1981a, 211–19) remarkable discussion of predicate-reference. Everything I am about to say is nothing more than a development – or in some places just a tidying up – of what Dummett

---

[1] Indeed, it is debatable whether Frege realised that this insight required him to draw a distinction between term-reference and predicate-reference. Heck and May (2006) think that he did; Furth (1968) thought that he did not.

already said.[2] However, in an effort to keep the discussion as clear as possible, I will not offer an extended commentary on Dummett's discussion in the main text. For all of its insights, Dummett's discussion was much more complicated than it needed to be, and included a number of distracting elements which did not need to be there.[3] (It probably goes without saying that something Dummett wrote was brilliant but difficult.) I will, then, largely relegate discussion of Dummett to footnotes, safe in the knowledge that his influence on this chapter will be unmissable.

6.1 Predicate-Reference and Satisfaction

My initial proposal is that Fregean realists should use the following to express predicate-reference:

(S) $\forall y(y$ satisfies $x \leftrightarrow Yy)$.[4]

If they accept this proposal, this is how they will specify what 'x is a horse' refers to:

(1) $\forall y(y$ satisfies 'x is a horse' $\leftrightarrow y$ is a horse).

On this proposal, then, all that Fregean realists mean when they say that a predicate refers to a property is that a predicate has a satisfaction condition.[5] Now, this might seem like an extremely odd thing to say. The idea that we should use satisfaction conditions to account for the semantic roles of

---

[2] I should also like to acknowledge the influence of Furth 1968.

[3] Most notable here is Dummett's reliance on what we might call *predicate-radicals*, which are expressions like 'tall', 'a horse', 'laughing'. According to Dummett (1981a, 214), or at least Dummett's Frege, predicate-radicals are just predicates, and 'the copula is a mere grammatical device, with no content'. But as far as I can tell, these predicate-radicals are not really needed. All that speaks in favour of including them is that predicate-radicals can appear as the grammatical subjects in sentences, and predicates proper cannot (Frege 1879, §9; Dummett 1981a, 216). And while that can be pedagogically helpful, that help is totally offset by the confusion that predicate-radicals have brought with them (see Dudman 1976, §II; Wiggins 1984, 316–7; Russinoff 1992, 75–7; Gaskin 1995, 164; Wright 1998, 77–81).

[4] Strictly speaking, we should read 'x predicate-refers to Y' as: x is a predicate $\wedge \forall y(y$ satisfies $x \leftrightarrow Yy)$. Without the 'x is a predicate' conjunct, every non-term would automatically predicate-refer to the empty property, because nothing satisfies a non-predicate. However, this extra conjunct can be safely omitted whenever it is clear that we are in fact dealing with a predicate.

[5] The same proposal, or at least very similar proposals, have been made by: Furth (1968, 45), Heck and May (2006, 10–12, 2013, 844–7), Noonan (2006, 168) and Jones (2016, §2). Dummett (1981a, 213–18) made a slightly different recommendation: '$\forall y(y$ is what x stands for $\leftrightarrow Yy)$', where the 'is' is the 'is' of predication, not identity. However, it seems to me that Dummett's 'is what x stands for' is best thought of as the result of binding the variable Y in '$\forall y(y$ satisfies $x \leftrightarrow Yy)$' with a second-order definite description operator. If that is right, then Dummett's stand-in differs from (S) only by containing a redundant second-order generalisation.

predicates is very familiar, but it is normally presented as an *alternative* to thinking of predicates as referring expressions. Rather than accounting for the role of a predicate by picking out something in the world for it to refer to, we do it simply by stating the conditions under which an object would satisfy that predicate. So with what right can the Fregean realists now co-opt (S) as their expression for predicate-reference?

The best way to answer this question is to turn it around. Why is it so tempting to insist that instances of (S) do *not* attribute referents to predicates? The answer is, I believe, that (S) does not have a gap for a *singular term* which refers to a property. And this answer is perfectly reasonable if we assume that properties are objects (or that they would have to be objects if they were anything at all). But this will not impress a Fregean realist. For her, predicates *and only predicates* can refer to properties. So of course there are no gaps in (S) for *singular terms* which refer to properties. However, there is a gap for a *predicate* in (S), and thus by the Fregean realist's lights, an instance of (S) expresses a relation between a predicate and a property. For example, a Fregean realist will read (1) as expressing a relation between the predicate 'x is a horse' and the property that 'x is a horse' stands for, just as,

(2) 'Socrates' refers to Socrates,

expresses a relation between the term 'Socrates' and the object that 'Socrates' stands for. Of course, the Fregean realist reads (1) in this way only because she takes it for granted that, *in some sense*, predicates are referring expressions – all we are currently trying to do is spell out the exact nature of the relation between predicate and property – and we have not yet seen any reason to agree with the Fregean realist on this. We will come back to this fundamental issue in Chapter 7. But all that matters now is that for a Fregean realist, (S) *does* express a word-world relation, between a predicate and a property.

But why should a Fregean realist take *this* word-world relation to be predicate-reference? Well, pretty much all of Chapter 4 was spent belabouring the relationship between disquotation and the intentionality of reference, and so the first thing to say is that (S) *does* allow us to disquote predicates. (1) is an example of this sort of disquotation, and everyone agrees that (1) is true; it is guaranteed to be by the fact that 'x is a horse' has any satisfaction condition at all. And, of course, the same goes for every other predicate. Thus, (S) satisfies at least one necessary condition for expressing our intentional concept of predicate-reference.

Nonetheless, it is natural to object that (S) is too *coarse-grained* to express predicate-reference. Consider the following two instances of (S):

(3a) $\forall y(y$ satisfies 'x is a unicorn' $\leftrightarrow y$ is a unicorn)

(3b) $\forall y(y$ satisfies 'x is an even prime number greater than 2' $\leftrightarrow y$ is a unicorn).

There are no unicorns and there are no even prime numbers greater than 2, so (3a) and (3b) are both true. Thus, if Fregean realists used (S) to express predicate-reference, they would be forced to say that 'x is a unicorn' and 'x is an even prime number greater than 2' co-refer. This result would strike many realists as intuitively absurd. However, while there may be some justice to the objection that (S) is too coarse-grained, this is not a judgement that should be left up to intuition. We need to ask: for what purpose is (S) too coarse-grained? And to answer this question, we need to get clearer on what it is that we want our notion of predicate-reference to do.

It will be useful to start by thinking about *term*-reference. As everyone has remarked at some time or another, co-referring terms are intersubstitutable *salva veritate* in extensional contexts. Of course, we do not say this because we have tried substituting lots of co-referring terms in lots of extensional contexts, and found that all of these substitutions were truth-preserving. We say it because term-reference plays a particular role in our semantic theorising. Roughly, once we have said which object a given term refers to, we have said all that there is to say about that term's *semantic role* in extensional contexts – i.e., about the role that that term plays in determining the truth-values of the extensional sentences in which it appears. For example, 'Socrates' helps to determine the truth-value of 'Socrates is wise' simply by referring to Socrates: 'Socrates is wise' is true iff the referent of 'Socrates' – i.e., Socrates – satisfies 'x is wise'.

(S) clearly plays a similar role in extensional contexts.[6] If two predicates have materially equivalent satisfaction conditions, then they are intersubstitutable *salva veritate* in extensional contexts. And, again, this intersubstitutability is a consequence of the theoretical role that satisfaction plays. Roughly, once we have said which satisfaction condition a given predicate has, we have said all that there is to say about that predicate's semantic role in extensional contexts. For example, 'x is a horse' helps to determine the truth-value of 'Shergar is a horse' simply by being satisfied by, and only by,

---

[6] Really, I should say that *the relationship picked out by* (S) plays a similar role, but that strikes me as a little pedantic.

horses: 'Shergar is a horse' is true iff the referent of 'Shergar' satisfies 'x is a horse' – i.e., iff it is a horse.

So we can disquote a predicate with an instance of (S), and an instance of (S) is all we need to characterise a predicate's semantic role in extensional contexts. This seems warrant enough to conclude that if we only had to deal with extensional contexts, then (S) would be the proper expression of predicate-reference. But of course, in reality, we also have to deal with a huge variety of intensional contexts, and it is in relation to these contexts that (S) starts to appear too coarse-grained. For example, the fact that two predicates are materially equivalent is no guarantee that they will have the same semantic role in modal contexts: '$\Diamond \exists x(x$ is a unicorn)' is true (I assume), but '$\Diamond \exists x(x$ is an even prime number greater than 2)' is not. Now, as it happens, modal contexts are not too hard to deal with. All we need to do is swap (S) for something along these lines:

(Modal-S) $\forall w \forall y(y$ satisfies x relative to $w \leftrightarrow Yy$ at w).[7]

And even if we make this swap, it will *still* be right to say that what it is for a predicate to refer is for it to have a satisfaction condition; the only relevant difference between (S) and (Modal-S) is how coarsely they individuate those satisfaction conditions.

Unfortunately, however, modal contexts are only the tip of the intensional iceberg. There are also *hyper-intensional* contexts, like 'Sharon believes that...' and 'Sharon wonders whether...', to deal with. In contexts like these, substituting one predicate for another can change the truth-value of a sentence, even if they are co-extensive relative to every world. For example, 'Sharon wonders whether Hesperus is Phosphorus' can be true even if 'Sharon wonders whether Hesperus is Hesperus' is false, despite the fact that 'x is Hesperus' and 'x is Phosphorus' are co-extensive relative to every world.

It is undeniably difficult to offer an account of predicate-reference that can handle hyper-intensional contexts. But it is also difficult to offer an account of *term*-reference which can handle those contexts. It seems to me, then, that the best way to make progress on predicate-reference is to set hyper-intensional contexts to one side for now, and save them for another time. In fact, for the time being, it would be best to temporarily set aside *all* forms of intensionality and focus just on extensional contexts. That way, we will not be distracted by the challenges that intensionality poses

---

[7]   It is crucial here that whether y satisfies x relative to w does not depend on how people use x in w. So, for example, if a is a horse at w, then a satisfies 'x is a horse' relative to w, since we use 'x is a horse' to mean x *is a horse*, even if people in w use 'x is a horse' to mean x *is a cow*.

for reference in general, and we can instead centre all of our attention on *predicate*-reference in particular.

So until further notice, it will be my policy to focus on extensional contexts. Consequently, I will assume that (S) is the Fregean realists' expression for predicate-reference. There are two attitudes we could take to this policy. We could think of (S) as an approximation to predicate-reference that comes close enough for extensional contexts. Or we could take a more pluralistic attitude and deny that we are limited to only *one* conception of predicate-reference. Why not say that (S) expresses one conception of predicate-reference, suitable for extensional languages, and (Modal-S) expresses another, suitable for modal languages? Of course, these different conceptions of *predicate-reference* will be associated with different conceptions of *property*, but we will come to that in the next section.

6.2 Properties Are Satisfaction Conditions

In this section, I want to shift focus from predicate-reference to the referents of predicates, which up until now I have been calling 'properties'. What, according to a Fregean realist, do predicates refer to? Given what I just said in the last section, the answer to this question might seem obvious: if (S) expresses predicate-reference, then predicates surely refer to their satisfaction conditions. (This also seems like the right thing to say if we use (Modal-S) to express predicate-reference.) But things are not quite that simple. At least on the face of it, '( ) is a satisfaction condition' appears to be a first-level predicate, 'x is a satisfaction condition'; the gap marked x is a gap for singular terms, not predicates.[8] And according to Fregean realism, terms cannot refer to properties. So we cannot really say that predicates refer to satisfaction conditions. If we tried, the best we could do is something ungrammatical, like:

(4) # $\forall y(y$ satisfies 'x is a horse' $\leftrightarrow y$ is a horse) $\wedge$ is a horse is a satisfaction condition.

But worse, by the very same token, we cannot really call the referents of predicates 'properties' either: at least on the face of it, '( ) is a property' appears to be a first-level predicate, 'x is a property'. At this point, we are coming up against Frege's notorious concept *horse* paradox, which I briefly

---

[8] Van Inwagen (2004, 175–82) believes that properties are satisfaction conditions (or 'assertibles') in this first-level sense. It is important to be clear that this view is not a version of Fregean realism, for the reason about to be explained.

outlined in the Introduction. However, I do not want to get caught up in a full discussion of the paradox right now; that can wait until Chapter 9. For the time being, it will suffice just to explain what Fregean realists must do to respond to the problem at hand. They must acknowledge that, strictly speaking, it is misleading to call the referents of predicates 'properties', or 'satisfaction conditions', and come up with something better.

In particular, what the Fregean realists need is a second-level predicate of the form '$P(\mathbf{X})$', instead of a first-level predicate like 'x is a property'. So rather than saying 'The property *horse* is a property', Fregean realists would say something of the form: P(is a horse). Dummett was the first to explain clearly that this is what Fregean realists need, and he (1981a, 216) suggested that they choose '$\forall x(\mathbf{X}x \vee \neg\mathbf{X}x)$' for the job.[9] Dummett defended this choice by appealing to the following analogy. The first-level predicate 'x is an object' can be completed by, and only by, singular terms. Moreover, the result of completing this predicate with a referring singular term is always true. Similarly, the second-level predicate '$\forall x(\mathbf{X}x \vee \neg\mathbf{X}x)$' can be completed by, and only by, first-level predicates. Moreover, the result of completing this second-level predicate with a first-level predicate that has a determinate satisfaction condition is always true.

However, I am not completely satisfied by Dummett's suggestion. In the first place, as Wright (1998, 78–9) pointed out, it builds the law of the excluded middle into the very notion of a property; this probably would not have worried Frege, who was firmly committed to the law, but it may still worry some of the rest of us.[10] And perhaps more importantly, all that Dummett's justification really guarantees is that '$\forall x(\mathbf{X}x \vee \neg\mathbf{X}x)$' has the right *extension* to characterise the referents of predicates.[11] But whether '$\forall x(\mathbf{X}x \vee \neg\mathbf{X}x)$' can replace 'x is a property' is not just a question of extension; it is also a question of *sense*. To put it loosely, we do not just want a second-level predicate that is true of every property, but one which *says of a property that it is a property*. As I say, this is just a loose statement of what

---

9   Actually, that is not quite right. What Dummett actually recommended was that we use '$\mathbf{X}$ is something which everything either is or is not', where $\mathbf{X}$ marks a gap for one of Dummett's predicate-radicals (see fn. 3). So rather than saying 'The property *horse* is a property', we would say 'A horse is something which everything either is or is not'. However, as I mentioned in fn. 3, there is no real need to use a predicate-radical here. If we wanted to avoid all use of a formalisation, we could just say: everything either is a horse or is not a horse. The only benefit of using Dummett's formulation is that 'a horse' appears as the grammatical subject, but that is only a heuristic benefit, and only a slight one at that.

10 Wright followed up on his objection by suggesting that we use 'either there is no x such that $\mathbf{X}x$, or it is possible that there is some x such that $\mathbf{X}x$' to characterise the referents of predicates. However, I think that this suggestion is open to the same objection that I am about to present against '$\forall x(\mathbf{X}x \vee \neg\mathbf{X}x)$'.

11 '$\forall x(\mathbf{X}x \vee \neg\mathbf{X}x)$' also has the right Carnapian intension, but that still is not enough.

we want, but I will not try to tighten it up now; the requirement I have in mind should become clear when I present the second-level predicate which satisfies it.

Our route to this second-level predicate will be slightly indirect. Let's temporarily set aside the question of how Fregean realists should characterise the referents of predicates; we will carry on calling them 'properties' for now. Instead, I want to ask how Fregean realists should individuate properties. This has always been a troubling question for realists, but it takes on an extra significance in the current context. When we talk about identity, we are ordinarily talking about the relation expressed by the first-level predicate '$x = y$'. But predicates cannot be substituted into the gaps in a first-level predicate, and so we cannot use '$x = y$' to express identities between properties. Nonetheless, if Fregean realism is to count as any kind of *realism*, it must surely offer some way of expressing these identities. (It would be a mistake to *completely* abandon Quine's slogan: no entity without identity.)

Fregean realists need another distinction, then, this time between identity for objects and identity for properties: whereas the identity relation for objects is expressed by '$x = y$', the identity relation for properties can only be expressed by a second-level predicate of the form '$I(\mathsf{X}, \mathsf{Y})$'. In fact, Frege (1891–5, 175–7) himself saw the need for this distinction. He suggested that we use,

(I) $\forall x(\mathsf{X}x \leftrightarrow \mathsf{Y}x)$,

to express identity for properties. So rather than saying 'The property *horse* is not identical to the property *dog*', Frege would have us say:

(5) $\neg\forall x(x \text{ is a horse} \leftrightarrow x \text{ is a dog})$.

Frege defended this choice by appealing to the following analogy: if '$a = b$' is true, then 'a' and 'b' are intersubstitutable *salva veritate* in extensional contexts; similarly, if '$\forall x(Fx \leftrightarrow Gx)$' is true, then '$Fx$' and '$Gx$' are intersubstitutable *salva veritate* in extensional contexts. Now, this analogy is undoubtedly important and well worth noting, but if Fregean realists use (S) to express predicate-reference, then we can actually offer something a bit more definitive. If (S) expresses predicate-reference, then to say that two predicates co-refer – i.e., refer to one and the same thing – is to say that they have materially equivalent satisfaction conditions. It follows that '$\forall x(\mathsf{X}x \leftrightarrow \mathsf{Y}x)$' must express identity between properties.[12]

[12] Furth (1968, 44–5) offers a similar argument, but what he started with was not quite (S), and so what he ended up with was not quite (I).

We can now return to '$P(\mathbf{X})$', the second-level predicate that Fregean realists will use to characterise the referents of predicates. Given that they use (S) to express predicate-reference, I think that Fregean realists should take '$P(\mathbf{X})$' to be:

(P) $\exists Y \forall x (\mathbf{X}x \leftrightarrow Yx)$.

So rather than saying 'The property *horse* is a property', Fregean realists should say:

(6) $\exists Y \forall x (x$ is a horse $\leftrightarrow Yx)$.[13]

This suggestion is not open to either of the objections that I levelled against Dummett's suggestion of '$\forall x (\mathbf{X}x \lor \neg \mathbf{X}x)$'. First, using '$\exists Y \forall x (\mathbf{X}x \leftrightarrow Yx)$' to characterise the referents of predicates does not build the law of the excluded middle into the very notion of a property: '$P \leftrightarrow P$' is classically *and intuitionistically* valid. Second, there is reason to think that '$\exists Y \forall x (\mathbf{X}x \leftrightarrow Yx)$' has the right *sense*, and not just the right *extension*, to characterise the referents of predicates. Plausibly, we should understand 'x is an object' as '$\exists y (x = y)$'; roughly, this predicate says of an object that it is identical to something in the domain of the first-order quantifiers – i.e., the domain of objects. And as we have already seen, if (S) expresses predicate-reference, then '$\forall x (\mathbf{X}x \leftrightarrow Yx)$' expresses identity for properties. So, roughly, '$\exists Y \forall x (\mathbf{X}x \leftrightarrow Yx)$' says of a property that it is identical to something in the domain of the second-order quantifiers – i.e., the domain of properties. At any rate, this is the intuitive gloss for Fregean realists to put on '$\exists Y \forall x (\mathbf{X}x \leftrightarrow Yx)$'; we will look more closely at the way in which Fregean realists should understand second-order quantification in Chapter 7.

Of course, this is all based on the assumption that Fregean realists use (S) to express predicate-reference, and as I made clear at the end of the last section, this may not be an assumption that we want to make outside of extensional contexts. When it comes to modal contexts, for example, they might prefer to use (Modal-S) instead. If they do, then they should obviously use

(Modal-I) $\Box \forall x (\mathbf{X}x \leftrightarrow Yx)$,

to express identity for properties,[14] and

---

[13] Mendelsohn (1981, 80) also makes this suggestion, and at one point, Dummett (1981a, 219) comes close to making it too.

[14] In a recent and impressive paper, Dorr (2016) systemically explores the logic of property identifications, which are canonically expressed in the form 'To be F is to be G'. As Dorr (pp. 68–70)

(Modal-P) $\exists Y \Box \forall x (Xx \leftrightarrow Yx)$,

to characterise the referents of predicates. Now, as I also made clear at the end of the last section, we are not forced to think of (S) and (Modal-S) as being in competition with one another. Instead, we can say that they express *different* conceptions of predicate-reference, one suitable for extensional contexts and another suitable for modal contexts. Similarly, we are not forced to think of (P) and (Modal-P) as being in competition either. Instead, we can say that they express different conceptions of what it is to be the referent of a predicate, each corresponding to a different conception of predicate-reference.

6.3   The Property/Object Distinction

We started the last section with the simple thought that if (S) – or (Modal-S) – expresses predicate-reference, then predicates refer to their satisfaction conditions. But as we have seen, it is deeply misleading to say that 'x is a horse' refers to its satisfaction condition, or even that it refers to a property. If Fregean realists want to state clearly what sort of thing it is that they think 'x is a horse' refers to, they must say:

(7) $\exists X (\forall y (y$ satisfies 'x is a horse' $\leftrightarrow Xy) \wedge \exists Y \forall x (Xx \leftrightarrow Yx))$.[15]

However, I have to admit that I don't find sentences like (7) very easy to read at a glance. I think it would be a good idea, then, if Fregean realists stuck for the most part to the misleading formulation with which we began: predicates refer to their satisfaction conditions. Or just as good: properties are satisfaction conditions. Yes, this is misleading, but so long as we remember that this is just a loose and convenient way of speaking, a mere abbreviation of the much more complicated truth, then we will not actually be misled. So Fregean realists would not be doing anything wrong if they said,

(8)   'x is a horse' refers to the property *horse*,

explains, there are strong pressures pushing us to equate property identification with (Modal-I). However, Dorr (§§8–9) also explains how (and why) we might try to resist these pressures, and I strongly encourage any Fregean realists who want to individuate their properties more finely than (Modal-I) to read these sections of Dorr's paper. Importantly, however, a Fregean realist could not just help themselves to Dorr's work and say no more about it. They would also need to offer an account of predicate-reference which coheres with Dorr's fine-grained individuation of properties. I have no idea what such an account should look like.

[15]   If Fregean realists use (Modal-S) instead of (S), then instead of (8), they should have: $\exists X (\forall w \forall y (y$ satisfies 'x is a horse' relative to $w \leftrightarrow Xy$ at $w) \wedge \exists Y \Box \forall x (Xx \leftrightarrow Yx))$.

so long as they did not let themselves get suckered in by its superficial form. Really, (8) can be used to say what 'x is a horse' refers to *only when* it is used as a snappier version of:

(1) $\forall y(y$ satisfies 'x is a horse' $\leftrightarrow y$ is a horse).

Most importantly, Fregean realists must not let the loose way of speaking make them forget that according to their own view, it is *nonsense* to say that a property is an object. Properties are the referents of predicates; objects are the referents of terms; and, as we saw in §4.6, for the Fregean realist, it is nonsense to say that a term might co-refer with a predicate. But this is easily obscured when we indulge in the loose use of the word 'property'. Then there seems to be absolutely no problem with saying that a property is an object. But Fregean realists must remember that for them, trying to say that a property is an object is a matter of trying to bind both of the free variables (the big X and the little x) in the following formula with a single existential quantifier:

(9) $\exists Y \forall y(Xy \leftrightarrow Yy) \wedge \exists y(x = y)$.

But that is impossible (see §4.6), and so it is impossible to say that a property is an object. And, of course, it is equally impossible to say that a property is a particular kind of object: it is nonsense to say that a property is a set, or a mereological sum, or any other kind of object you like. And for that matter, it is also nonsense to identify an individual property with some object*s*, in the plural.

To put the point in its most general form: Fregean realists must reject as nonsense *any* attempt to say of an object what can be said of a property, or *vice versa*.[16] First-level predicates say things of objects; so since it is non-sensical to suppose that a property is an object, it is nonsensical to imagine that a first-level predicate could say something of a property. Second-level predicates, on the other hand, say things of properties; so since it is non-sensical to suppose that an object is a property, it is nonsensical to imagine that a second-level predicate could say something of an object. Properties and objects are in this sense *incomparable*: we have a way of saying things about objects, and a way of saying things about properties, but these two ways cannot be mixed and matched.[17]

---

[16] This is the root of the concept *horse* paradox, which I will discuss in Chapter 9.
[17] For essentially this argument, see Dummett 1981a, 177–8.

CHAPTER 7

Fregean Nominalism

We now understand Fregean realism pretty well: we know exactly what a Fregean realists mean when they say that predicates refer to properties, and we know not to take the surface form of the way they speak too seriously. But we still haven't seen a complete argument *for* Fregean realism. Back in §4.5, I argued that we have a choice: either draw the Fregean realists' distinction between term-reference and predicate-reference, or just deny that predicates refer. So far, we have focussed exclusively on the first option, but now it is time to consider the second.

Let's call anyone who thinks that predicates are not referring expressions a *nominalist*.[1] (This is a very narrow use of a very broad term; we will look at another kind of nominalism in §10.1.) Given the course that the book has taken so far, you might have expected this chapter to be spent presenting some kind of argument in favour of Fregean realism and against nominalism. But I have no such argument to offer. I don't think that there could be one. That is not because I think there is some sort of inevitable stalemate. It is because, in the end, I just cannot see any real difference between nominalism and Fregean realism. We can make out a substantial disagreement between nominalists and realists *only if we assume that properties are supposed to be a kind of object*. But that is an assumption which the Fregean realists reject as sheer nonsense, and thus there is no more disagreeing to do.

7.1 Two Different Ways of Reading (S)?

Nominalists and realists are meant to disagree over whether predicates are referring expressions. Now, if the realists thought that properties were

---

[1] These nominalists include Quine (1948, 9–11; 1960, §49), Devitt (1980) and Davidson (2005, ch. 7). To be clear, nominalists in my sense do not doubt that predicates form a significant semantic category; they just deny that predicates refer to anything. As I made clear in §3.5, this discussion is very much being carried out within our scheme of terms and predicates.

objects (call that *traditional realism*),[2] then I suppose it would be fairly easy to see what the disagreement would amount to. The traditional realist would make claims like this

(1) 'x is a horse' refers to the property *horse*,

and she would mean it in exactly the way that its form suggests: there is an object, called 'the property *horse*', and it is referred to by the predicate 'x is a horse'. The nominalist would deny (1), presumably on the grounds that she did not believe in this object.

But the Fregean realist does not want to say (1). Or at least, if she does, then she does not want you to take it too seriously. She thinks that,

(S) $\forall y(y$ satisfies x $\leftrightarrow$ Y$y)$,

expresses predicate-reference (at least in extensional contexts). So all a Fregean realist would mean by (1) is this:

(2) $\forall y(y$ satisfies 'x is a horse' $\leftrightarrow y$ is a horse).

Now, clearly, *that* is not something that any nominalist would ever want to deny. More than that, historically, it was the nominalists who stressed that we can account for the semantic roles of predicates in terms of their satisfaction conditions.[3] Of course, these nominalists face the same difficulties with hyper-intensional contexts as the Fregean realists (see §6.1), but as before, we can all agree to focus on extensional contexts for now.

Straightaway, then, the gap between nominalism and Fregean realism is a lot narrower than the gap between nominalism and traditional realism. But surely there *is* still a gap? Don't the nominalists and Fregean realists understand (S) in different ways? For a Fregean realist, (S) expresses a relation between a predicate and a property: (2) tells us that a given property is the referent of 'x is a horse'. But for a nominalist, (S) expresses no such relation: (2) just tells us how to decide whether a given object satisfies 'x is a horse'.

However, we know by now to be wary when a Fregean realist tells us that (S) expresses a relation between a predicate and a property. We know that we must not take her quite at her word. So what exactly does the difference between the two ways of reading (S) amount to?

---

[2] There have been too many traditional realists to list – there have been almost as many traditional realists as there have been realists – but here are three recent examples: Hale (2010), Wright (1998) and MacBride (2011a). However, I should mention that Hale and Wright would probably resist the label. See Chapter 8 for further discussion.

[3] See Quine 1960, §20 and §49; Devitt 1980, 96; Davidson 2005, 159–61.

7.2 Against a Quinean Suggestion

Here is one familiar suggestion, descending from Quine.[4] The difference between the ways in which nominalists and Fregean realists read (2),

(2) $\forall y(y$ satisfies 'x is a horse' $\leftrightarrow y$ is a horse),

is reflected in the different generalisations that they are willing to make. In particular, Fregean realists are happy to infer the following *second-order*[5] generalisation from (2):

(3) $\exists Y \forall y(y$ satisfies 'x is a horse' $\leftrightarrow Yy)$.

They are happy to make this inference because, by their lights, if (2) is true then the second-level predicate '$\forall y(y$ satisfies "x is a horse" $\leftrightarrow Yy)$' is *true of something*. The point to stress here is that for a Fregean realist, second-order quantification is wholly analogous to first-order quantification: first-order quantifiers quantify over a domain, and that domain is a collection of objects each of which could be referred to by a singular term; and in an exact analogy, second-order quantifiers quantify over a domain, and that domain is a collection of properties each of which could be referred to by a predicate.[6] Nominalists, on the other hand, refuse to admit that this generalisation is legitimate: although (2) is true, '$\forall y(y$ satisfies "x is a horse" $\leftrightarrow Yy)$' is not true *of* anything, and more generally, there are no properties for second-order quantifiers to quantify over.

I think that this Quinean suggestion is all wrong. That is because I am a *neutralist* about second-order quantification. According to neutralism, second-order quantification is *ontologically neutral* in the following sense: second-order quantification cannot generate an ontological commitment to a kind of entity that is not already generated by the use of predicates. (The same goes, mutatis mutandis, for every kind of quantification, but I want to focus on the second-order case.) Neutralism thus stands opposed to the Quinean idea that every kind of quantification is automatically quantification *over a domain of entities*. MacBride, who first coined the term 'neutralism', put it like this:

---

4 See Quine 1939, 704–8; 1951a, 93–4; 1953b, 145–6; 1970, 67; 1980b, 167.
5 For the purposes of this book, *second-order quantification* is quantification into the positions of first-level predicates. In general, the relation between the order of a quantifier and the level of a predicate is as follows: nth-order quantifiers are $(n + 1)$-level predicates and bind variables in the position of $(n - 1)$-level expressions (treating singular terms as level 0).
6 Not that it is always necessary to explicitly state what the second-order domain is. In full extensional second-order logic, the second-order domain is determined by the first-order domain: for any objects in the first-order domain, there is a property in the second-order domain that is instantiated by all, and only, those objects.

the role of a quantifier that binds a position X is to generalize upon the
semantic function of the category of constant expressions that occupy X;
how a quantifier generalizes depends upon *what* semantic function the corresponding category of constant expressions perform. (MacBride 2006, 445)

On the neutralist picture, we cannot just assume that second-order quantifiers quantify over anything. It is true that first-order quantifiers *quantify
over* objects, but that is only because singular terms *refer to* objects; the
first-order quantifiers are generalising upon the semantic function of the
singular terms. In exactly the same way, whether or not second-order quantifiers quantify over anything depends entirely on whether or not predicates
refer to anything: if predicates refer, then the second-order quantifiers will
quantify over the things that they can refer to; but if predicates do not
refer, then the second-order quantifiers will generalise upon their semantic
function in some other way.

If neutralism is right, then the disagreement between nominalists and
Fregean realists cannot be a disagreement about the step from (2) to (3).
When we combine nominalism with neutralism, we reach the conclusion
that second-order quantification is ontologically innocent: predicates do
not refer to anything, and so second-order quantifiers do not quantify over
anything. Given neutralism, then, nominalists have nothing to fear from
second-order quantification. They are just as free as Fregean realists to infer
(3) from (2).

So now we must ask again: what are the nominalists and Fregean realists
disagreeing about? It might be tempting to answer that they are disagreeing about how to understand (3): the Fregean realists read the second-order
quantifier in (3) as ranging over a domain of properties, and the nominalists
do not. But this answer gets us nowhere. On the neutralist picture, a disagreement about whether second-order quantifiers quantify over anything
is just a disagreement about whether predicates refer to anything. And that
is exactly where we began! We started off down this road precisely because
it is hard to see what is actually at stake when a nominalist and a Fregean
realist argue about predicate-reference.

The upshot of all of this is that if neutralism is true, then the disagreement between nominalists and Fregean realists cannot be, at bottom, a disagreement about second-order quantification. But why should we accept
neutralism? I have to admit, I have no knockdown argument. I can't really
imagine what a knockdown argument for neutralism would look like.
Nonetheless, I think that neutralism has a plausible ring about it. In fact,
to my mind, neutralism is one of those ideas which strikes you as obviously true the moment you first hear it. I suspect that it would have been

orthodoxy if it had not been for Quine's (e.g., 1970, 66–8) forceful polemics against second-order quantification. It certainly seems no coincidence that neutralism has started to make substantial gains now that Quine's influence is less keenly felt: neutralism, or something near enough, has been advocated by Prior (1971, ch. 3), Boolos (1985), Rayo and Yablo (2001), Williamson (2003, 458–60; 2013, §5.9) and Wright (2007).

But while neutralism may be growing in popularity, it is probably not yet mainstream enough for me to assume it without further comment. So over the next two sections, I will try to motivate neutralism. (If it turns out that I am pushing at an open door, then all the better.) As I said, I have no knockdown arguments to give. Instead, my aim is just to make neutralism look as natural and attractive an approach to second-order quantification as possible.

7.3   Non-Nominal Quantification

We can make neutralism feel a bit more familiar by looking at quantification in English. Of course, it will not help much to look at first-order quantification in English: it is (relatively) uncontroversial that first-order quantification is ontologically committing, but it is also uncontroversial that (at least some) terms are referring expressions. However, English appears to contain a number of *non-nominal* quantifiers – i.e., quantifiers that bind variables which are not in term-position – and examining them is quite instructive.[7] This point was very well made by Prior, who probably deserves to be known as the father of neutralism:

> We form colloquial quantifiers, both nominal and non-nominal, from the words which introduce questions – the nominal 'whoever' from 'who', and the non-nominal 'however', 'somehow', 'wherever', and 'somewhere' from 'how' and 'where'. No grammarian would seriously regard 'somewhere' as anything but an adverb; 'somewhere', in 'I met him somewhere', functions as the adverbial phrase 'in Paris' does in 'I met him in Paris'. We could also say 'I met him in some place', and argue that people who use such locutions are 'ontologically committed' to the existence of places as well as ordinary objects; but we don't have to do it that way. Similarly, no grammarian would count 'somehow' as anything but an adverb, functioning in 'I hurt him somehow' exactly as the adverbial phrase 'by treading on his toe' does in 'I hurt him by treading on his toe'. Once again, we might also say 'I hurt him in some way', and argue that by so speaking we are 'ontologically

---

[7]   For a helpfully broad range of examples of non-nominal quantification, see Sainsbury 2018, 46.

committed' to the real existence of 'ways'; but once again, there is no need to do it this way, or to accept this suggestion. (Prior 1971, 37)

Prior is arguing for more than neutralism about the adverbial quantifiers 'somewhere' and 'somehow': he does not just think that they are ontologically *neutral*; he thinks that they are ontologically *innocent* – i.e., that they carry no ontological commitments at all. However, it is also clear that the reason Prior thinks adverbial quantifiers are ontologically innocent is that he thinks adverbial constants, like 'by treading on his toe', are ontologically innocent too. So Prior is a neutralist about adverbial quantifiers, albeit a neutralist with nominalist prejudices. And it seems to me that neutralism about averbial quantifiers is overwhelmingly plausible: it would be very weird to think that you commit yourself to the existence of *ways* when you say 'I hurt him somehow', but you do not similarly commit yourself when you say 'I hurt him by treading on his toe'.

It seems, then, that English includes some ontologically neutral, non-nominal quantifiers. Unfortunately for us, however, it is not at all clear that English includes any second-order quantifiers – i.e., quantifiers which bind variables in *predicate*-position. We do say things like 'There is something that Wittgenstein was and Russell wasn't, namely Austrian', but the quantifier is here binding a variable in the position of the copula-free adjective 'Austrian', not the full predicate 'is Austrian'. We might try to finesse this difficulty by claiming that there is no semantic difference between 'Austrian' and 'is Austrian', on the grounds that the copula is semantically empty,[8] but it is not entirely obvious that this is true. A number of philosophers[9] have insisted that 'Austrian' and 'is Austrian' have quite different meanings: they claim that 'is Austrian' is incomplete in a sense in which 'Austrian' is not. Now, I do not want to suggest that these philosophers are right,[10] but the point remains that it would be highly controversial to equate the copula-free 'Austrian' with the predicate 'is Austrian'.

So, unless we want to take a controversial stance on the role of the copula, it seems that we cannot use observations about non-nominal quantification in English to offer any direct argument for neutralism about second-order quantification. Nonetheless, that does not mean that these observations are useless. We can still use them to provide some *indirect* support for neutralism. The fact that there seem to be non-nominal quantifiers undermines the old Quinean doctrine that all quantification must be quantification

---

[8] This is what Dummett (1981a, 213–6), Krämer (2014a, 168) and Rieppel (2016) do.
[9] E.g., Dudman 1976, 83–4; Wiggins 1984; Wright 1998, 77–81.
[10] For the record, I think that they are wrong, for precisely the reasons that MacBride (2006, 440–1) gives.

into term-position. Now, natural English may not contain any second-order quantifiers, but that gives us no reason to think that they could not be intelligibly added to the language, or included from the start in a formal system.[11] And if the other non-nominal quantifiers are ontologically neutral, why wouldn't the second-order quantifiers be neutral too?

7.4 Set-Theoretic Semantics

The previous section may be enough to soften some people up to neutralism, but there is still a big obstacle to overcome. Let's put natural languages like English to one side and focus on a formal second-order language, $\mathcal{L}$. If we want $\mathcal{L}$ to be more than an uninterpreted bunch of symbols, then at some point we will need to give it a semantics. And in the standard Tarskian semantics, we assign sets to second-order variables. So isn't it just obvious that on the Tarskian semantics, the second-order quantifiers quantify over those sets, just as the first-order quantifiers quantify over the objects assigned to the first-order variables?

Now, even if the answer to this question were 'yes', that would not be the death of neutralism. It would just mean that the neutralists had to cook up a new kind of semantics. The obvious idea would be to give a higher-order semantics in the style of Boolos (1985), which I outline in the appendix to this chapter (§7.A). Alternatively, we might give up on traditional semantic theorising altogether and try an inferentialist alternative (see Wright 2007).

But, more importantly, I think it would be a mistake to assume that second-order quantifiers quantify over sets just because we assigned sets to second-order variables. After all, we also assign sets to *predicates*, and few philosophers would want to say that it automatically follows that predicates *refer* to those sets, in the sense that using a predicate is a way of *talking about* the set assigned to it. Indeed, this was a point on which Quine (the arch-nominalist) was very clear. Although he wanted to deny that predicates refer to sets, he saw that he was not thereby forced to

> deny that there are certain sets connected with [predicates] otherwise than in the fashion of being [referred to]. On the contrary, in that part of the theory of reference which has to do with sets there is occasion to speak of the *extension of* a general term or predicate – the set of all things of which the predicate is true. One such occasion arises when in the theory of reference we treat the topic of validity of schemata of pure quantification theory …

---

[11] Williamson (2003, 459) makes just this point.

The general theory of quantificational validity thus appeals to sets, but the individual statements represented by the schemata of quantification theory need not; the statement '$(\exists x)(x$ is a dog . x is black)' involves, of itself, no appeal to the abstract extension of a predicate. (Quine 1951a, 95)[12]

But if we are not forced to say that predicates refer to the sets that they are assigned, why do we have to say that second-order quantifiers quantify over the sets that are assigned to the variables they bind?

To pursue this point further, it will be helpful to depart very slightly from the standard Tarskian semantics. I do not intend to go far. I just want to use a minor variation of the Tarskian semantics which will probably be familiar to anyone who has taught an introductory logic class.[13] To be clear, I do not think that there is really anything special about this variation; it will just allow me to make my points a little more easily than I otherwise could.[14]

Let's start by giving this semantics for the first-order fragment of $\mathcal{L}$. An *interpretation* of $\mathcal{L}$ is any ordered pair $\langle D, v \rangle$, where D is any set, and v is a function which maps singular terms of $\mathcal{L}$ to members of D and n-adic predicates to subsets of D^n.[15] Truth on an interpretation is then recursively defined as follows:

> Let $\mathcal{I}$ be any interpretation, Φ, Ψ and Ξ be any formulae of $\mathcal{L}$, α be any first-order variable of $\mathcal{L}$, and β be any individual constant of $\mathcal{L}$ that does not appear in Φ.
>
> (a) If Φ is a (atomic) n-adic predicate, F^n, followed by n singular terms, $a_1...a_n$, then Φ is true on $\mathcal{I}$ iff $\langle v(a_1), \ldots, v(a_n) \rangle \in v(F^n)$.
> (b) If $\Phi = \ulcorner \neg\Psi \urcorner$ then Φ is true on $\mathcal{I}$ iff Ψ is not true on $\mathcal{I}$.
> (c) If $\Phi = \ulcorner \Psi \wedge \Xi \urcorner$ then Φ is true on $\mathcal{I}$ iff Ψ is true on $\mathcal{I}$ and Ξ is true on $\mathcal{I}$.

---

[12] For the sake of conformity with my own terminology, I have replaced every occurrence of 'class' in the preceding quotation with 'set'. I have also replaced one occurrence of 'named' with 'referred to', as indicated in the text. I do not believe that this alteration has done any violence to Quine's meaning: if Quine wanted his claim that extensions are not 'named' by predicates to carry any philosophical significance, then he must surely have meant *referred to*. A nearly identical passage appears in Quine (1953a, 115). See also Quine (1970, 67).
[13] For example, it is the semantics which Mates gives in his textbook *Elementary Logic* (1972, ch. 4).
[14] Having said that, Evans (1977, 476) did once claim that this kind of semantics should be preferred to a standard Tarskian semantics on the grounds that it places whole sentences at the centre of our semantic theorising; in this respect, it obeys Frege's Context Principle, which tells us never to ask after the meaning of a word outside of the context of a sentence.
[15] D^n is defined recursively as follows: $D^1 = D$, and $D^{n+1} = D^n \times D$. The base clause requires that we identify each object a with its 1-tuple $\langle a \rangle$. Importantly, however, this does not amount to identifying each object with its singleton: 1-tuples are just degenerate cases of ordered sequences, which for simplicity we identify with the objects they are 1-tuples of.

(d) If $\Phi = \ulcorner \exists \alpha \Psi \urcorner$ then Φ is true on $\mathcal{I}$ iff $\Psi[\alpha/\beta]$ is true on some β-variant of $\mathcal{I}$.

(e) If $\Phi = \ulcorner \forall \alpha \Psi \urcorner$ then Φ is true on $\mathcal{I}$ iff $\Psi[\alpha/\beta]$ is true on every β-variant of $\mathcal{I}$.

$\Psi[\alpha/\beta]$ is the result of replacing every occurrence of α in Ψ with β; for example, 'Fx'['x'/'a'] is 'Fa'.[16] A β-variant of an interpretation $\mathcal{I}$ is an interpretation that differs from $\mathcal{I}$ only by assigning a different object to β, if it differs at all.

As Boolos (1975, 514–15) observed, it is very easy to extend this β-variant semantics to cover the second-order quantifiers.[17] We do not need to change our account of what an interpretation is in any way. All we need to do is add a couple of clauses:

> Let A be any n-adic second-order variable of $\mathcal{L}$, and B be any atomic n-adic predicate of $\mathcal{L}$ that does not appear in Φ.[18]

(f) If $\Phi = \ulcorner \exists A \Psi \urcorner$ then Φ is true on $\mathcal{I}$ iff $\Psi[A/B]$ is true on some B-variant of $\mathcal{I}$.

(g) If $\Phi = \ulcorner \forall A \Psi \urcorner$ then Φ is true on $\mathcal{I}$ iff $\Psi[A/B]$ is true on every B-variant of $\mathcal{I}$.

A *B-variant* of $\mathcal{I}$ is, of course, an interpretation that differs from $\mathcal{I}$ only by assigning a different set of n-tuples to B, if it differs at all.

Now I want to ask: what, if anything, do the second-order quantifiers quantify over on the B-variant semantics? At first, it might still seem obvious that the answer is: sets! After all, '$\exists X Xa$' is true on $\mathcal{I}$ iff $\ulcorner Ba \urcorner$ is true on some B-variant of $\mathcal{I}$, and the B-variants of $\mathcal{I}$ differ from one another by assigning different *sets* to B. (That is certainly how Boolos (1975, 511) saw things.) But that is much too quick.

Let's take a step back, and ask: what does it mean to say that the *first-order* quantifiers quantify over *objects* on the β-variant semantics? The answer is, I think, that a certain relation holds between using a first-order quantifier and saying something about an object. As I emphasised in §4.2, term-reference is an intentional concept: if a referring term is used in a sentence, then that sentence says something *about* the object referred to by that term. So '$\exists x Fx$' is true on $\mathcal{I}$ iff $\ulcorner F\beta \urcorner$ is true on some β-variant of $\mathcal{I}$, and on each β-variant,

---

[16] Just to be clear, the notion of substitution involved here is the *simple-substitution* of Chapter 1, not *sense-substitution*. Simple-substitution may not be much use in natural languages, but we are dealing with a formal language now, and it suffices for our purposes here.

[17] This point is also made by Rosefeldt (2008, 322–3).

[18] If any predicates are being treated as logical constants – for example, '$x = y$' – then B must be a predicate that is not a logical constant.

⌜$F\beta$⌝ says something about the object referred to by β. It is this point of contact between using a first-order quantifier and *talking about* objects that makes it appropriate to say that first-order quantifiers quantify over objects.

Does an analogous relation hold between using a second-order quantifier and saying something about a set? Well, it would if predicates *referred to* the sets that they are assigned, as some traditional realists have maintained. As I insisted in §4.3, predicate-reference is just as intentional as term-reference: if predicates referred to sets, then you would say something about a set when you used a predicate in a sentence. In that case, the following principle would hold: '$\exists X \, Xa$' is true on $\mathcal{I}$ iff ⌜Ba⌝ is true on some B-variant of $\mathcal{I}$, and on each B-variant, ⌜Ba⌝ says something about the set referred to by B.

But if predicates do not refer to the sets that they are assigned, then there is no analogy: '$\exists X \, Xa$' is true on $\mathcal{I}$ iff ⌜Ba⌝ is true on some B-variant of $\mathcal{I}$, but on no B-variant does ⌜Ba⌝ say something about the set assigned to B. There would then be no point of contact between using a second-order quantifier and *talking about* sets, and so it would be quite inappropriate to say that second-order quantifiers quantify over sets.[19]

So second-order quantifiers quantify over sets if and only if predicates refer to sets. And, of course, this point can be generalised. I assigned sets to predicates, but if you would rather assign them something else, then that is fine too. In fact, there is no need to embed the semantics in set theory at all. This is worth emphasising, because all set-theoretic semantics face well-known difficulties when it comes to absolutely unrestricted quantification over all objects; the most elegant way of overcoming those difficulties is by thinking of interpretations as higher-order entities rather than set-theoretic constructs.[20] But however exactly you conceive of interpretations, you have to agree that they somehow attribute satisfaction conditions to predicates; all that changes from one conception to another is how they do it. In general terms, then, we can define a B-variant of an interpretation $\mathcal{I}$ as any interpretation which differs from $\mathcal{I}$ only by attributing a different satisfaction condition to B, if it differs at all. With this generic definition of a B-variant, we can use clauses (f) and (g) to extend *any* semantic theory for a first-order language to include second-order generalisations.[21]

The important, wholly general, point is this. Whatever ontological force the second-order quantifier in '$\exists X \, Xa$' has must be traced back to the

---

[19] I first argued for this in Trueman (2013a). Krämer (2014a, 206–8) independently reached a very similar conclusion.

[20] See Williamson 2003; Rayo 2006; Linnebo and Rayo 2012, appendix B; Button and Walsh 2018, §12.A.

[21] See the appendix to this chapter, §7.A, for a higher-order implementation of the B-variant semantics.

ordinary predicate B. If B is a referring expression, then that quantifier quantifies over the things that B can refer to, in the sense that '$\exists X\, Xa$' says something *about* those things. But if it is not the job of B to refer to anything, then the quantifier does not quantify over anything at all.[22]

7.5 Quantification over Satisfaction Conditions

I hope that I have said enough to make neutralism seem compelling. In what follows, I will simply take it for granted. Now I want to bring everything back to the dispute between nominalists and Fregean realists.

To begin with, they should now agree with each other that it is a mistake to say that second-order quantifiers quantify over sets. That is because they both reject the idea that predicates refer to sets: the Fregean realists think it is a mistake to say that predicates refer to objects, including sets, and the nominalists think it is a mistake to say that predicates refer to anything at all.

But don't they still disagree over what the second-order quantifiers *do* quantify over? Nominalists do not think that predicates refer to anything, and so they will say that the second-order quantifiers do not quantify over anything. But the Fregean realists think that predicates refer to properties – i.e., satisfaction conditions. As a result, they will say that the second-order quantifiers quantify over satisfaction conditions: '$\exists X\, Xa$' is true on $\mathcal{I}$ iff $\ulcorner Ba \urcorner$ is true on some B-variant of $\mathcal{I}$, and on each B-variant, $\ulcorner Ba \urcorner$ says something about the satisfaction condition referred to by B.

Things are not so simple. For the Fregean realists, the claim that 'predicates refer to their satisfaction conditions' is a loose and potentially misleading way of speaking. If we keep things simple and stick with the set-theoretic version of the B-variant semantics, a Fregean realist should really specify the referent of B on a given interpretation with an instance of:

(4) $\quad \forall y \in D(y \in v(B) \leftrightarrow Yy).$[23]

According to Fregean realism, (4) expresses the intentional concept of predicate-reference: if B is used in a sentence, then that sentence says

---

22 The preceding is, I think, a spelled-out version of one of Prior's (1971, 42–3) arguments for neutralism.

23 Recall that for the time being, we are individuating satisfaction conditions extensionally. It should also be mentioned that, for all I have said so far, this method of specifying the referent of a predicate will only work for *simple* predicates, because only simple predicates have been assigned extensions. However, it would be easy to lay down some recursive stipulations which would allow (4) to apply to complex predicates too.

something about the condition Y. So if a Fregean realist wanted to say what the second-order quantifier quantifies over, she would have to use a second-order quantifier herself and say something like:

(5) '$\exists X\, Xa$' is true on $\mathcal{I}$ iff $\ulcorner Ba \urcorner$ is true on some B-variant of $\mathcal{I}$, and on each B-variant, $\exists Y \forall y \in D(y \in v(B) \leftrightarrow Yy)$.

But given neutralism, which we are now taking for granted, (5) is not something that a nominalist need disagree with: from a nominalist point of view, '$\exists Y \forall y \in D(y \in v(B) \leftrightarrow Yy)$' is just another ontologically innocent second-order generalisation.

7.6   Beyond Nominalism and Realism

What is there for nominalists and Fregean realists to disagree about? They are supposed to disagree about whether or not predicates are referring expressions, but what does that disagreement really amount to? I have argued that Fregean realists should use (S) to express predicate-reference (in extensional contexts). So if a Fregean realist wanted to tell us what 'x is a horse' refers to, she would just say:

(2) $\forall y(y$ satisfies 'x is a horse' $\leftrightarrow y$ is a horse).

No nominalist would ever deny that (2) is true. And given neutralism, no nominalist need even deny that (2) entails,

(3) $\exists Y \forall x(x$ satisfies 'x is a horse' $\leftrightarrow Yx)$,

or that this entailment proceeds in exactly the way that the Fregean realists describe. At this point, it seems very doubtful that anything of substance is left for them to disagree about.

Of course, it should be remembered that we have so far been focussing on extensional contexts. We have said nothing whatsoever about what to do with hyper-intensional contexts. I suppose it might be suggested that when we do come to deal with hyper-intensional contexts, we will find something substantial for nominalists and Fregean realists to disagree about. But it is hard to imagine what that might actually be. Nominalists and Fregean realists agree over how to deal with the extensional cases, and neither party seems to have more resources available to them than the other. It seems inevitable, then, that any way of dealing with hyper-intensional contexts that works for one of them will work for the other too.

In the end, I think that the difference between nominalism and Fregean realism comes down to just this. There are some important analogies between term-reference and (S):

(S) $\forall y(y \text{ satisfies } x \leftrightarrow Yy)$.

Term-reference has the right form for disquoting terms, and (S) has the right form for disquoting predicates; we can use term-reference to give a semantics for terms and first-order quantifiers, and we can use (S) to give a semantics for predicates and second-order quantifiers. Fregean realists are impressed by those analogies, so impressed that they think of (S) as another kind of reference. But where there are analogies, there are disanalogies too, and it is the disanalogies that impress the nominalists. Now, we have not really taken the time to look at the differences between term-reference and (S), but there certainly are some. To give just one example: there are meaningful singular terms which do not refer to any object, but it is arguable that *every* meaningful predicate has a satisfaction condition.

So the Fregean realists think that term-reference and (S) are similar enough to both count as kinds of reference, although, of course, they must also acknowledge that there are important differences between the two. The nominalists, on the other hand, think that term-reference and (S) are just too different to count as two kinds of reference, although, of course, they must also acknowledge that there are important analogies between them. I think it is pretty clear that there is nothing in a disagreement like this.[24] The nominalist and the Fregean realist agree on everything of substance; however far the analogies go, they go precisely that far for both of them.

There is to be no vindication of Fregean realism over nominalism, nor of nominalism over Fregean realism. There is no opposition to be had at all. Rather, Fregean realism, when its implications are followed out strictly, coincides with a kind of nominalism. We could just as well have called Fregean realism 'Fregean *nominalism*', or just plain 'Fregeanism', if we had liked. Now, as it happens, I am more impressed by the analogies between term-reference and (S) than the disanalogies, and so I will continue talking in a realist mode. But as we can now see, that is just a way of speaking. Nothing I will say should trouble the conscience of a good, honest nominalist.

---

[24] This also seems to be Dummett's considered view of things. After presenting a number of disanalogies between term-reference and predicate-reference, including the one mentioned above, Dummett (1981a, 243) originally concluded that 'Frege's attribution of reference to incomplete expressions appears in the end unjustified'. However, on later reflection, he wrote that 'this conclusion now seems to be too strong: it would have been better to locate the disanalogy and pass on' (Dummett 1981b, 164).

7.A Appendix: Second-Order Semantics

In §7.4, I defended *neutralism*, the thesis that second-order quantification does not introduce ontological commitment to any kind of thing that is not already introduced by the use of predicates. One pressing worry for neutralism is that on the standard set-theoretic semantics, it just seems obvious that the second-order quantifiers quantify over sets. I used a particular implementation of the set-theoretic semantics, which I called the *B*-variant semantics, to argue that the second-order quantifiers quantify over sets *only if* predicates refer to sets.

It is important to emphasise, however, that the *B*-variant semantics is not inherently set-theoretic. As I explained at the end of §7.4, we can use a version of the *B*-variant semantics to extend *any* semantics for a first-order language to include the second-order quantifiers. This is important to emphasise because, otherwise, someone might come away with the (admittedly quite odd) idea that my defence of neutralism would not survive if we abandoned standard set-theoretic semantics. In this appendix, then, I will illustrate this important point by presenting a version of Boolos' (1985) second-order semantics, reworked in *B*-variant terms.[25]

The first thing we need to do is give a second-order definition of what we mean by an 'interpretation':

> An *interpretation* of language $\mathcal{L}$ is any first-level dyadic relation I such that:
> (i) $\forall x(x$ is an individual constant in $\mathcal{L} \rightarrow \exists! y\, I(x,y))$;
> (ii) $\forall x \forall y(x$ is an n-adic atomic predicate in $\mathcal{L} \rightarrow (I(x,y) \rightarrow y$ is an ordered n-tuple$))$.

The idea is that if an individual constant bears I to an object, then that constant refers to that object; and if a predicate bears I to an ordered n-tuple of objects, then that predicate is true of those objects in that order. As condition (ii) makes clear, this semantics is not entirely free of set theory. But it is nowhere near as set-theoretic as the standard semantics: there is no requirement that the domain be a set, or that the extensions of predicates be sets either. Boolos (1985, 336) also helped himself to exactly this much set theory. Button and Walsh (2018, §12.A) have presented a method for entirely eliminating set theory from our semantics, but applying that method here would require moving into a fourth-order meta-language. So,

---

[25] See also Rayo and Uzquiano 1999; Williamson 2003, 453–4.

to keep things simple, we will follow Boolos' lead and make free use of n-tuples.

We can now recursively define 'true on I' for the first-order fragment of $\mathcal{L}$ as follows:

> Let I be any interpretation, Φ, Ψ and Ξ be any formulae of $\mathcal{L}$, α be any first-order variable of $\mathcal{L}$, and β be any individual constant of $\mathcal{L}$ that does not appear in Φ.
>
> (a) If Φ is a (atomic) n-adic predicate, F^n, followed by n singular terms, $a_1 \ldots a_n$, then Φ is true on I iff $\exists x_1 \ldots \exists x_n (I(a_1, x_1) \wedge \ldots \wedge I(a_n, x_n) \wedge I(F^n, \langle x_1, \ldots, x_n \rangle))$.
> (b) If $\Phi = \ulcorner \neg \Psi \urcorner$ then Φ is true on I iff Ψ is not true on I.
> (c) If $\Phi = \ulcorner \Psi \wedge \Xi \urcorner$ then Φ is true on I iff Ψ is true on I and Ξ is true on I.
> (d) If $\Phi = \ulcorner \exists \alpha \Psi \urcorner$ then Φ is true on I iff $\Psi[\alpha/\beta]$ is true on some β-variant of I.
> (e) If $\Phi = \ulcorner \forall \alpha \Psi \urcorner$ then Φ is true on I iff $\Psi[\alpha/\beta]$ is true on every β-variant of I.

A β-variant of I is any interpretation which differs from I only over what it relates β to, if it differs at all.[26]

To extend this definition to deal with second-order quantifiers in $\mathcal{L}$, we just need to add these clauses:

> Let A be any n-adic second-order variable of $\mathcal{L}$, and B be any atomic n-adic predicate of $\mathcal{L}$ that does not appear in Φ.
>
> (f) If $\Phi = \ulcorner \exists A \Psi \urcorner$ then Φ is true on I iff $\Psi[A/B]$ is true on some B-variant of I.
> (g) If $\Phi = \ulcorner \forall A \Psi \urcorner$ then Φ is true on I iff $\Psi[A/B]$ is true on every B-variant of I.

A B-variant of I is any interpretation which differs from I only over what it relates B to, if it differs at all.[27]

This second-order version of the B-variant semantics is, in one regard, a significant improvement over the set-theoretic version presented in §7.4. The set-theoretic semantics could not handle absolutely unrestricted first-order quantification: on that semantics, first-order quantification is always quantification over a *set* of objects, and there is no universal set. In stark contrast, the second-order semantics *always* interprets first-order

---

[26] I.e., J is a β-variant of I iff: J is an interpretation of $\mathcal{L} \wedge \forall x (x \neq \beta \rightarrow \forall y (J(x, y) \leftrightarrow I(x, y)))$.
[27] I.e., J is a B-variant of I iff: J is an interpretation of $\mathcal{L} \wedge \forall x (x \neq B \rightarrow \forall y (J(x, y) \leftrightarrow I(x, y)))$.

quantification as absolutely unrestricted. Unfortunately, however, this second-order semantics still faces limitations of its own: as Williamson (2003, 457) observed, it cannot handle absolutely unrestricted second-order quantification. We can get around this problem by ascending to an (at least) third-order semantics,[28] but we will not pursue that point here. My aim in this appendix is just to make it clear that none of my arguments in §7.4 depended on a set-theoretic approach to semantics. For that purpose, it will suffice to show that the Boolos-style semantics is just as neutralist as the set-theoretic semantics.

Suppose you were a certain kind of traditional realist who thought that each predicate plurally referred to all of the n-tuples it bears I to. That is, suppose you thought that if a predicate is used in a sentence, then that sentence says something *about* all the n-tuples which that predicate bears I to. In that case, you should think that the second-order quantifiers quantify over pluralities of n-tuples, in the sense that using a second-order quantifier is a way of talking about those pluralities.

But suppose instead that you were a Fregean realist and so rejected the idea that predicates refer to n-tuples as nonsense. In that case, you would also reject the idea that second-order quantifiers quantify over pluralities of n-tuples: using a second-order quantifier is *not* a way of talking about n-tuples. You would instead stand by the idea that the second-order quantifiers quantify over satisfaction conditions. You would then explain that the satisfaction condition of predicate B on interpretation I is properly specified with an instance of:

$$(4') \ \forall y(I(B, y) \leftrightarrow Yy).$$

As a Fregean realist, you would think that $(4')$ expresses an intentional relation: if B is used in a sentence, then that sentence says something *about* condition Y. So you would insist that when we use the second-order quantifiers, we thereby *say something about* the satisfaction conditions that B takes on each B-variant of I. Of course, you would also admit that this is a slightly loose way of speaking, and explain that you can only really say what the second-order quantifiers quantify over by *using* a second-order quantifier yourself. And at this point, it would become impossible to distinguish yourself from a nominalist who denies that predicates refer, and so maintains that the second-order quantifiers do not quantify over anything at all.

---

[28] See Rayo 2006; Linnebo and Rayo 2012, appendix B. Linnebo and Rayo assume that they have access to a second-level *ordered-pair* function; Button and Walsh (2018, §12.A) do without this assumption, but in a fifth-order semantics.

As I hope all of this makes clear, *nothing* in the dialectic of this chapter would change if we swapped the standard set-theoretic version of the *B*-variant semantics for the second-order version. It would still be right to say that the second-order quantifiers cannot introduce new kinds of ontological commitment. Whatever ontological force the second-order quantifiers have would still have to be traced back to the ordinary predicate *B*. And, of course, the same would be true on absolutely any version of the *B*-variant semantics.

CHAPTER 8

Some Alternatives

So far, I have developed and argued for Fregean realism. I have done my best to put this view in a good light, but there has been a shadow over things: the concept *horse* paradox. The paradox runs like this. If Fregean realism is right, then it is nonsense for terms and predicates to co-refer, even for 'x is a horse' and 'the property *horse*'. But surely these two must co-refer: not only do they really *look* like they do, but many have worried that if pairs like this are not allowed to co-refer, then we will not have the words to articulate Fregean realism in the first place.

I will finally confront the paradox in the next chapter, but before that, I want to look at some alternatives to Fregean realism. These alternatives are designed to allow terms to refer to properties[1] and thereby dodge the concept *horse* paradox altogether. Now, in a sense, I have nothing new to say in this chapter. I have already given my argument *for* Fregean realism, and that is my argument *against* its alternatives, too. However, I still think it is worth seeing exactly where Fregean realism disagrees with those alternatives. If nothing else, that will hopefully go some way to convincing you that the concept *horse* paradox really cannot be avoided.

8.1 Wright's Ascription

In what must be one of the best papers dealing with the concept *horse* paradox, Wright (1998) traces the paradox back to the *Reference Principle*:

(RP) Co-referring expressions are everywhere intersubstitutable *salva congruitate*.[2]

---

[1] This is not quite true of Wiggins' proposal, which I will discuss in §8.4; but as we will see, Wiggins' proposal doesn't really count as an *alternative* to Fregean realism.

[2] Hale and Wright offer a couple of different formulations of the Reference Principle in a later paper (Hale and Wright 2012, 93 and 105). I explain why I do not think we should use these formulations in Trueman 2015, 1902–3.

The concept *horse* paradox seems to be just one short step from (RP): terms and predicates are not everywhere intersubstitutable *salva congruitate*, and so (RP) tells us that they do not co-refer. Now, since Wright wanted to sidestep the paradox, we might have expected him simply to reject (RP). But that is not what he does. Instead, Wright (1998, 84–90) tries to defang (RP) by distinguishing between two kinds of reference: term-reference, which he simply calls *reference*, and predicate-reference, which he calls *ascription*.[3] When we read 'refers' as 'term-refers', then all that (RP) entails is that terms and predicates never *term-refer* to the same thing. But of course not: predicates are not in the business of term-referring to anything! Similarly, what we might call the *Ascription Principle*,

> (AP) Co-ascribing predicates are everywhere intersubstitutable *salva congruitate*,

entails that terms and predicates never *ascribe* the same thing. But of course not: terms are not in the business of ascribing anything! The crucial thing is that neither of these principles, taken separately or put together, entails that no term term-refers to something which some predicate ascribes. So for Wright, the way out of the concept *horse* paradox is to recognise that while 'x is a horse' and 'the property *horse*' do not co-refer, 'the property *horse*' does refer to what 'x is a horse' ascribes.[4]

It is impossible to miss the similarities between Wright's approach and my own. Wright's Reference Principle has appeared a number of times in my discussion. And just like Wright, I was forced to draw a distinction between two kinds of reference: term-reference and predicate-reference (which we could have called 'ascription' if we had liked). But there are also some differences between our approaches, and they count for more than the similarities.

First, and most important of all, Wright's ascription is a relation of a different *type* from my predicate-reference: whereas Wright's ascription is expressed by a first-level predicate, 'x ascribes y',[5] my predicate-reference is expressed by a mixed-level predicate, of the form 'x predicate-refers to Y'. This difference is absolutely crucial. In §4.6, we saw that it was impossible to say that a term term-refers to the same thing that a predicate predicate-refers to. We would need to bind *both* the variables in,

---

[3] This idea has recently been developed further by Liebesman (2015) and, in a slightly different direction, by Rieppel (2016).
[4] See Hale and Wright 2012, 106–7.
[5] See Hale and Wright 2012, 118–19.

'The property *horse*' term-refers to $y \wedge$ 'x is a horse' predicate-refers to Y,

with a single existential quantifier, and that is impossible: those variables, y and Y, are of different types. But by reading his 'ascribes' as the first-level 'x ascribes y', Wright faces no such difficulty. At least on point of grammaticality, there is nothing wrong with:

$\exists y$('The property *horse*' term-refers to $y \wedge$ 'x is a horse' ascribes y).

But, of course, I did not insist on using 'x predicate-refers to Y' just to make a rod for my own back. As we saw in Chapter 4, there is an essential relationship between reference – all types of reference – and disquotation. In particular, I argued in §4.3 that nothing can express predicate-reference unless it allows us to disquote predicates. And we cannot use Wright's first-level 'x ascribes y' to disquote a predicate: the second argument place, marked y, is a gap for terms, and predicates cannot be substituted for terms. What we need is an expression whose second gap is custom built for predicates, which is just what we have in our 'x predicate-refers to Y'.

There is another important difference between Wright's treatment of the concept *horse* paradox and my own. For Wright, (RP) was the true source of the paradox: it was the first principle from which the paradox sprang. But I have not given (RP) such a fundamental role. Instead, I took the path I just recounted: I used the relationship between reference and disquotation to argue that predicate-reference must be expressed by something of the form 'x predicate-refers to Y', and thus that it would be impossible to say that a term term-refers to the same thing that a predicate predicate-refers to. It was only *after* presenting that argument that I showed how we could generalise it into an argument for the following version of (RP):

(RP$_3$) If it makes sense to say that α refers$_\alpha$ to what β refers$_\beta$ to, then α and β are everywhere sense-intersubstitutable.

This principle goes further than (RP) and (AP), as Wright understands them: Wright insisted that those principles do not have the power to rule out the possibility that a term and a predicate might pick out the same thing, in their own special ways; (RP$_3$) does.

8.2   Hale's Primary/Secondary Distinction

Like Wright, Hale (2010, 414–15) thinks that (RP) is the ultimate source of the concept *horse* paradox. But unlike Wright, Hale does not think that the principle is sacrosanct, and he solves the paradox by simply rejecting it. This, Hale argues, has the virtue of allowing us to use just one reference relation for all types of expression: 'x is a horse' and 'the property *horse*' not only refer to the very same thing, but they do so in the very same sense of 'refer'. Nonetheless, Hale also thinks that our practice of referring to properties with predicates is somehow more basic than our practice of referring to them with singular terms:

> Where there are expressions of different logical types having reference to entities of a given kind, we distinguish between *primary* and *secondary*, or derivative, modes of reference to them. For example, while we *can* refer to properties by means of (complex) singular terms (such as terms of the form: the property of being something that ϕs), the basic mode of reference is by means of the incomplete predicate '$\phi(\ldots)$'. (Hale 2010, 415–16)[6]

What exactly is this distinction between primary and secondary modes of reference meant to achieve? Well, in the first place, it gives Hale the means to keep hold of the Fregean slogan 'No property is an object' even while he insists that properties can be referred to by terms. He (Hale 2010, 416; Hale and Wright 2012, 117) does this by redefining 'object' and 'property' as follows: an *object* is anything that is *primarily* referred to by a singular term, and a *property* is anything that is *primarily* referred to by a predicate. However, this strikes me as preserving the letter of Frege's slogan at the cost of its spirit. In this book, then, I will stick to the original Fregean definitions of 'property' and 'object'.

But this is not to say that Hale's primary/secondary distinction is an idle wheel. Recall that for Hale, (RP) is a fundamental assumption of the concept *horse* paradox: there is no argument *for* the principle. That is why he thinks that all he has to do to block the paradox is reject (RP). However, there is no denying that (RP) has a lot of intuitive pull, and so merely denying the principle, and saying no more about it, would inevitably feel deeply unsatisfying. This is where Hale's distinction comes in. For Hale, there is a kernel of truth in (RP): it holds for primary modes of reference, but not for secondary ones. In other words, (RP) is really just an overgeneralisation of the following, restricted principle:

---

[6] Hale presents the same solution to the concept *horse* paradox in *Necessary Beings* (2013, §§1.7–1.10). He further explains the idea that terms refer to properties only 'derivatively' in Hale and Wright (2012), §VIII. And in a joint paper, Hale and Linnebo (2020) develop some of the formal details of Hale's view.

(RP$_h$) If two expressions *primarily* refer to the same thing, then they are everywhere intersubstitutable *salva congruitate*.[7]

It seems to me that this is a plausible enough suggestion if you started off with Hale's view of (RP): an intuitively compelling, but ultimately unargued-for, premise. But that is not how I want you to see (RP). In Chapter 4, I used the relationship between reference and disquotation to argue that it makes no sense to say that a term and a predicate co-refer; then, in Chapter 5, I generalised that argument into an argument for my version of the Reference Principle, (RP$_3$). So if Hale's primary/secondary distinction is to excuse us from accepting that principle, it must do so by somehow disrupting those arguments. How might it do that?

I can just about imagine someone suggesting the following: Although there is an important relationship between reference and disquotation, it applies only to *primary* reference, not *secondary* reference. That would be enough to break my argument for (RP$_3$). However, it is important to note that this suggestion misunderstands *both* my argument *and* Hale's primary/secondary distinction. First, the relationship between disquotation and reference in my argument has nothing to do with Hale's primary/secondary distinction. I argued that there is an intimate connection between disquotation and the intentionality of reference. And no relation deserves to be called 'reference', not even 'secondary reference', unless it is intentional. Second, if we grant that primary reference is inherently tied up with disquotation, then we would still end up saying that primary predicate-reference can only be expressed by something of the form 'x predicate-refers to Y', not by 'x refers to y'. We would, then, still be left with a proliferation of reference relations of different logical types, which Hale explicitly set himself against.

I can think of no better way in which we might try to use Hale's distinction between primary and secondary modes of reference to undermine my argument for (RP$_3$). Since it did not work, I take it that that argument stands as firmly as it ever did (however firmly that turns out to be).

8.3 MacBride's Impure Reference

We come now to MacBride's (2011a) solution to the concept *horse* paradox. It starts from the very same place as Hale's and Wright's: the Reference Principle. And like Hale, MacBride wants to defuse the paradox without

---

[7] See Hale 2010, 416; Hale and Wright 2012, 116–17; Hale and Linnebo 2020, §5.10.

introducing different types of reference for different types of expression. But rather than relying on Hale's primary/secondary distinction, he introduces his own distinction between *purely* and *impurely* referring expressions. Roughly, a *purely* referring expression is an expression which refers and does nothing else. A little more precisely: the semantic role of a purely referring expression is exhausted by its referring to whatever it refers to; that is all there is to its contribution to the truth-values of the sentences in which it appears.[8] An *impurely* referring expression is an expression which refers but *also* does something else; there is more to its semantic role than reference.

According to MacBride, predicates are *impurely* referring expressions: in the sentence 'Shergar is a horse', 'x is a horse' refers to the property *horse*, *and* applies that property to Shergar. Moreover, this fact is meant to explain why we cannot grammatically intersubstitute 'x is a horse' and 'the property *horse*', even though they co-refer:

> Any attempt to substitute (e.g.) 'flying', 'the property of flying' or even 'the reference of "ξ flies"' for the verb 'ξ flies' misfires, at best transforming a sentence into a list. But this doesn't betoken an absence of co-reference between these expressions. Regardless of whether names or other singular phrases in ordinary language are purely referring expressions, predicates always do more: they also contribute in their own distinctive way towards the representation of how the properties or relations they signify are exhibited. Whereas a monadic predicate such as 'ξ flies' comes equipped with a rule for interpreting the representational significance of flanking it with a singleton occurrence of a name, a dyadic predicate such as 'ξ kissed ζ' comes with an order sensitive rule for interpreting the significance of flanking it with occurrences of right and left-flanking names etc. By contrast singular phrases don't come equipped with any such rule. Singular phrases can't be substituted for predicates because they're incapable of discharging the further semantic function predicates perform, viz. representing how the objects picked out by flanking names exhibit the properties or relations predicates signify. But this doesn't prevent singular phrases from picking out what predicates signify. (MacBride 2011a, 308–9)

---

[8] A nice question: are we forced to think of purely referring expressions on the Millian mould? Or, to put it the other way around: can we apply the sense/reference distinction to purely referring expressions? As far as I can tell, MacBride does not answer this question. However, my hunch is that we *can* apply the sense/reference distinction here. To say that an expression is a purely referring expression is to say that its *semantic role* (i.e., its contribution to the truth-values of the sentences in which it appears) is exhausted by its referring to whatever it refers to. But at least in ordinary contexts, the sense of an expression is no part of its semantic role. The sense of an expression is something over and above its semantic role.

MacBride's solution to the concept *horse* paradox is, then, to restrict (RP) to purely referring expressions:

(RP$_m$) If two expressions *purely* refer to the same thing, then they are everywhere intersubstitutable *salva congruitate*.

What is more, MacBride presents an independent motivation for restricting (RP) in this way. As I noted in §1.1, there seems to be a range of natural language counterexamples to (RP). Here is one of them:

(1) I am Rob
(2) # Me am Rob.

(2) is ungrammatical, even though (1) is grammatical and 'I' and 'me' co-refer (in any given context). I dealt with this counterexample to (RP) by pointing out that it relied on a relatively crude conception of substitution, and offering a more sophisticated one: *sense-substitution*. But MacBride (2011a, 305) offers another solution. Rather than tweaking our notion of substitution, we just need to replace (RP) with (RP$_m$) and then deny that 'I' and 'me' are purely referential. What more do these expressions do than refer? At this point, MacBride invokes the *thematic role* approach to case, a mainstay of empirical linguistics.[9] According to this approach, when you use the word 'I' in a sentence, you not only refer to yourself but also indicate that you are the *Agent* of the event described by the sentence; so if you say 'I phoned Sharon', you indicate that you are the Agent who did the phoning. By contrast, when you use 'me', you indicate that you are the *Patient* of the event; if you say 'Sharon phoned me', you indicate that you are the Patient who was phoned. This difference between 'I' and 'me' is, MacBride claims, a difference in their *descriptive content*:

> pronouns embody *descriptive* content about whether a referent of a given occurrence of a pronoun is the Agent or the Patient of the action expressed by the corresponding active verb. (MacBride 2011a, 305)

So that is what 'I' and 'me' do over and above referring: they describe their referents as playing a particular thematic role in the event at hand.

8.3.1 *Impure Reference and Case*

Let's start by looking at MacBride's way of dealing with the 'I'-'me' counterexample to (RP), and save our questions about predicate-reference for

---

[9] For an introduction to thematic role analysis, see Larson and Segal 1995, §12.3.

later. To my mind, it is fairly unnatural to think of differences in case as reflecting differences in descriptive content. Indeed, as I said in §1.3, I think that 'I' and 'me' have *the very same sense* as each other. Here's an imaginary story to soften you up to this way of seeing things.

There is a group of philosophers who have got into the convention of marking the different gaps in predicates with different styles of brackets; so instead of writing 'x loves y', they write '( ) loves [ ]'. When they want to make a sentence out of one of these predicates, they write the terms *into* those brackets; so instead of 'Daniel loves Simon', they write '(Daniel) loves [Simon]'. One day, this community realises that this convention has introduced a certain degree of redundancy into their language. They have two ways of telling which argument place a given term is written into: they can use word order, or they can look at the style of bracket surrounding the term. Some bright spark proposes to eliminate this redundancy by reading nothing into word order. This proposal is accepted, and so '(Daniel) loves [Simon]', '[Simon] loves (Daniel)', '[Simon] (Daniel) loves', etc., all come to mean the same thing: that Daniel loves Simon.

In this imaginary language, the different brackets, ( ) and [ ], behave a lot like different case markers in highly inflected languages, such as Latin: ( ) is like the nominative case marker, and [ ] is like the accusative case marker. But it would be a mistake to think that '(Daniel)' and '[Daniel]' are impurely referring terms. They are not terms at all: the unbracketed 'Daniel' is. The brackets are used in our conventions for interpreting predicates; they mark the argument places of predicates. The curved brackets around 'Daniel' in '[Simon] (Daniel) loves' are just there to indicate that 'Daniel' is in the first argument place of 'loves'. To suggest that they somehow affected the sense of the term 'Daniel' itself would be like suggesting that in plain English, 'Daniel' has different senses in 'Daniel loves Simon' and 'Simon loves Daniel'. It seems to me that, from a logical point of view, the same could be said about case in English. The case of an expression simply tells us which argument place that expression belongs in. We may not be able to straightforwardly detach the case from 'I' and 'me', but no matter: although we have no neutral, uncased version of 'I' or 'me', we can still think of them as instances of the same term in different cases.[10]

Of course, I do not intend these rudimentary reflections to constitute anything like a theory of case, or even the beginnings of one. For that, we would need to turn to empirical linguistics. But it is important to note that this broad way of thinking about case can be made to fit very well with the

---

[10]   Thanks to Michael Potter for first putting me onto this line of thought.

thematic role analysis; indeed, it can be made to fit better than MacBride's. Consider the following two sentences:

(3a) I phoned Sharon
(4a) Sharon phoned me.

On one way of implementing the thematic role analysis, these sentences become something like this:

(3b) $\exists e(\text{phoning}(e) \land \text{Agent}(i, e) \land \text{Patient}(a, e))$
(4b) $\exists e(\text{phoning}(e) \land \text{Agent}(a, e) \land \text{Patient}(i, e))$.

The 'I' and 'me' in (3a) and (4a) have both been formalised with exactly the same symbol, 'i', in (3b) and (4b). To this extent, it seems that the analysis is treating 'I' and 'me' as semantically equivalent. The sense in which the case of 'I' indicates that its referent is the Agent in (3a) has nothing to do with the descriptive content of 'I'. What is indicated is which predicate 'i' should be substituted into in (3b): it should go into 'Agent(x, e)'. Of course, the predicate 'Agent(x, e)' describes the referent of 'I' as being the Agent of event e, but that descriptive content belongs to that predicate, not to the term 'I'. Exactly the same remarks apply to 'me': the sense in which the 'me' in (4a) indicates that its referent is the Patient is just that it tells us that the 'i' in (4b) should be plugged into the predicate 'Patient(x, e)'.

8.3.2   Impure Reference and Predicates

We turn now to the issue that really matters to us: predicate-reference. We need to ask two questions. First, are predicates impurely referential? And second, if they are impurely referential, does that fact somehow permit terms and predicates to co-refer?

The second of these questions is the easiest to answer. It would make no difference at all to the argument of Chapter 4 if predicates were impurely referential. At no point in that argument did I assume that predicates referred *and did nothing else*. All that my argument required was that *one* of the things that predicates did was refer, whatever else they did as well. From there, the relationship between reference and disquotation kicks in and forces us to draw my distinction between term-reference and predicate-reference, which then makes it impossible to say that a term and a predicate might co-refer.

But what about the first question? Are predicates impurely referential? MacBride (2011a, 309–10) thinks that they must be, because otherwise there would be no explaining the difference between a sentence and a list: the reason that 'Shergar is a horse' is an articulate sentence rather than a mere list is that 'x is a horse' not only refers to the property *horse*, but also *applies* it to Shergar as well. Maybe you should find this line of reasoning compelling if you think that predicates refer in the same sense as singular terms, so that predicate-reference is a relation between two objects – a predicate and a special object called a 'property'. But if my argument from Chapter 4 stands, that is not how we should think of predicate-reference. We should instead think of predicate-reference as being expressed by a predicate of the form 'x predicate-refers to Y'. In particular, I argued in §6.1 that we should think of predicate-reference as being expressed by:

(S) $\forall y(y \text{ satisfies } x \leftrightarrow Yy)$.

When we think of predicate-reference in this way, we are not forced to say that predicates are impurely referential. Or, at least, we are not forced to say that *just* to account for the difference between a sentence and a list. Predicates do apply properties to objects, but it is a mistake to think that this is something they do *over and above* merely referring to those properties: the applying is built into the kind of referring that predicates do from the very start.

8.4 Wiggins, Strawson and the Copula

So far, all of the alternatives to Fregean realism that we have looked at have agreed on one thing: that in some sense or other, predicates stand for properties. But I want to end this chapter with something different. Wiggins (1984) has argued that we should stop the concept *horse* paradox in its tracks by denying that predicates stand for anything. Instead, Wiggins divides 'Shergar is a horse' into three components: 'Shergar', which refers to Shergar; '(a) horse', which refers to *horse*; and the copula 'is', which says of Shergar and *horse* that the former falls under the latter. According to Wiggins, this is essentially how we should analyse every subject-predicate sentence, although the job of the copula is sometimes taken over by finite verb endings, and sometimes it is not explicitly marked at all.[11]

It is worth noting how similar Wiggins' view is to Strawson's (1974, ch. 1). According to Strawson, the semantic labour involved in the sentence 'Shergar is a horse' divides in three ways: one expression refers to the individual

---

[11] For example, in '1 + 2 = 3', there is no copula or anything like a finite verb ending.

Shergar; one expression refers to the property *horse*;[12] and one indicates that the first two expressions are *propositionally combined* in such a way that the whole sentence is true if and only if Shergar instantiates *horse*. Unlike Wiggins, Strawson did not (or, at least, did not originally) assign these jobs to 'Shergar', '(a) horse' and 'is'. Instead, Strawson (29–31) claimed that we put the words 'is a horse' to double duty: we use them both to refer to *horse* and to indicate propositional combination. Importantly, however, Strawson did not think that predicates were impurely referential in MacBride's sense. For Strawson, predicates have only one job: referring to properties. It is just that we happen to use one and the same *string of words* – in this case, 'is a horse' – both as a predicate and as an indicator of propositional combination. We could use a notation in which the three jobs were clearly separated,

ass(Shergar, *horse*),

where '*horse*' merely refers to *horse*, and 'ass(x, y)' indicates propositional combination (Strawson 1974, 25 and 30). At this point, the parallels between Wiggins' and Strawson's views are easy to see. And, in fact, Strawson (1987) later wrote an article in which he expressed his general agreement with Wiggins.[13]

So what is wrong with views like Wiggins' and Strawson's? Nothing. But, then, they are not really *alternatives* to Fregean realism; they are versions of it. That might seem like an absurd claim, so let's approach it step by step. First off, we need to note that Wiggins' copula and Strawson's 'ass' are, by our criteria, types of predicate. Back in Chapter 2, I explained that, for my purposes, a predicate is any expression which *says something of* something else. And that is just what Wiggins and Strawson tell us that 'is' and 'ass' do: in 'Shergar is a horse' and 'ass(Shergar, *horse*)', 'is' and 'ass' both say of Shergar and *horse* that the former falls under the latter.[14]

Now, Strawson explicitly resisted this way of thinking about 'ass':

> It is to be remembered that 'ass' merely represents the function of propositional combination; it is not to be thought that 'ass' itself represents a concept-specifying expression, e.g. an expression specifying the concept of assignment or that of exemplification or that of application. (Strawson 1974, 26)

---

[12] Strawson prefers to use the word 'specifies' rather than 'refers' in relation to predicates; I will not worry about that terminological nicety here.
[13] Strawson's one reservation was over Wiggins' claim (1984, 320–1) that an expression like '(a) horse' cannot co-refer with an expression like 'the property *horse*'.
[14] Frege (1892a, 192–3) makes exactly this point about this kind of approach to predication.

But all that Strawson is really denying here is that 'ass' refers to anything, not that it is a predicate. So in our terminology, Strawson is simply a *nominalist* when it comes to the predicate 'ass(x, y)'. The same is true of Wiggins and 'is'. Wiggins (1984, 318) is explicit that the copula does not refer to anything. But that does not mean that 'is' is not a predicate; it just means that Wiggins is a nominalist about that predicate. And, in fact, Strawson and Wiggins are both nominalists of a very familiar kind. In effect, they account for the semantic roles of 'ass' and 'is' in terms of their satisfaction conditions: an object and a property satisfy 'ass'/'is' iff the former falls under the latter (Strawson 1974, 21–2; Wiggins 1984, 318).

So Strawson and Wiggins are happy to agree that 'is' and 'ass' have satisfaction conditions. However, in Chapter 6, I argued that all that Fregean realists mean when they say that predicates refer to properties is that they have satisfaction conditions; and then, in Chapter 7, I used this fact to collapse the distinction between nominalism and Fregean realism. (Admittedly, I focussed on monadic predicates, but the same goes for dyadic predicates too.[15]) Thus Wiggins and Strawson are Fregean realists after all: their 'is' and 'ass' do refer, in the only sense that predicates can.

Of course, not all Fregean realists will agree with Wiggins and Strawson. They are claiming that 'Shergar is a horse' can be divided into three semantically significant components: on Wiggins' taxonomy, 'Shergar', '(a) horse', and the copula 'is'. Other Fregean realists (like Frege himself: 1892a, 182) will insist that there are only two significant components here: 'Shergar' and 'x is a horse'. For the most part, I have spoken as if the latter group of Fregean realists are right, and I will give my reasons for preferring their view of things in §10.1. But nothing I have said so far really turned on that: we could just as well be Fregean realists of the Wiggins-Strawson stripe.

But hold on: won't we get into serious trouble if we think of the copula (or 'ass') as standing for a relation, even in the Fregean realist's attenuated sense of 'stands for a relation'? If 'is' stood for a relation, then it would have to be the relation of *instantiation*. But then 'Shergar is a horse' would say that Shergar instantiates *horse*. And by analysing 'Shergar is a horse' in this way, we would have taken the first step down *Bradley's Regress*. Next we

---

[15] Actually, things are slightly complicated by the fact that, for Wiggins (1984, 320–1), '(a) horse' is not a term, and so 'is' is not a *first-level* dyadic predicate. However, I take it that the point I am making is not affected by this complexity. Moreover, it is arguable that by Wiggins' own lights, it was a mistake to insist that 'horse' is not a term: Wiggins' aim was to dodge the concept *horse* paradox, but if 'horse' is nowhere intersubstitutable with a term, then it will still be nonsense to say that 'horse' refers to an object. Someone who shared Wiggins' aims would, then, be better off saying that 'horse' is a term. For an example of someone developing Wiggins' theory in this direction, see Gaskin 1995, 164 and 171.

would end up analysing 'Shergar instantiates *horse*' as: Shergar and *horse* together instantiate instantiation. And then on we would go, giving more and more complex analyses, starting with 'Shergar is a horse' but never ending.

It is exactly this sort of worry that made Wiggins (1984, 318) and Strawson (1974, 22) deny that 'is' and 'ass' refer to anything. But Fregean realists have nothing to fear from Bradley's Regress. That regress simply cannot get going if we steadfastly refuse to blur the distinction between properties and objects. Or, at least, that is something I will be arguing for in §10.2.

CHAPTER 9

The Concept Horse *Paradox*

I cannot put it off any longer. It is time to confront the concept *horse* paradox. Just to remind you, the paradox first came up in Frege's theorising about the relation between bits of language and bits of the world. Frege thought that terms and predicates were both types of referring expression, but that they refer to different types of thing: terms refer to *objects*, predicates refer to *properties*, and no property is an object. (It is known as the 'concept *horse* paradox' because, for some reason, Frege decided to call properties 'concepts'.) At this point, however, Frege's theorising seemed to trip up over itself. If properties are not objects, then no term can refer to a property, not even terms like 'the property *horse*'. Thus Frege was led to the bizarre-sounding conclusion that the property *horse* is not a property.[1]

We are in essentially the same predicament as Frege. The only difference is that Frege claimed that it was *false* to say that a property is an object, whereas I argued that it is *nonsensical*. (And, as we will see in §9.2, even that difference will end up collapsing under its own weight.) So, for us, it is just nonsense to imagine that a term might refer to a property, including 'the property *horse*'. Thus we are led to the bizarre-sounding conclusion that it is nonsense to say that the property *horse* is a property.

Put like that, my view (*Fregean realism*) hardly sounds coherent at all. I did my best to explain clearly what this view amounts to in Chapters 6 and 7, but I shied away from the concept *horse* paradox whenever we ran into it. In this chapter, I will look at a number of problems which this paradox throws up and deal with them as best as I can. In some cases, this will be straightforward enough: we will hardly need to do anything more than remind ourselves of what was said in previous chapters. But not all of the problems are disposed of so easily.

---

[1] The locus classicus of this paradox is, of course, 'On concept and object' (Frege 1892a).

9.1   The Property *Horse* Is Not a Property?

It is not hard to pinpoint the source of the discomfort that we feel when we are first presented with the concept *horse* paradox. The planet Neptune is a planet, the volcano Vesuvius is a volcano, and so the property *horse* must surely be a property![2] That much seems incontrovertible. But we have controverted it anyway.

Taken out of context, this might sound like a devastating objection to Fregean realism. But as we saw in Chapter 6, the Fregean realists are only speaking loosely when they say that predicates refer to 'properties'. On the face of things, '( ) is a property' looks like a first-level predicate, 'x is a property', but Fregean realists insist that the referents of predicates are properly characterised by a second-level predicate, of the form '$P(X)$'. I recommended that they use '$\exists Y \forall x(Xx \leftrightarrow Yx)$' for this purpose (see §6.2). So rather than saying,

(1a) The property *horse* is a property,

a Fregean realist should strictly say:

(1b) $\exists Y \forall x(x$ is a horse $\leftrightarrow Yx)$.

However, (1b) is not an easy thing to say, and so, for the most part, the Fregean realists are well advised to keep speaking loosely and stick to (1a). It is just up to us not to take the surface form of what they say too seriously: when they say (1a), they mean (1b).

So the Fregean realists are actually free to agree that (1a) is true, so long as they do not take its surface form too seriously. But what if they *do* take it seriously? Well, when we read (1a) like that, 'the property *horse*' appears as a term, and '( ) is a property' as a first-level predicate. Now, a Fregean realist is not automatically obliged to object to the very use of terms like 'the property *horse*'. All a Fregean realist is obliged to do is dismiss as non-sense the idea that 'the property *horse*' refers to a property, *in the Fregean realist's sense of 'property'*.[3] And as I just emphasised, this sense of 'property' is properly expressed by the *second-level* predicate '$\exists Y \forall x(Xx \leftrightarrow Yx)$'. So whatever it is that the *first-level* predicate 'x is a property' expresses, it is not that. Consequently, the truth-value of (1a) on a strict reading is not really any of a Fregean realist's business.[4]

---

[2] See Frege 1892a, 185; Wright 1983, 15–22.
[3] Having said that, in §10.1, I will recommend that Fregean realists avoid using terms like these. However, it is important to recognise that this recommendation is an addition to what is strictly required by Fregean realism.
[4] This point has its origins in Parsons 1986, 452–4.

In order to get something which has any chance of causing trouble for a Fregean realist, we need to take the surface form of (1a) just *half* strictly. We need to read 'the property *horse*' strictly, as a real singular term, and '( ) is a property' loosely, as the Fregean realist's snappy but misleading rendering of '$\exists Y \forall x (Xx \leftrightarrow Yx)$'. And yes, read like that, (1a) is nonsense. But that should no longer seem strange. Trying to read (1a) like that is the same as trying to substitute a term into a second-level predicate, and that is impossible.

This is all well and good, but isn't there still something weird about saying that it is nonsensical for 'the property *horse*', thought of as a genuine singular term, to refer to a property? After all, that term was custom built for the job! At this point it simply is not good enough to point out that it is only nonsense to say that 'the property *horse*' refers to a property *in the Fregean realist's sense of 'property'*. The objection is that the term 'the property *horse*' was introduced to refer to one of the Fregean realist's properties. So what *exactly* went wrong?

I am tempted to take a very short line with this objection. I argued that it is nonsense for a term to refer to a property in Chapter 4.[5] If my argument stands, then 'the property *horse*' cannot refer to a property, even if that is what we introduced it to do. We wanted 'the property *horse*' to do something impossible, and we were inevitably disappointed. However, perhaps we can make things clearer by comparing 'the property *horse*' to 'the volcano Vesuvius'. We read the latter term as a contracted version of 'the *x* such that *x* is a volcano and *x* = Vesuvius'. Read like that, it is easy to see why it must refer to a volcano, if it refers to anything at all. But it is impossible to expand 'the property *horse*' in a similar way. If we tried, we would end up with something like 'the *x* such that *x* is a property and *x* = *horse*'. The first thing that looks odd here is '*x* = *horse*', but let's not worry too much about that. The real obstacle is that this expansion treats '( ) is a property' as a first-level predicate. But if we want to insist that '( ) is a property' is here being used in the Fregean realist's sense, then it must be taken as a shorthand for the *second-level* predicate '$\exists Y \forall x (Xx \leftrightarrow Yx)$'.

It is, then, easy enough to recover from the initial shock of the concept *horse* paradox. Unfortunately, however, the paradox does not end here, and things only get more difficult.

---

[5] I actually argued that it is nonsense for a term and a predicate to co-refer, but that comes to the same thing.

9.2   Categorial Differences

It has been suggested that the concept *horse* paradox illustrates a serious difficulty that Fregean realists face when they try to articulate their own position.[6] Fregean realists want to say all sorts of things about properties, but doing so appears to require referring to them with singular terms. Here are some examples:

(1a) The property *horse* is a property
(2a) The property *horse* is not identical to the property *dog*
(3a) 'x is a horse' refers to the property *horse*.

However, as I explained in Chapter 6, and then repeated just a moment ago, this is nothing but a loose way of speaking, and the Fregean realists can stop speaking loosely whenever they like. Instead of (1a)–(3a), they can say:

(1b) $\exists Y \forall x(x$ is a horse $\leftrightarrow Yx)$
(2b) $\neg \forall x(x$ is a horse $\leftrightarrow x$ is a dog)
(3b) $\forall y(y$ satisfies 'x is a horse' $\leftrightarrow y$ is a horse).

But is it really true that the Fregean realists can rewrite *everything* they want to say about properties in this way?[7] In §6.3, I argued that if Fregean realism is right, then we must reject as nonsense any attempt to say of an object what can be said of a property, and *vice versa*. According to Fregean realism, then, it is impossible to compare properties and objects. But don't the Fregean realists *want* to compare them?

Consider the following claim:

(4a) No property is an object.

Since Chapter 4, I have been careful not to assert (4a). According to Fregean realism as I have laid it out, it is *nonsense*, not false, to say that a property is an object. But Frege himself asserted (4a) all the time. And there is an obvious problem with asserting that. If it were true, then we could still run a version of the argument from §6.3 to show that we must reject any attempt to say of a property what can be said of an object: all we have to do is replace formulations like 'it is nonsense to say that...' with straightforward negations. Indeed, Frege himself was well aware of this fact:

6   For example, see Hale and Wright 2012, 95–8 and 103–4.
7   In what follows, I focus on what I take to be the most serious expressibility challenges facing the Fregean realists. Linnebo (2006) presents a number of related expressibility challenges for philosophers he calls *type theorists*, but Krämer (2014b) has already met these additional challenges. See also Jones 2016.

> I do not want to say it is false to say concerning an object what is said here concerning a concept [i.e. property]; I want to say it is impossible, senseless to do so. (Frege 1892a, 189)

> concepts cannot stand in the same relations as objects. It would not be false, but impossible to think of them as doing so. (Frege 1891–5, 175)

But in that case, if (4a) were true, then (4a) would itself be nonsense: we *can* say of an object that it is an object, and so we cannot say it of a property!

I do not think that we have just revealed any kind of confusion in Frege's own thought. I think it just shows that he *was* a Fregean realist in my sense, and when he said (4a), he was just speaking loosely, as Fregean realists tend to do. What Frege really wanted to assert was:

(4b) It is nonsense to say that a property is an object.

But now a difficult question: is (4b) really any better than (4a)? On the face of it, (4b) appears to be *using* the sentence 'a property is an object': (4b) looks like the result of substituting 'a property is an object' for '*P*' in 'It is nonsense to say that *P*'. But in that case, (4b) is *itself* a bit of nonsense, on a par with:

\# It is nonsense to say that fribble frabble bibble babble.

Here is a quicker way of putting the same problem: to say that properties and objects are incomparable is *still* to draw a comparison between them. Fregean realism thus appears to be a self-stultifying doctrine.

There is only one way to avoid this conclusion. We must insist that, despite surface appearances, we do not *use* the sentence 'a property is an object' in (4b). The most obvious way of trying to implement this thought is by simply *mentioning* the sentence instead:

(4c) It is nonsense to say 'A property is an object'.

But this is still not quite right. To say that a sentence is nonsense is not to say that there is something inherently wrong with it. Nonsensical sentences do not have special nonsensical meanings. Rather, to say that a sentence is nonsense is just to say that the rules of our language do not determine a meaning for it.[8] (4c) is, then, just an empirical claim to the effect that,

---

[8] This is the *austere* conception of nonsense, rightly insisted upon by the so-called *resolute* readers of the *Tractatus*. See §9.4 for discussion.

as things stand, we have no use for 'A property is an object' in our language. This claim may well be true, but that could change at any moment. (Suppose that we stipulated that 'property' is to mean the same as 'dog', and 'object' is to mean the same as 'mammal'.) Worse than that, it may not even be true: as I acknowledged in §9.1, for all the Fregean realists care, there may already be perfectly meaningful uses of 'x is a property' as a first-level predicate.

Clearly (4c) cannot be what the Fregean realists mean when they assert (4b). They are trying to get at something much deeper than that. They want to deny the existence of a certain thought. Which thought? We want to say: the thought that a property is an object! But the problem with that is obvious. We have ended up trying to express the very thought whose existence we wanted to deny.

The Fregean realists are in a tight spot here, but fortunately, there is a way out. Although the Fregean realists must not try to get at the thought they are rejecting by expressing it, they *can* get at it by describing the way in which it would be put together, if it existed. We are using '( ) is an object' and '( ) is a property' with certain senses: '( ) is an object' characterises the referents of terms, and '( ) is a property' characterises the referents of predicates. What the Fregean realists deny is that we could build a thought by combining these senses with the sense of an existential quantifier. '( ) is an object' is a first-level predicate, but the Fregean realists insist that when we use '( ) is a property' to characterise the referents of predicates, it must be read as a second-level predicate. And it is impossible to make a thought by combining the senses of a first-level predicate, a second-level predicate and an existential quantifier.

At no point in any of this do the Fregean realists need to express the thought whose existence they want to deny. They just need to describe a way of trying to put that thought together and then deny that any thought can be put together in that way. There is thus no risk of self-stultification here. Still, this way of expressing things reifies senses a little bit too much for my tastes. Happily, however, we can use my sense-substitution to eliminate this reification:

> (4d) Given what we are using these expressions to mean, it is impossible to sense-substitute 'X is a property' into the gap in '∃x(Xx ∧ x is an object)'.

This is how I think we should understand (4b). And what is more, it is easy to see why we would find (4b) a natural way of expressing (4d). In (4b), we display our best, but inevitably unsuccessful, attempt to perform the sense-substitution that (4d) declares to be impossible. In what follows, then, I will continue to make free use of the locution 'It is nonsense to say that. . .', on the understanding that what I say should be understood on the model of (4d).[9]

9.3   Categorial Similarities

Properties and objects cannot be compared. That means two things. First, we cannot say that properties are in any way *different* from objects. We focussed on that in the last section: it is wrong to say that properties are not objects; it is *nonsense* to say that properties are objects, and by that I mean something along the lines of (4d). But second, we also cannot say that properties are in any way *similar* to objects. And that throws up a much harder problem.

According to Fregean realism, it is a mistake to think that *Property* and *Object* are two species of a common genus, *Entity* or *Thing*. Given what Fregean realists mean by 'property' and 'object', it is straightforwardly non-sensical to imagine that there could be a single domain which contained properties and objects. But at the same time, it is very tempting to complain that, at some level, the Fregean realists *must* secretly be thinking of proper-ties and objects as two kinds of 'thing'. After all, they think that terms and predicates are both types of referring expression. Admittedly, they think that terms and predicates refer in different ways, but they are still meant to be two different ways of referring. In other words, term-reference and predicate-reference *are* two species of the genus *Reference*. But why do they count as two species of this genus? One part of the answer is that they have some formally similar properties; for example, you can use term-reference to disquote terms, and predicate-reference to disquote predicates. But the other part of the answer must surely be that they are both word-world rela-tions – i.e., relations between bits of language and things in the world: term-reference relates terms to objects, and predicate-reference relates predicates to properties. However, if the Fregean realists give this answer, then they will have to admit that they are thinking of properties and objects as two kinds of 'thing' which can stand on the world-end of a word-world relation.[10]

---

[9] What I have said here was very much influenced by Moore (2003, 186–9).
[10] Exactly the same objection could be put in terms of existence or identity: Why do '$\exists x \ldots x \ldots$' and '$\exists X \ldots X \ldots$' count as expressing two kinds of existence? Part of the answer must be that they are both quantifiers that range over a domain of things. Why do '$x = y$' and '$\forall x(Xx \leftrightarrow Yx)$' count as expressing two kinds of identity? Part of the answer must be that they both express relations which a thing can only bear to itself.

What are the Fregean realists to do? Well, I think that they should just concede that term-reference and predicate-reference cannot be thought of as two species of the genus *Reference*. This might have seemed like more of a concession than any Fregean realist could afford to make. What exactly would it leave of the *realism* in Fregean realism? However, in Chapter 7, I argued that there is no real difference between Fregean realism and a kind of nominalism. The only reason I have called it Fregean 'realism' and not 'nominalism' is that I am at home with the realist's way of speaking, but this really is just a way of speaking. What is actually said is something that a nominalist could happily say too. Properly understood, Fregean realism *transcends* the nominalist/realist distinction.

Of course, this is not to say that the Fregean realist should *deny* that predicate-reference is a word-world relation. The point is just that what it means to call predicate-reference a word-world relation is quite different from what it means to call term-reference a word-world relation. Roughly, to say that term-reference is a word-world relation is to say that from a sentence of the form ' "*a*" refers to *y*', you can infer '∃*y*("*a*" refers to *y*)'; and to say that predicate-reference is a word-world relation is to say that from a sentence of the form '∀*y*(*y* satisfies "*Fx*" ↔ *Yy*)', you can infer '∃*Y*∀*y*(*y* satisfies "*Fx*" ↔ *Yy*)'. Fregean realists should, then, carry on insisting that predicate-reference is a word-world relation, and as we saw in Chapter 7, nominalists should agree with what the Fregean realists mean, even if they don't like putting it that way.

This deals with the objection as I have so far presented it, but now things get a bit trickier. The argument that I gave *for* Fregean realism was clearly guided by the idea that term-reference and predicate-reference are two types of reference. (That's the title of Chapter 4!) Fregean realists may be happy to disown this idea as something that they have outgrown, but in doing so, they will also have to disown the very argument for their position.

This is clearly a precarious dialectical position, but in the end, it is a stable one. We started off speaking unreflectively about the idea that predicates are 'referring' expressions. Our choice of words was not accidental. We took it for granted that predicates did essentially the same thing as singular terms: they both stood for things in the world. However, when we looked more closely, we saw that we could not quite say that. If we were to have any chance of preserving the idea that terms and predicates are two types of referring expression, then we had to say that terms and predicates refer in two different ways. But once we drew the needed distinction, we *still* could not say that term-reference and predicate-reference are two types of reference. There is no harm in speaking like a realist, but we must not take that way of speaking too seriously. This may at first make it sound like our whole project was a failure, but that is not the right way of thinking about things. What we can now see clearly is that if we try to work through the idea that predicates are referring expressions in all of its details, then we end up with the very same view we would have ended up with if we had started off trying to work through the idea that predicates are *not* referring expressions. That is a uniquely satisfying resolution to the nominalist/realist debate about predicate-reference.

9.4   Saying and Showing

Much of what I just said will be familiar to anyone who knows Wittgenstein's *Tractatus*. In the *Tractatus*, Wittgenstein appears to present a theory of how language relates to the world; but then, at the end of the book, he reveals that the whole theory is, *by its own lights*, nonsensical. Wittgenstein infamously instructs his reader to 'throw away the ladder after he has climbed up it' (1922, 6.54). I have given essentially the same instruction. This is no coincidence. As Geach (1976) has convincingly argued, Wittgenstein's conviction that we inevitably speak nonsense when we try to articulate a philosophical vision of the relation between language and world was born out of his reflections on the concept *horse* paradox. In this section, I will connect my discussion of Fregean realism's apparently self-destructive nature to some of the extensive literature dealing with Wittgenstein's *Tractatus*.

It is now standard practice to distinguish between two interpretations of the *Tractatus*: the *traditional* and the *resolute*. According to the traditional interpreters, although Wittgenstein thought that the *Tractatus* was a tissue of nonsense, he still thought that it conveyed some kind of insight. Plainly, it cannot *say* anything insightful, since it does not say anything at all, but it still gets something insightful across. It can do this because the nonsense in the *Tractatus* is an attempt to say what is properly *shown* by the meaningful use of our language. This attempt ends up in nonsense because what can be shown cannot be said. However, we can reach a deeper appreciation of what is shown by working through Wittgenstein's failed attempts to say it.[11]

---

[11]   The traditional interpreters are often said to include Anscombe (1959), Geach (1976) and Hacker (1972). However, as Sullivan (2003, 199–204) points out, it is not at all clear whether this is a fair way of understanding Anscombe and Geach. We will return to Geach's views on saying and showing shortly.

The resolute readers think that this is a serious misreading of the *Tractatus*. Yes, there are many remarks in the book dealing with the saying/showing distinction, but those remarks are just rungs on the ladder that we are meant to kick away. Really, there is nothing which can be shown but not said. To think otherwise would be to believe in a realm of ineffable quasi-truths, and that is just incoherent. Relatedly, there is no special kind of nonsense which can be described as an attempt to say what can only be shown. To think otherwise would be to believe that certain nonsensical sentences have meanings of a sort, just the wrong sort of meanings to be meaningful, to *say* something. But really, nonsense is just nonsense, squiggles on a page for which we have not yet fixed any meaning.[12]

The traditional and resolute interpretations are often presented as if they were not only mutually exclusive but also mutually exhaustive: you have to read the *Tractatus* in exactly one of these two ways. However, as Moore (2003) and Sullivan (2002, 2003) have made very clear, the space of possible interpretations is not really as limited as that.[13] We can have the best of both worlds. The resolute reading is absolutely right to insist that nonsensical sentences are just sentences we have not fixed a meaning for. (I insisted on just the same thing in §9.2.) But that does not mean that we have to reject the idea that some things are shown by our use of language, or that we can use nonsensical sentences to convey those things.

As I mentioned earlier, the resolute readers dismiss the idea that anything can be shown on the following grounds: according to the *Tractatus*, what is shown cannot be said, and so anything that was shown would have to be some sort of ineffable quasi-truth;[14] but the whole idea of something which is enough like a proposition to be true but not enough like one to be effable is incoherent. However, this quick dismissal smuggles in the unwarranted assumption that anything which could be shown would have to count as being 'true' in some sense. And why assume that? It certainly is not built into the *ordinary* usage of the word 'show'. I can show you a horse, but horses are not the sort of thing that can be true or false.

---

[12] The canonical resolute texts are Diamond 1991; Crary and Read 2000. Kremer (2001) offers a particularly interesting development of the resolute reading.

[13] The rest of this chapter owes a great debt to these papers by Moore and Sullivan.

[14] Outside of the context of the *Tractatus*, I do not think that there is any problem with the idea that some truths are shown *and* said. For example, in §4.2, I pointed out that ' "Socrates" refers to Socrates' is true iff ' "Socrates" refers to y' is true of the referent of 'Socrates', even though that is not what this sentence *says*. I am at least half-tempted to say that the truth of this sentence *shows* that ' "Socrates" refers to y' is true of the referent of 'Socrates'. However, I will set this kind of case aside, since I want to focus on things which can *only* be shown, not said.

Of course, we cannot leave things here, with a simple observation about the ordinary use of 'shows'. We need to offer some account of what is shown but not said by our meaningful use of language. One natural suggestion, which can be traced back to Geach (1976), is that what is shown is *how* to do certain things.[15] What we learn when we are shown something is not *that* things are a certain way, but *how* to do certain things; we are left with non-propositional *know-how*, not propositional *know-that*.[16]

This sort of approach may or may not be enough to account for all the uses to which Wittgenstein wanted to put his notion of *showing*.[17] But it certainly is an approach to showing that I would like to take in my defence of Fregean realism. I want to say that our meaningful use of language shows us how to do something: it shows us *how to use our language meaningfully*.

That may strike you as trivial, but I would prefer to call it demystifying. In general, a good way of showing me how to do something is by simply doing it in front of me. So a good way of showing me how to use an expression meaningfully is by simply using it meaningfully in front of me. Of course, there are other ways of getting me to understand how to use an expression. You could tell me *that* it is used in this or that way. But what you would tell me is not the very same thing you would show me by using the expression meaningfully: what you tell me is a truth, but what you show me is a technique.

Very well, let's all agree that our meaningful use of language shows us how to use our language meaningfully, and that this is a non-propositional kind of showing: *show-how*, not *show-that*. How is this meant to be of any help to the Fregean realists? Well, although they have no choice but to dismiss their own argument for Fregean realism as nonsensical, they can still insist that it helps us to grasp something which is properly shown, not said. It helps us to grasp how to use the word 'refers' in relation to predicates, and it does so by being a case study in how *not* to use it. The way we speak can

---

[15] This approach was subsequently developed by Moore (1997, 189), who thought that we are shown how to understand things.

[16] There is an ongoing controversy over whether *knowing-how* really is a different kind of knowing from *knowing-that*. (For one side of the controversy, see Ryle 1945–6, 1949, ch. II. For the other, see Stanley and Williamson 2001.) My remarks in this section clearly presuppose that there is an important difference between these kinds of knowledge. Unfortunately, however, it is beyond the scope of this book to offer any defence of that presupposition here. But importantly, if it turns out that this presupposition is a mistake, then that would not be too serious a blow for my project. It would just mean that we cannot use the saying/showing distinction in the way that I suggest to shed light on the Fregean realist's delicate dialectical predicament.

[17] I am optimistic that it is, but there is room for doubt. For example, Morris and Dodd (2007, esp. 263) think that we are not shown *how to do* things, we are just shown *things*: for them, showing is a route to knowledge-*of* (or *acquaintance*), not knowledge-*how*.

make it seem as if 'refers' can be applied to predicates in just the way that it can be applied to terms. The sentence 'Predicates refer to properties' looks for all the world like it was built in exactly the same way as 'Terms refer to objects'. The Fregean realists reveal that this is a mistake by speaking as if it were not one. They show us the mess we get into when we try to speak like that. They present us with what looks like an argument, whose interim conclusion is that we must draw a distinction between term-reference and predicate-reference, and whose final conclusion is that we cannot count both of them as two kinds of 'reference'. This is a self-undermining conclusion, and our only option is to dismiss the whole 'argument' as a load of nonsense. But working through the 'argument' was not a waste of time. The Fregean realists' failed attempt to say anything was instructive. We now know *how* to use the word 'refers' in relation to predicates: we can say ' "x is a horse" refers to a property' if we like, but that just means the same as '$\exists Y \forall y (y$ satisfies "x is a horse" $\leftrightarrow Yy)$'. So even though the Fregean realists have not *said* anything in their nonsensical argument, they have helped us to see more clearly what is *shown* by our meaningful use of language.

What is more, by working through the Fregean realists' case study, we become better at spotting this kind of nonsense when we see it. And as I will try to show in the next chapter, it comes up again and again in the form of puzzles and paradoxes which have bedevilled the metaphysics of properties. Geach (1976, 58) once claimed that we could set an exam to test whether a student had learnt the know-how Frege was trying to convey with his nonsensical remarks about properties and objects. This exam would test the student's ability to use Frege's *Begriffschrift*, or the modern equivalent. But that is the wrong kind of exam. (I am not sure I would try to teach elementary formal logic by making my students read 'On concept and object'.) The exam should be in metaphysics, and it should test the student's ability to dissolve pseudo-problems.

CHAPTER 10

The Metaphysics Exam

Up until now, I have been trying to convince you that you *have* to be a Fregean realist. In this chapter, I will try to convince you that you *want* to be one. I will argue that Fregean realism offers easy solutions to a range of metaphysical puzzles. All of these puzzles rely in one way or another on the assumption that properties are objects. If we refuse to grant that assumption, then they cannot even get started.

10.1   The Problem of Universals

If Fregean realism is right, then it does not make sense for terms and predicates to co-refer; for example, it does not make sense for 'x is wise' to co-refer with 'wisdom'. But it does not automatically follow that terms like 'wisdom' do not refer to anything at all.[1] You might still insist that they refer to certain property-like objects – call them *universals*.[2]

To be absolutely clear, Fregean realism does not by itself tell us anything about whether or not universals exist. But while the base model of Fregean realism might be silent on this issue, I would like to add the rejection of universals as an optional extra. Universals come with a host of metaphysical puzzles – we will be looking at a number of those puzzles in this chapter – and so it would be better to do without them. Of course, it goes well beyond what I can do in this section to show once and for all that we really *can* do without them.[3] But what I can do is show that the master argument for universals, often known as the *Problem of Universals*, has no force for a Fregean realist.

---

[1]   At least for a while, Frege (1892a) himself thought that nominalised predicates referred to objects which went proxy for properties. For a detailed theory of predicate nominalisation along these lines, see Chierchia and Turner 1988.
[2]   For the great modern defence of universals, see Armstrong 1978a, 1978b.
[3]   For one recent attempt to show that we can do without universals (and propositions and numbers), see Hofweber 2016b.

10.1.1   Universals and Ontological Commitment

Here is one presentation of the Problem of Universals, due to Armstrong:

> its premiss is that many different particulars can all have what appears to
> be the same nature. … The conclusion of the argument is simply that in
> general this appearance cannot be explained away, but must be accepted.
> There is such a thing as identity of nature. (1978a, xiii)

Presented like this, the argument starts with truths of the following form:

(1) *a* and *b* share the characteristic *F*
(2) *a* and *b* are both *F*
(3) *a* and *b* have something in common.

It is then pointed out that (1) and (2) at least seem to imply that *a* and *b* have
something in common, and (3) explicitly says that they do. The argument
ends by claiming that this *something* is a universal.

That is the argument in outline, but how are we meant to fill in the
details? There are two broad strategies: first, we might argue that (1)–(3) are
ontologically committed to universals; second, we might argue that universals
are involved in the *truthmakers* for (1)–(3). I will focus on the argument from
ontological commitment in this subsection, and I will turn to the argument
from truthmaking in §10.1.2.

If we take its surface form seriously, (1) seems to be committed to a universal, referred to by 'the characteristic *F*'. But I am a Fregean realist, and
Fregean realists have a habit of not taking the surface form of sentences
like this too seriously. I think we should take (1) to be nothing more than
a fancy notational variant of the much plainer (2). What, then, are the
commitments of (2)? Well, I take it that (2) is just shorthand for:

(4) *a* is *F* and *b* is *F*.

And presumably, the commitments of (4) are just the union of the commitments of its two conjuncts. So all we need to do is determine the commitments of sentences of the following form:

(5) *a* is *F*.

But now that we are down to sentences of this form, like 'Socrates is wise'
and 'Shergar is a horse', it is easy to deny that there is any commitment to
universals. We are committed to ordinary particulars alright, like Socrates
and Shergar, but why think that we are committed to universals as well?

So far, I have followed in the footsteps of Devitt's (1980) *ostrich nominalist*.[4] However, I would now like to deviate a little from the path that Devitt laid out. According to Devitt, (5) is *only* committed to the particular referred to by '*a*'. I think things are a little more complicated. I am a Fregean realist, and so I think that we have two completely different concepts of existence: one expressed by the first-order quantifier, $\exists x \ldots x \ldots$, and one by the second-order quantifier, $\exists X \ldots X \ldots$.[5] These different concepts of existence are aligned to different concepts of ontological commitment. I agree with Devitt that the only *first-order* commitment of (5) is the particular referred to by '*a*'. But I also think that there is a *second-order* commitment to a property referred to by '*x* is *F*'. These two commitments are revealed when we put the truth condition for (5) like this:

$$\exists X \exists x (`a\text{' refers to } x \wedge \forall y(y \text{ satisfies `}x \text{ is } F\text{' } \leftrightarrow Xy) \wedge Xx).$$

Now we come to (3), and unfortunately, Devitt offers us no guidance on how to handle this one. It is at this point, however, that Fregean realism earns its keep. If we read its quantifier as first-order, then (3) is surely committed to the existence of universals. But things are different if we read the quantifier as second-order, so that (3) becomes:

(6) $\exists X(Xa \wedge Xb)$.

Traditionally, philosophers who reject universals have been wary of second-order quantification because they have worried that it was itself a form of quantification over universals.[6] But for a Fregean realist, this worry is based on a kind of category error. Second-order quantifiers do not quantify over universals; they quantify over properties in the Fregean realist's sense – i.e., satisfaction conditions. So if a Fregean realist reads (3) as (6), then even (3) does not introduce a commitment to universals.[7]

---

4 Devitt (1980, 94) resisted this label, since it was originally intended as a term of abuse by Armstrong (1978a, 16–17). However, the ostriches have come to own the name.
5 I am here speaking as a Fregean *realist*. As I explained in Chapter 7 (and §9.3), there is no substantive difference between a Fregean realist and a Fregean *nominalist*, who denies that $\exists X \ldots X \ldots$ expresses existence. Importantly, though, that does not mean there is anything wrong with talking about second-order existence. The point is just that we need to understand such talk as the realist gloss on something which could also be said by a nominalist.
6 Peacock (2009, 208) argues that an ostrich nominalist should avoid (6) because it appears to quantify over universals.
7 We might want to take a leaf out of Lewis' book (1983; 1986c, §1.5) and restrict the quantifier in (6) to *natural* properties, so that (6) implies that *a* and *b* resemble each other in some robust sense. However, we do not need to worry about that here, since restricting the range of satisfaction conditions we are quantifying over need not introduce a commitment to universals.

10.1.2   Universals and Truthmaking

So far, we have thought of the Problem of Universals as an argument about *ontological commitment*. But as I mentioned earlier, that is not the only way to think of it. We can also think of it as an argument about *truthmakers*.[8] Now, I should put my cards on the table. I do not believe in truthmakers. A truthmaker for a proposition is meant to be an entity whose existence some-how *explains* why that proposition is true; the proposition is true *in virtue of* the existence of its truthmaker.[9] But I do not think that propositional truth can be explained in this way. In fact, I do not think that it is possible to give any general, one-size-fits-all explanation of why true propositions are true. I will give my reasons for this later, in §14.6. For now, though, I want to set all of my doubts about truthmakers to one side. What I want to show in this subsection is that even if they buy into truthmaking, Fregean realists should not feel forced to admit universals into their ontology.

The new version of the Problem of Universals begins with propositions of the following forms:[10]

(1) ⟨*a* and *b* share the characteristic *F*⟩
(2) ⟨*a* and *b* are both *F*⟩
(3) ⟨*a* and *b* have something in common⟩.

We now ask what the truthmakers for these propositions are. As Rodriguez-Pereyra (2002, 40–1) points out, we can simplify our question. First, (1) and (2) are both equivalent to:

(4) ⟨*a* is *F* and *b* is *F*⟩.

So any truthmakers for (4) will do as truthmakers for (1) and for (2). (3), on the other hand, is an existential generalisation of (4): (3) says that *a* and *b* have some property or other in common, whereas (4) says that they have *F* in particular in common. So any truthmakers for (4) will also be truthmakers for (3), as will be the truthmakers for ⟨*a* is *G* and *b* is *G*⟩, and the truthmakers for ⟨*a* is *H* and *b* is *H*⟩, and so on. All that is left to do now is to find truthmakers for truths of form (4). But (4) is a conjunction, and so is made true by whatever makes its conjuncts true. This last task therefore reduces to the task of finding truthmakers for truths of this form:

---

[8]   Truthmaker variants of the Problem of Universals have been given by Armstrong (1989, 88–9; 2004, 39–42) and Rodriguez-Pereyra (2000; 2002, chs. 2–3).
[9]   See Armstrong 2004; Rodriguez-Pereyra 2005, 18.
[10] In this section, I will follow the common convention of abbreviating 'the proposition that *P*' as '⟨*P*⟩'.

(5) $\langle a$ is $F\rangle$.

So we are left looking for truthmakers for simple predications like $\langle$Socrates is mortal$\rangle$, $\langle$Socrates is a philosopher$\rangle$, $\langle$Plato is mortal$\rangle$, etc.

Why might we think that the hunt for these truthmakers will uncover universals? The best way to see why is to start with what Rodriguez-Pereyra (2002, 43–6) calls *truthmaker ostrich nominalism*. According to this position, it is ordinary objects which make the instances of (5) true: Socrates makes $\langle$Socrates is mortal$\rangle$ true, Plato makes $\langle$Plato is mortal$\rangle$ true, and so on.[11] (This position gets its name because it takes the broad strategy of the ostrich nominalist and applies it to the truthmaker variant of the Problem of Universals.) Rodriguez-Pereyra argues that truthmaker ostrich nominalism is untenable on the following grounds. Socrates is not only called upon to make $\langle$Socrates is mortal$\rangle$ true. He is also called upon to make $\langle$Socrates is a philosopher$\rangle$ true. But, Rodriguez-Pereyra argues, that cannot be right: 'x is mortal' and 'x is a philosopher' are not even co-extensive, and so whatever makes $\langle$Socrates is mortal$\rangle$ true must be distinct from what makes $\langle$Socrates is a philosopher$\rangle$ true.

So it takes more than Socrates to make $\langle$Socrates is mortal$\rangle$ true. In particular, Rodriguez-Pereyra (2002, 45) tells us that $\langle$Socrates is mortal$\rangle$ is made true by the *fact that Socrates is mortal*; similarly, $\langle$Socrates is a philosopher$\rangle$ is made true by the *fact that Socrates is a philosopher*. What is more, Rodriguez-Pereyra (2002, 45–6) insists that these facts must display a certain kind of multiplicity. We cannot claim, as van Cleve (1994, 589) once did, that Socrates is the sole constituent of the fact that Socrates is mortal and of the fact that Socrates is a philosopher. There must be something extra, something that is involved in the fact that Socrates is mortal, but which is *not* involved in the fact that Socrates is a philosopher. Otherwise, there would be no way to distinguish between these two facts. And from here, it is just one more small jump to suggest that this extra thing is the universal *mortality*.

How convincing is this as an argument for the existence of universals? Well, that largely depends on whether there are any other good suggestions about what differentiates the fact that Socrates is mortal from the fact that

---

[11] Something like this view was advocated by Parsons (1999). However, it is should also be noted that Parsons was working with a non-standard conception of truthmaking. On Parson's (1999, 326–7) conception, to say that entity *e* is a truthmaker for $\langle P \rangle$ is *not* to say that $\langle P \rangle$ is true in virtue of *e*'s mere existence; rather, it is to say that $\langle P \rangle$ cannot become false without a change in *e*'s intrinsic properties.

Socrates is a philosopher.[12] And Fregean realism has a way of distinguishing these facts without introducing universals. According to Fregean realism, the fact that Socrates is mortal does not involve the universal mortality; it involves the Fregean property *is mortal*. Admittedly, this Fregean property cannot be involved in the fact that Socrates is mortal in exactly the same way as Socrates is. Socrates is an object, and whatever can be said of an object cannot be said of a property. But that does not mean it is not involved in that fact in some other way. I will say more about what this amounts to in §11.4, but for now, the following will do: the fact that Socrates is mortal is the fact we express with the sentence 'Socrates is mortal'; in the course of expressing this fact with this sentence, we predicate something of the object Socrates, and this gives us a sense in which that object is involved in that fact; equally, we predicate the property *is mortal* of something, and this gives us a sense in which that property is involved in that fact. We can now distinguish the fact that Socrates is mortal from the fact that Socrates is a philosopher: although they both involve the same object, Socrates, they involve different Fregean properties: *is mortal* and *is a philosopher*.

What we are left with, then, is a descendent of truthmaker ostrich nominalism which is immune to Rodriguez-Pereyra's attack. We begin by conceding that it is not really Socrates which makes ⟨Socrates is mortal⟩ true, but the fact that Socrates is mortal. Nonetheless we insist that Socrates is the only *object* that is involved in that fact.[13] Taken as a first-order generalisation over objects, van Cleve was quite right to say:

> the fact that *a* is *F* has *a* as its sole constituent, and the difference between this fact and the fact that *a* is *G* is not a difference in their constituents. (Van Cleve 1994, 589)

But this does not make the difference between the fact that Socrates is mortal and the fact that Socrates is a philosopher mysterious, as Rodriguez-Pereyra complained. That's because there is also a property involved in the fact that Socrates is mortal, in some second-level sense of 'involved', which is not involved in the fact that Socrates is a philosopher. So, taken as a second-order generalisation over properties, it would also be right to say:

> the fact that *a* is *F* has *F* as its sole constituent, and the difference between this fact and the fact that *b* is *F* is not a difference in their constituents.

---

[12] Rodriguez-Pereyra (2002) himself thinks that we can do without universals by pursuing a version of resemblance nominalism.

[13] Or at least, it is the only object involved on the relevant decomposition. The point of this qualification will become clear in §11.4, but for now, I will leave it to one side.

And, of course, this does not introduce some new mystery about how the fact that Socrates is mortal differs from the fact that Plato is mortal: they differ because they involve different objects, in the first-level sense of 'involve' suitable for objects.

10.2   Bradley's Regress

Here is *Bradley's Regress*:

> Suppose that Socrates is wise. For Socrates to be wise, it is not enough that Socrates and wisdom both exist. They need to bear some kind of relation to each other. Call that relation 'instantiation'. So for Socrates to be wise is for Socrates to instantiate wisdom. But for Socrates to instantiate wisdom, it is not enough that Socrates, wisdom and instantiation all exist. They need to bear some kind of relation to each other. Call it 'instantiation$_2$'. So for Socrates to be wise is for Socrates and wisdom to instantiate$_2$ instantiation. But at this point it is clear that we have started down an infinite regress.

I think it is fair to say that in the eyes of many philosophers, Bradley's Regress is *the* problem in the metaphysics of properties.[14] As MacBride (2005a, 603–4) puts it: 'It is an adequacy constraint on an account of instantiation that it shows either (a) Bradley's regress can be avoided or (b) it is a regress that need not be avoided.' Unfortunately, very few accounts of instantiation actually meet this adequacy constraint. But my aim in this section is to show that Fregean realism does: if Fregean realism is right, then Bradley's Regress simply cannot get going.

I will begin in §10.2.1 by trying to get clearer on why we might think that Bradley's Regress is vicious. Then, in §10.2.2, I will consider three familiar, but unsuccessful, strategies for dealing with the regress. Finally, in §§10.2.3–10.2.4, I will present the Fregean realist response; as we will see, it combines the three familiar strategies into a single satisfying solution.

10.2.1   What Makes Bradley's Regress Vicious?

You might think that Bradley's Regress is vicious just because it is ontologically extravagant: somehow, the mere fact that Socrates is wise has managed

---

[14]   Bradley (1893, 27–8) originally intended his regress only to show that there was something incoherent about relations. But later philosophers have co-opted it as a general problem for anyone who believes in properties or relations, whatever the adicity. Throughout this section, I will focus on monadic properties, but everything I say here applies mutatis mutandis to relations. (See §10.4 for the Fregean realist's take on relations.)

to force us to introduce infinitely many instantiation relations into our ontology.[15] However, as natural as this initial thought is, it is not all that forceful. First, it is by no means obvious that the regress does introduce infinitely many instantiation relations. It may be that we are dealing with exactly the same instantiation relation over and over, at every step in the regress: instantiation$_2$ is the very same relation as plain old instantiation, as is instantiation$_3$, instantiation$_4$ and so on. (Instantiation would have to be a multigrade relation, but there is nothing obviously incoherent about that.) And second, even if we did agree that Bradley's Regress introduces infinitely many instantiation relations, it simply is not clear why that would be so bad. Ontological economy may be a theoretical virtue, but it is not the only one. If someone presented a theory of properties which enjoyed a great many other virtues, like simplicity and explanatory power, then it may well be worth the infinitary ontological cost.

A much better suggestion is that Bradley's Regress gets its bite by frustrating a certain explanatory project. We want to offer an explanation of how properties and objects come together. Consider Socrates again. He was wise, but he was not immortal. So somehow, Socrates was bound up with the property of wisdom, but not with the property of immortality. We want to explain what that difference amounts to. But there only seems to be one explanation to give: Socrates bears a certain relation to wisdom that he does not bear to immortality. And now the regress kicks in. We have tried to explain how an object and a property got bound together by adding an instantiation relation into the mix. But that sheds no light on the matter at all, since we are now left wondering how the object, property and instantiation relation got bound together. And repeating this process infinitely many times will not help.[16] Priest gives a clear articulation of this point:

> If one is asked how to join two links of a chain together, it helps not one iota to say that one inserts an intervening link. (And adding that one might need an infinite number of such links merely makes the matter worse.) In vicious regresses of this kind (I do not think it is the only kind) the infinity has, in fact, precious little to do with matters. The point is that something has already gone wrong at the first step: a failure of explanation. (Priest 2014, 11)

---

[15] Armstrong (1989, 108) hints that this may be all that is wrong with a regress of instantiation relations when he says: 'The regress that results is either vicious or viciously uneconomical.'

[16] The idea that Bradley's Regress is vicious because it threatens to undermine an explanatory project is a fairly common one. See Armstrong 1978a, 70–1; Oliver 1996, 33; Dodd 1999a, 150–1; Lewis 2002, 6–7; MacBride 2011b; Peacock 2012; Priest 2014, 9–11.

The problem with Bradley's Regress is not really that it is an *infinite* regress. The problem is that it is a *futile* regress: no step in the regress takes us any closer to the explanation that we are after.

Bradley's Regress leaves us with just two options. We could start looking for an alternative account of how properties and objects get bound together, one which is not frustrated by the regress. Or we could just abandon that explanatory project altogether. That is, we could take Bradley's Regress as a proof that the project was ill founded from the get-go. Objects do get bound together with properties – after all, Socrates was wise – but there is no hope of explaining *how* that is possible.[17]

In the end, I think that the second option is inevitable: we say all that there is to say about how Socrates is bound together with wisdom when we say that Socrates is wise. But I do not think it would be satisfying to jump to that conclusion now. On the face of it, the question of how properties and objects get bound together appears to be a perfectly good one. In fact, it appears to be a compulsory question for any decent metaphysics of properties and objects. If we want to deny that this question can be answered, then we need to find some way of showing that it does not *need* to be.

I am sure it will come as no surprise to you that this is where I think Fregean realism comes in. I will shortly argue that Fregean realism frees us from the felt obligation to explain how properties and objects come together. But before that, I want to briefly sketch three familiar strategies for blocking Bradley's Regress. These are certainly not the only strategies that philosophers have tried. Bradley's Regress has become common property, and every metaphysician has their own response to it.[18] I have chosen to focus on these three strategies because, although they are unsatisfactory as they stand, they all point in the right direction. Now, this may initially seem a bit odd, because these strategies all appear to point in *different* directions. But as we will see, they are all incorporated into the Fregean realist response to Bradley's Regress.

---

[17] This is how Lewis (1983, 351–4) and Oliver (1996, 33) respond to the regress.
[18] For a range of responses to the regress that I have not discussed here, see Gaskin 1995, 2008; Baxter 2001; Vallicella 2000, 2002; Priest 2014. I find all of these responses more or less mind bending. By contrast, the Fregean realist response I am about to give strikes me as entirely straightforward. But then, I would say that.

Instantiation Is Not an Ordinary Relation

The first strategy is to accept that Socrates and wisdom are joined together by an instantiation relation, but then insist that instantiation is not an ordinary relation. Ordinary relations, like *loves* and *is older than*, need to be linked to their relata via an instantiation relation, but the instantiation relation itself links up with its relata directly, without mediation. The instantiation relation is, then, so different from ordinary relations that it is probably best not to call it a 'relation' at all. Better to call it something else, like a 'tie' or a 'nexus'. This strategy, or something like it, has been suggested by Strawson (1959, 167–79), Bergmann (1960) and an early timeslice of Armstrong (1978a, 108–11).

I think that there is insight in this strategy. As I will shortly argue, there is an instantiation relation which holds between Socrates and the property *is wise*, but it is of a fundamentally different type from ordinary relations like *loves*. However, until more is said, the strategy is deeply unsatisfying. It looks like little more than a change in terminology. No one really cares what you call instantiation. Call it a 'relation', or a 'tie', or whatever else you like. We are still stuck with exactly the same question. Somehow, Socrates, wisdom and instantiation have become bound together. How is that possible, if not by some relation (or tie or whatever) holding between them? Until we say more, we must surely agree with Lewis (2002, 7) that calling instantiation 'a "non-relational tie" [points] away from error, but not toward much of anything'.

Properties Are Unsaturated

On the second strategy, we do not try to block Bradley's Regress by saying that there is something special about the instantiation relation in particular. We do it by saying that there is something special about *every* property and relation. This strategy is often associated with the Fregean doctrine that all properties and relations are 'unsaturated'. According to Frege (1892a, 1891–5), properties come with gaps, which are just the right size and shape to be filled by objects. If this is how we think of properties, then we may well deny that there is any need for an instantiation relation at all. We do not need any relation to tie an object to a property. The object fits directly *into* the property itself.

Again, I think that there is real insight in this Fregean approach. There is something special about properties, and appreciating that fact is an important part of blocking Bradley's Regress. But, again, until we say much more, this strategy is pretty unsatisfying. First off, even Frege (1891–5, 173–4; 1906c, 296) admitted that calling properties 'unsaturated' was to speak in metaphor. We need to find some way of spelling that metaphor out in literal terms.[19] And just as important, we *still* seem to be stuck with the same question as before. Somehow, Socrates is bound up with the property *is wise* but not with the property *is immortal*. A Fregean will put this by saying that Socrates *saturates* the first of these properties but not the second. However, in doing so, they seem to be introducing a new relation, saturation, and Bradley's Regress beckons.[20]

Properties Are Ways

The third strategy was proposed by Seargent (1985, 110–16). According to Seargent, Bradley's Regress only comes up because we are speaking about properties in the wrong way. We speak about properties as if they were 'things', which is what makes Bradley's Regress seem inevitable: if properties are a kind of thing, then they must be things that are somehow related to the objects which instantiate them, and that is the first step in the regress. But there is a way out. We just need to stop speaking about properties as if they were *things*, and instead speak about them as *ways*. Being wise is not a thing which Socrates is related to; rather, being wise is a way that Socrates is. According to Seargent, if we start speaking in this way, we will no longer feel the need to introduce an instantiation relation to connect an object with its properties. In fact, doing so would be a kind of category error, since relations are there to relate one thing to another, not one thing to a way.

I certainly think that Seargent is on the right track. Bradley's Regress is just a product of our thinking and speaking about properties in the wrong way. But, again, we cannot just leave things here. Although Seargent's suggestion that properties are really 'ways' is suggestive, he does not explain exactly what that is supposed to mean. Nor does he explain what he means when he says that properties are *not* 'things'. Armstrong (1997, 30–1), for example, responded to Seargent by agreeing that properties are ways, but by denying that this meant that they are not things: for Armstrong, ways are just another kind of thing.

What we need, then, is a worked-out theory of what it means to say that a property is not a 'thing'. And this is exactly what Fregean realism provides. Properties are not 'things' in the sense that they are not *objects*. Properties can only be referred to by predicates, not singular terms. And once we accept that, we really will be in a position to block Bradley's Regress.

---

[19] This point is rightly emphasised by Hale and Wright (2012, 121).
[20] This point is made by Vallicella (2000, 242–3; 2002, 33–4) and MacBride (2005a, 606–7).

10.2.3   The Fregean Realist Response

As soon as you reject the idea that properties are objects, Bradley's Regress starts to look suspicious. We begin by saying that if Socrates *is wise*, then he must bear some kind of relation to *wisdom*. Right from the beginning, then, we seem to be speaking as if properties were objects – we seem to be speaking as if the predicate 'x is wise' co-referred with the term 'wisdom'. Admittedly, even Fregean realists sometimes speak as if properties were objects, since doing so allows them to express their thoughts much more easily than they otherwise could. But this way of speaking is acceptable only if it is possible to express those thoughts the long way round, without pretending that properties are objects. And crucially, Bradley's Regress is exactly the sort of thing that cannot be expressed without reifying properties.

Here are the first two steps of the regress:

(1) Socrates is wise
(2) Socrates instantiates wisdom.

I take it that for the purposes of Bradley's Regress, it is essential that 'wisdom' co-refers with 'x is wise'. After all, (2) is meant to articulate the relationship between Socrates and the property *wise* that is implicit in (1). Thus, (2) does appear to involve an illicit reification of that property: we are trying to refer to it with 'wisdom', which at least appears to be a singular term. If we want to deny that there is really any illicit reifying going on, we need to find some paraphrase of (2), in which we swap 'wisdom' for a predicate. As it happens, it is not too hard to find such a paraphrase. The natural suggestion would be (1) itself. But in that case, the step from (1) to (2) cannot be the first step in a regress. It can't be, because it isn't really a step at all. (2) is just a periphrastic restatement of (1).

Here is another way of reaching the same conclusion. We start by asking: how should we understand the word 'instantiates'? Should it be read as a first-level predicate, 'x instantiates y', or as mixed-level one, 'x instantiates Y'? Grammatical appearances obviously favour the former option. But if that is how we read it, then we could never use a sentence like (2) to express the relationship between Socrates and one of his properties: 'Socrates instantiates y' would be a first-level predicate true or false of objects, not properties.

So let's try reading 'instantiates' as a mixed-level predicate, 'x instantiates Y'. If this is how we read 'instantiates', then we will be forced to discard surface grammatical appearances and read 'wisdom' in (2) as a disguised predicate, 'x is wise'. It would be more perspicuous, then, to rewrite (2) as:

(2′) Socrates instantiates is wise.

Of course, this is ungrammatical as far as normal English goes, but there is no reason why we could not extend the language to include it. In fact, we can define this new 'x instantiates Y' as follows:

$$x \text{ instantiates } Y \leftrightarrow_{df} Yx.$$

In other words, 'x instantiates Y' is just a notational variant of 'Yx', which is the predicate you get when you take 'Socrates is wise' and replace both 'Socrates' and 'x is wise' with gaps of the appropriate sorts.[21] If this is how we read 'instantiates', then we can use it to express the relation that holds between Socrates and his properties. But, again, this is not the first step in a regress. If 'x instantiates Y' is just a notational variant of 'Yx', then (2′) is really just a notational variant of (1). In the step from (1) to (2′), our feet remain firmly where they were.

For a Fregean realist, then, Bradley's Regress is halted at the first step. What is more, we can see this response to Bradley's Regress as a development of the three responses outlined in §10.2.2. Like Seargent, the Fregean realist insists that a certain kind of category error lies behind Bradley's Regress. We are only confronted with a regress when we speak of properties as if they were objects. But they are not: we can only refer to properties with predicates. And that is the literal truth behind the metaphorical claim that properties are 'unsaturated'. Objects plug directly into 'unsaturated' properties in the following sense: if you want to articulate the relationship between Socrates and the property of being wise, then you can do no better than (1). This is not to say that there is anything wrong with (2). It is just that if you want (2) to express the relation between Socrates and *wise*, you need to read it as a mere periphrasis of (1) itself. Or another way of putting the same point: we must read 'instantiates' as 'x instantiates Y', which should then be taken as nothing but a typographical variant of 'Yx'. And now we can see what is so special about the instantiation relation: although instantiation is a perfectly good relation, it is not a *first-level* relation, like *loves* or *is older than*. We could signal this by calling instantiation a 'tie' if we liked, but it would be better to call it what it is: a *mixed-level* relation.[22]

---

[21] Frege tells us that we should express instantiation with 'Yx' in volume I of *Grundgesetze* (1893, §22).

[22] What if you believed in universals (in the sense of §10.1) and wanted to know how Socrates is related to his universals, rather than his properties? In that case, we should read (2),

(2) Socrates instantiates wisdom,

in exactly the way its form suggests: two terms, 'Socrates' and 'wisdom', plugged into a dyadic first-level predicate, 'x instantiates y'. This way of reading (2) may be inappropriate if we want to express the relation between Socrates and one of his (Fregean) properties, but it has just the right

10.2.4   Abandoning the Explanatory Project

In §10.2.1, I suggested that Bradley's Regress gets its bite by threatening to undermine a certain explanatory project: Socrates is somehow bound together with wisdom, and we want to explain how this is possible by saying that Socrates instantiates wisdom; but now the question is simply repeated, this time about how Socrates, wisdom and instantiation are all bound together.

At first, you might have hoped that Fregean realism could save this explanatory project: the threat to the project was Bradley's Regress, and now that regress has been blocked. But, in fact, Fregean realism is just as big a threat as the regress was. I just argued that if (2),

(2) Socrates instantiates wisdom,

is to have any chance of articulating the relationship between Socrates and the Fregean property of being wise, then it must be read as a mere periphrasis of (1):

(1) Socrates is wise.

But in that case, we obviously cannot offer (2) as some sort of explanation of the unity described in (1). Really, that would just be to attempt to explain how (1) could be true simply by repeating (1).

However, it is important to bear in mind that the Fregean realist is not *merely* denying that (1) can be explained with (2). They are also offering a new perspective, from which we will see no need to offer any such explanation. The belief that we need to give (2) as an explanation for (1) stems from the feeling that (1) leaves something unsaid: (1) seems to hint at a relation between property and object, whereas (2) comes out and says what it is. However, that whole way of looking at things presupposes that properties are objects. Once we reject that presupposition, we will see that (1) leaves nothing unsaid: if you want to express the relationship between Socrates and the property of being wise, then you cannot do any better than (1). For

---

shape for expressing the relation between Socrates and one of his universals. However, this still will not kick off an infinite regress. The next step in the regress is meant to be:

(3) Socrates and wisdom instantiate₂ instantiation.

But if this is to articulate the relation between Socrates, wisdom and instantiation implicit in (2), then we cannot read 'instantiation' as a genuine singular term: according to Fregean realism, no singular term can co-refer with the *predicate* 'x instantiates y'. It must be possible, then, to give (3) a more perspicuous paraphrase, which eliminates the apparent term 'instantiation'. And, of course, it is possible: we can take (3) to be nothing more than a periphrastic variant of (2). But in that case, the 'step' from (2) to (3) is no step at all.

a Fregean realist, then, Bradley's Regress is really just a pseudo-problem for a pseudo-explanation.[23]

10.3   Are Properties Immanent or Transcendent?

Philosophers often divide realists about properties into two camps: the *platonists* and the *aristotelians*. The platonists claim that properties somehow *transcend* the objects which instantiate them, whereas the aristotelians claim that properties are somehow *immanent* in those objects. Now, as the 'somehow's suggest, it is not entirely clear what these claims actually mean. However, much of the recent disagreement has focussed on the location of properties: according to the platonists, properties are not located anywhere in space or time; but according to the aristotelians, properties are co-located with the objects which instantiate them.

There is an obvious objection to aristotelianism. The property *horse* is supposed to be co-located with the objects which instantiate it. But there are lots of horses all over the globe. So the property *horse* must be located in many places at once! This conclusion has struck many philosophers as mind boggling.[24] It certainly runs counter to our ordinary thought about location. In ordinary contexts, there is no better way of proving that x is not identical to y than by showing that x and y were in different places at the same time. (That is how alibis work.) Maybe we could learn to live with the idea that properties flout the usual laws of location,[25] but it surely counts as a mark against this version of aristotelianism that it requires us to do so.

There are also objections to platonism. First off, there is a familiar *Access Problem*. According to platonism, properties exist outside of space and time. Presumably, this implies that properties have no causal powers. But if we cannot causally interact with properties, then how could we know anything about them? For that matter, how could we even refer to them in the first place?[26]

---

[23]   I believe that Dummett (1981a, 174–6) was making a similar point when he said that if we realise that properties are not objects, problems like Bradley's Regress will 'simply vanish'.

[24]   For a clear rejection of the intelligibility of multiply-located universals, see Lowe 2006, 98–9.

[25]   For two attempts to make sense of multiple-location, see MacBride 1998; Paul 2002. Concerns about the intelligibility of multiple-location have also loomed large in the literature on extended simples: McDaniel 2003, §IV; 2007; 2009a; Parsons 2004, esp. 177–8.

[26]   The Access Problem has its roots in the philosophy of mathematics, and the locus classicus is Benacerraf 1973, 671–3. Benacerraf originally focussed exclusively on the epistemological version of the Access Problem, but the semantic version has since risen in prominence, see Hale and Wright 2002, 113–19.

But the problems for platonism go beyond the Access Problem. If properties are a kind of abstract object, existing outside of space and time, then what are they to the concrete objects which instantiate them? Imagine we have two balls, *a* and *b*, that are exactly the same, except *a* instantiates *weighs 1 kg*, and *b* instantiates *weighs 10 kg*. This is a very concrete kind of difference: if you push them with the same force, then *a* will accelerate much more than *b*; if you hold them above your head, then *b* will tire your arm faster than *a*; if you drop them from the same height, then, well, they'll hit the ground at the same time, but *b* will land with a much louder thud. How could all of this come about just by virtue of one ball standing in a relation to one abstract object, and the other ball in that relation to a different one?[27]

So, there are good objections to both platonism and aristotelianism. I certainly would not want to suggest that any of these objections are conclusive. Maybe we could learn to live with platonism or with aristotelianism. But it would be better if we could choose a third option. And as Jones (2018) has forcefully argued, this is just what Fregean realism offers us. According to Fregean realism, it simply does not make sense to say that properties are, or are not, spatiotemporal. 'x is spatiotemporally located' is a first-level predicate, true or false of objects, and what can be said of an object cannot be said of a property. (Just imagine trying to plug a predicate into the gap in 'x is spatiotemporally located'. The best we could do would be some nonsense like 'is a horse is spatiotemporally located'.) So from a Fregean realist's point of view, platonism and aristotelianism should both be rejected as incoherent; they both mistakenly presuppose that it makes sense to talk about the locations of properties.

That's actually a little bit fast. All that really follows from Fregean realism is that it doesn't make sense to ask whether properties are spatiotemporally located in exactly the same first-level sense that objects are located. It might yet be that there is some analogous second-level sense in which it does make sense. But what would this analogous sense be? The obvious suggestion is to define what it means to say that a property X is located in region r as follows:

(1) $L(X, r) \leftrightarrow_{df} \exists x(Xx \land x$ is located in $r)$.

---

[27] I take it that this is a version of the Problem of Bare Particulars (Armstrong 1978a, 69). However, the crucial point is not that an object seems bare when it is considered in isolation from its properties – that version of the problem has been thoroughly debunked by Sider (2006). The problem is that objects *still* seem bare, even after they have been hooked up to abstract properties.

However, that is just a second-level version of the aristotelian view that properties are located wherever their instances are, and we have already seen how strange that view is. Importantly, however, this observation no longer cuts against aristotelianism alone. The point is that the second-level relation defined by (1) does not behave analogously to the paradigm first-level cases of location. We are no closer, then, to the second-level analogue of location that we need to make sense of *either* aristotelianism *or* platonism.

Fregean realists should therefore reject both aristotelianism and platonism. This point is worth emphasising, because it can be easy to mistake Fregean realism for a brand of platonism. After all, platonists and Fregean realists both agree that it is a mistake to say that properties are spatiotemporally located. They just disagree about what kind of mistake it is: the platonists think it is false, and the Fregean realists think that it is nonsense. But this is a hugely important difference. Consider the following *Location Principle*:

(LP) Everything is spatiotemporally located.

I do not know whether (LP) is true, but plenty of philosophers have been attracted to it. That's bad news for platonism, since it straightforwardly contradicts (LP). But as Jones (2018, 822) points out, Fregean realism does not contradict (LP). (LP) is a first-order generalisation over objects, not properties. And for all that Fregean realism says, it may well be that every object is spatiotemporally located. Now, you might worry that this is a bit of a cheat. The quantifier in (LP) is presumably meant to be absolutely general: *absolutely everything* is spatiotemporally located, and shouldn't that include properties? But, crucially, properties aren't the sort of thing that you can quantify over with a first-order quantifier. So (LP) cannot be applied to properties. This is not to say that the quantifier has been restricted somehow. On its most general reading, (LP) is true just in case 'x is spatiotemporally located' is true of *everything* that it can be meaningfully applied to; it has nothing to say about anything else.

If that does not yet make it clear how different platonism and Fregean realism are, then consider the Access Problem. At first, you might have thought that Fregean realism faces a version of this problem too. 'x has causal powers' is a first-level predicate, and so, according to the Fregean realists, it cannot be applied to a property. So Fregean realism rejects the idea that properties have causal powers. On the face of it, then, Fregean realism seems to make our ability to refer to, and know about, properties just as mysterious as platonism.

In reality, however, there is no Access Problem for the Fregean realists. The Access Problem relies on causal principles like these:

(CR) It is impossible to refer to anything which lacks causal powers.

(CK) It is impossible to know about anything which lacks causal powers.

But the quantifiers in both of these principles are first-order. They have to be, because 'x has causal powers' is a first-level predicate, true or false of objects. These principles might be true, unrestrictedly true of absolutely every object, without implying anything about our ability to refer to, or know about, properties. Here it may be useful to recall that the Fregean realists use '$\forall y(y$ satisfies x $\leftrightarrow Yy)$', or something very much like it, to express predicate-reference. If we wanted to say that a property has to have causal powers in order for us to refer to it, we would therefore have to say something like this:

(2) # $\forall Y(\exists x \forall y(y$ satisfies $x \leftrightarrow Yy) \rightarrow Y$ has causal powers).

But the consequent of (2) is nonsense: 'x has causal powers' is a first-level predicate, true or false of objects, and Y is a predicate-variable, ranging over satisfaction conditions. Of course, there are all sorts of ways of modifying (2) to make it make sense. Here is one example:

(3) $\forall Y(\exists x \forall y(y$ satisfies $x \leftrightarrow Yy) \rightarrow \exists z(Yz \wedge z$ has causal powers).

On the face of it, (3) is a not implausible causal principle governing predicate-reference: we cannot refer to a property unless we can causally interact with some instance of it. If we decide to accept (3), then we will face an Access Problem for certain properties, like *is prime*: no object with causal powers is prime. Importantly, however, this would be a merely local Access Problem, not a general difficulty for our ability to refer to any property at all.

If you *still* aren't quite convinced that Fregean realism is not a brand of platonism, then perhaps this final point will settle it. I mentioned earlier that by treating properties as abstract objects, platonists make it difficult to see what relevance they could possibly have to the objects which instantiate them. But Fregean realists do not have any such problem. As I explained in §10.2.3, when Fregean realists say that *a* instiates the property *weighs 1 kg*, they do not mean that *a* bears a relation to some abstract object. They just mean that *a* weighs 1 kg.

10.4 Converse Relations

Relations come in pairs: *taller* and *shorter*; *older* and *younger*; *left* and *right*. Each relation is the *converse* of its partner. In general, relations are distinct from their converses: if Simon bears the *is older than* relation to Daniel, then he cannot also bear the *is younger than* relation to him; that seems enough to show that they are two different relations. But at the same time, there is a peculiar intimacy between a relation and its converse: if Simon bears the *is older than* relation to Daniel, then Daniel must bear the *is younger than* relation to Simon. Some philosophers have found this very puzzling. Why would nature double up on her relations like this?

Williamson (1985) responded by denying that relations are distinct from their converses: *is younger than* is the very same relation as *is older than*, despite the fact that Simon seems to bear only one of them to Daniel. And Fine (2000) went even further, denying that relations have converses in the first place. In this section, I will present the Fregean realist response. I will begin in §10.4.1 by arguing that, from the Fregean realist perspective, relations *obviously* have converses, and (non-symmetric) relations are *obviously* distinct from their converses. Then I will consider Williamson's argument in §10.4.2, and Fine's in §10.4.3.

10.4.1 Fregean Realism about Relations

In all of my presentations of Fregean realism so far, I have focussed on monadic properties, but Fregean realism naturally extends to properties of higher adicities. Monadic properties are the satisfaction conditions of monadic predicates (i.e., predicates with just one argument place). And by exactly the same token, dyadic relations are the satisfaction conditions of dyadic predicates (i.e., predicates with two argument places). We can express the relationship between a dyadic predicate and the relation it stands for with something like the following:

(S^2) $\forall y \forall z(y$ and z, in that order, satisfy x $\leftrightarrow$ R$yz)$.[28]

The x marks a gap for a term referring to a dyadic predicate, and the R marks a gap for a dyadic predicate.[29] So if we wanted to specify which relation 'x loves y' refers to, we would say:

---

[28] Strictly, (S^2) is only really fit for extensional contexts. If we wanted a notion of dyadic-predicate-reference suitable for modal contexts, we should probably trade it in for (Modal-S^2): $\forall w \forall y \forall z(y$ and z, in that order, satisfy x relative to $w \leftrightarrow$ Ryz at $w)$.

[29] As a result, Fregean realists should insist that it is nonsense to say that a relation is an object, or that a dyadic relation is a monadic property.

$\forall y \forall z (y$ and z, in that order, satisfy 'x loves y' $\leftrightarrow y$ loves z).

The Fregean realist conception of relations is, then, every bit as abundant as the Fregean realist conception of properties. *Every* dyadic predicate with a satisfaction condition automatically refers to a relation. It immediately follows that every relation has a converse. Given a relation R, we can always introduce a predicate which refers to its converse, '$\check{R}xy$', just by stipulating:

$$\check{R}xy \leftrightarrow_{df} Ryx.$$

So every relation has a converse. And as a general rule, relations tend to be distinct from their converses. To see this, we need only note that if we use (S^2) to express dyadic-predicate-reference, then we should use the following to express identity between dyadic relations:

(I^2) $\forall x \forall y (Rxy \leftrightarrow Sxy)$.[30]

(Like R, S here marks a gap for dyadic predicates.) It is now easy to argue that symmetric relations are identical to their converses, but non-symmetric relations are not. A relation, R, is symmetric just in case for all x and y, Rxy iff Ryx. Since $\check{R}xy$ iff Ryx, it immediately follows that R is the same relation as $\check{R}$ iff R is symmetric.[31]

All of this is entirely straightforward from the Fregean realist perspective. What we need to do now is get clearer on why other philosophers have been so puzzled by converse relations.

10.4.2 *Williamson's Linguistic Argument*

Williamson believes that every relation is identical to its converse.[32] He (1985, 252–4) argues for this via a *reductio ad absurdum*. Suppose that some relation is distinct from its converse. For the sake of having an example, let that relation be *kicks*. Now imagine a language, L_1, which uses the predicate 'K' to refer to this relation. In particular, 'Kab' says in L_1 that a kicks b. L_1 is here imposing a convention on the significance of word order: when we

---

[30] If we were using (Modal-S^2) to express dyadic-predicate-reference, then we would use (Modal-I^2) to express identity for relations: $\Box \forall x \forall y (Rxy \leftrightarrow Sxy)$.

[31] And if we were using (Modal-I^2), then a relation will be identical to its converse iff it is necessarily symmetric.

[32] Or at least, he did in 1985. In *Modal Logic as Metaphysics* (2013, 263–4), Williamson takes a much more Fregean view of properties and relations. There he commits himself to the idea that (Modal-I^2) is the proper expression of identity between relations. Presumably, Williamson has come to accept that non-symmetric relations are distinct from their converses (in the only sense of 'distinct' which can be applied to relations).

write 'K' followed by two terms, the referent of the first term is said to be the kicker, and the referent of the second term is said to be the kicked. But that convention is inessential, and we could imagine a language, L_2 which reverses it: the referent of the *second* term is said to be the kicker, and the referent of the *first* term is said to be the kicked. In L_2, then, '*Kab*' says that *b* kicks *a*. We can sum up the difference between L_1 and L_2 like this:

L_1: 'K' refers to the *kicks* relation, and '*Kab*' says that *a* stands in that relation to *b*.

L_2: 'K' refers to the *kicks* relation, and '*Kab*' says that *b* stands in that relation to *a*.

But now consider a third language, L_3, which is exactly like L_2, except 'K' stands for the converse of *kicks*, *is kicked by*:

L_3: 'K' refers to the *is kicked by* relation, and '*Kab*' says that *b* stands in that relation to *a*.

L_1 and L_3 are meant to be different languages: in L_1, 'K' refers to *kicks*, and in L_3, 'K' refers to *is kicked by*. However, it is fairly clear that there would be no way to tell whether a linguistic community was speaking L_1 or L_3: either way, they would both be saying that *a* kicks *b* when they say '*Kab*'. We are thus led to a new indeterminacy of reference: in general, there is no telling whether you are referring to a given relation and using one convention regarding word order, or referring to the converse relation and using a different convention. Williamson (1985, 255) recommends that we stop this indeterminacy argument in its tracks by identifying *kicks* with *is kicked by*. L_1 and L_3 are not really two different languages: 'K' refers to the same relation in both languages, and both languages follow a convention according to which the first term in '*Kab*' refers to the kicker, and the second to the kicked.

You might well suspect that Williamson's cure to this new indeterminacy is worse than the disease. As Williamson (1985, 256–62) readily acknowledges, the decision to identify every relation with its converse will require a serious rethinking of our whole approach to relations. But I do not want to pursue that point here. What I want to do is explain where Williamson's argument breaks down, from a Fregean realist's point of view.

Williamson's argument crucially assumes that there are two variables which can be varied independently: first, there is the relation that 'K' refers to; second, there is a convention about how to understand the whole sentence '*Kab*'. But according to Fregean realism, these are not independent variables. The reference relation for dyadic predicates is expressed by:

(S_1^2) $\forall y \forall z(y$ and z, in that order, satisfy x $\leftrightarrow$ Ryz).

(The reason for adding the numerical subscript will become clear shortly.) So if you want to say that 'K' – or, more properly, 'Kxy' – refers to the *kicks* relation, then you must really say something like this:

(1) $\forall y \forall z(y$ and z, in that order, satisfy 'Kxy' $\leftrightarrow$ y kicks z).

Specifying the referent of 'Kxy' in this way is already enough to settle the truth condition for 'Kab'. Truth and satisfaction are interlocking concepts: 'Kab' is true iff the referent of 'a' and the referent of 'b' satisfy 'Kxy', in that order. So, given (1), 'Kab' is true iff a kicks b. Equally, to say that 'Kxy' refers to the *is kicked by* relation, we would need to say:

$\forall y \forall z(y$ and z, in that order, satisfy 'Kxy' $\leftrightarrow$ y is kicked by z).

But this would leave 'Kab' with a different truth condition: 'Kab' is true iff a is kicked by b. In short, changing the referent of 'Kxy' from a relation to its converse *automatically* changes the meaning of 'Kab'. So if 'Kab' says that a kicks b, then 'Kxy' must refer to *kicks*, not *is kicked by*.

    At this point, you may want to complain on Williamson's behalf. We can swap *kicks* for *is kicked by*, and then compensate for that swap as follows:

(2) $\forall y \forall z(y$ and z, in that order, satisfy 'Kxy' $\leftrightarrow$ z is kicked by y).

Now the truth condition of 'Kab' is as it was: 'Kab' is true iff b is kicked by a – i.e., iff a kicks b. But while that is certainly true, it is important to recognise that (2) is not an instance of (S_1^2): the y and the z are in the same order on both sides of (S_1^2), but not on both sides of (2). So, if we are using (S_1^2) to express dyadic-predicate-reference, then (2) does not say that 'Kxy' refers to *is kicked by*, or to anything else for that matter.

    However, what now becomes clear is that our decision to use (S_1^2) to express dyadic-predicate-reference was somewhat arbitrary. It would have been just as good to use:

(S_2^2) $\forall y \forall z(y$ and z, in that order, satisfy x $\leftrightarrow$ Rzy).

If we had, then it would have been (2) that specified the referent of 'Kxy', not (1). In fact, there is even more space for variation. I have so far assumed that truth and satisfaction are connected as follows: 'Kab' is true iff the referent of 'a' and the referent of 'b' satisfy 'Kxy', in that order. But we could introduce a new satisfaction relation, satisfaction*, which relates to truth like this: 'Kab' is true iff the referent of 'b' and the referent of 'a' satisfy* 'Kxy', in *this* order.

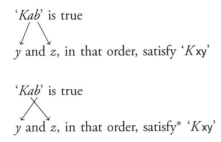

Using this new satisfaction*, we can offer two more expressions that we might have used to express dyadic-predicate-reference:

(S_3^2) $\forall y \forall z(y$ and z, in that order, satisfy* x $\leftrightarrow$ Ryz)
(S_4^2) $\forall y \forall z(y$ and z, in that order, satisfy* x $\leftrightarrow$ Rzy).

If we wanted to specify what 'Kxy' refers to by these standards, we would say:

(3) $\forall y \forall z(y$ and z, in that order, satisfy* 'Kxy' $\leftrightarrow y$ is kicked by z)
(4) $\forall y \forall z(y$ and z, in that order, satisfy* 'Kxy' $\leftrightarrow z$ kicks y).

We are, then, confronted with a choice between four ways of expressing dyadic-predicate-reference, (S_1^2)–(S_4^2). Every one of them will work as well as every other.[33] On some choices, (S_1^2) and (S_4^2), we end up saying that 'Kxy' refers to *kicks*, and on others, (S_2^2) and (S_3^2), we end up saying that it refers to *is kicked by*. But this is not to say that there is any kind of indeterminacy about what 'Kxy' refers to. It is not as though (S_1^2)–(S_4^2) are in competition with each other. There are no inscrutable facts about which relation is the *real* reference relation, or about which relation 'Kxy' *really* refers to.

---

[33] You might want to object at this point. Back in Chapter 4, I argued that there is an essential relationship between reference and disquotation. But it seems that neither (S_2^2) nor (S_3^2) will allow us to disquote 'x kicks y', since the following are both false:

$\forall y \forall z(y$ and z, in that order, satisfy 'x kicks y' $\leftrightarrow z$ kicks y)
$\forall y \forall z(y$ and z, in that order, satisfy* 'x kicks y' $\leftrightarrow y$ kicks z).

Importantly, however, this objection is mistaken. As I emphasised in §4.3, disquotation should be characterised in terms of *sense-substitution*. And it seems to me that we are entirely free to say that the *object-language* predicate 'x kicks y' has the same sense as the *metalanguage* predicate 'x is kicked by y'. If we do, then the following will count as instances of disquotation:

$\forall y \forall z(y$ and z, in that order, satisfy 'x kicks y' $\leftrightarrow z$ is kicked by y)
$\forall y \forall z(y$ and z, in that order, satisfy* 'x kicks y' $\leftrightarrow y$ is kicked by z).

The important point, then, is just that different conceptions of *sense* go with different conceptions of *reference*.

(S_1^2)–(S_4^2) simply provide us with different senses in which dyadic predicates can be said to refer to relations. For practical purposes, it is helpful to settle on just one of these senses, and we have settled on (S_1^2). But any of them would do. In the end, 'Kxy' refers to *kicks* and also refers to *is kicked by*, just in different senses of 'refers'.

10.4.3   Fine's Metaphysical Argument

Fine (2000, 2–7) has an argument which is meant to show that relations do not have converses. This argument rests on two premises:

> *Identity.* Any completion of a relation is identical to a completion of its converse.
> *Distinctness.* No complex is the completion of two distinct relations.

A *completion* of a dyadic relation R is what you get when you combine R with two objects in the right way. For example, the completion of *loves* by Daniel and Simon (in that order) is Daniel's loving Simon. Fine is intentionally unspecific about what completions are. You can think of them as states of affairs or facts or propositions; whichever you choose, Fine thinks that *Identity* and *Distinctness* will both be true.

Let's start with *Identity*. Suppose that Daniel loves Simon. It follows automatically that Simon is loved by Daniel. But it would be very strange to say that these are two different states of affairs (or facts or propositions): Daniel's loving Simon, and Simon's being loved by Daniel. As Fine (2000, 3) puts it, it is much more natural to say that there is just one state of affairs 'out there in reality', which we can choose to describe one way or the other.

But turn now to *Distinctness*. It is very tempting to think of completions as a kind of complex, which are somehow built out of objects and relations. Exactly how they are built out of objects and relations is up for grabs, but there is a strong inclination to insist that something like this must be right. And for Fine (2000, 3), it is a short step from here to *Distinctness*. He finds it very hard to see how a single complex could be built out of two distinct relations. Wouldn't that be like saying that we could make *one and the same* table either by sticking some legs onto one tabletop, or by sticking them onto another?

Taken together, though, *Identity* and *Distinctness* appear to lead to a contradiction: Daniel's loving Simon is both identical to, and distinct from, Simon's being loved by Daniel. The only way to block this contradiction is by denying that *loves* has a distinct converse, *is loved by*. That is the negative component of Fine's (2000) paper. The rest of it is spent working out a positive proposal about how we should think of relations if we want to avoid introducing converses into our ontology. However, we will not look at that positive proposal here. Our only interest is in where Fine's argument against converse relations goes wrong, from a Fregean realist's point of view.[34]

Fregean realists should have no quarrel with *Identity*. I will develop a Fregean account of states of affairs in Chapter 11, but here is a short précis. States of affairs are not a kind of object. Rather, states of affairs are the truth conditions of whole sentences, like 'Daniel loves Simon' and 'Simon is older than Daniel'. From this Fregean realist perspective, *Identity* seems like an overwhelmingly plausible principle. Even if 'Daniel loves Simon' and 'Simon is loved by Daniel' are not quite synonymous, they are surely close enough to count as having the same truth condition by any reasonable standard.

Distinctness, however, has no pull. Fine motivated this principle by thinking of states of affairs as complexes, built out of relations and objects in something like the way that a table is built out of some legs and a tabletop. But thinking about states of affairs in this way clearly presupposes that states and relations are kinds of object. We can grant that the satisfaction condition of 'x loves y' is in some sense a 'constituent' of the truth condition of 'Daniel loves Simon' (see §11.4), but it is clearly nothing like the sense in which a tabletop is a constituent of a table. We cannot, then, let our ordinary intuitions about complex objects guide us when we are dealing with states of affairs. Instead, we can treat the fact that 'Daniel loves Simon' and 'Simon is loved by Daniel' evidently refer to the same state of affairs as a standing refutation of *Distinctness*.[35]

Of course, this response to Fine will not be truly sastisfying until we have the full Fregean realist account of states of affairs. But presenting that account is the central task of the next chapter.

---

[34] For interesting discussions of Fine's positive proposal, see MacBride 2007, 2014, 13–14.
[35] In addition to his metaphysical argument, Fine (2000, 6–7) also has a back-up linguistic argument. Fine asks us to imagine a language in which people do not use the sentence 'Daniel loves Simon' to say that Daniel loves Simon. Instead, they write 'Daniel' on one side of a heart-shaped piece of card, and 'Simon' on the other. One of these sides is coloured red, the other coloured black, and it is understood that the name written on the red side is the name of the person said to be the lover, and the name written on the black side is the name of the person said to be the beloved. Fine insists that it would be obviously absurd to say that this heart-shaped card stands just for *loves* or just for *is loved by*. We must say either say that it refers to both of them or to neither of them. Fine plumps for the second option, but Fregean realists should plump for the first: it is easy to see how we could apply my response to Williamson to this case, and say that the heart-shaped card refers to both relations, but in two different senses of 'refers'.

States of Affairs

Fregean realism is a doctrine about properties. According to that doctrine, we cannot think of properties as objects that can be referred to with singular terms; properties are really just the satisfaction conditions of predicates. In this chapter, I will argue that this account of properties naturally leads to a corresponding account of *states of affairs*. According to that account, states are the *truth conditions* of sentences.

This chapter is primarily intended to prepare the way for Chapters 12–14. In those chapters, I will argue that we ought to push the frontiers of Fregean realism even further, this time to include propositions. I will recommend that we think of propositions in exactly the same way as states of affairs: as the truth conditions of sentences. As we will see, this way of thinking about states and propositions has important consqequences for our understanding of truth. But before we can get to any of that, we need to start with the states of affairs.

11.1 Fregean Realism about States of Affairs

A state of affairs is what you get when you combine a monadic property with an object: when you combine the property *is wise* with Socrates, you get the state of affairs *Socrates is wise*. Equally, you can make a state of affairs by combining a *dyadic* relation with *two* objects: combine *loves* with Daniel and Simon (in that order), and you end up with the state of affairs *Daniel loves Simon*. As a general rule, an *n*-adic property is an entity which becomes a state of affairs when it is combined with *n* objects. Or to put it the other way around, an *n*-adic property is what you get when you take a state of affairs and remove *n* objects.

But still, what *exactly* is a state of affairs? Well, according to the general rule I just gave, a state of affairs is a 0-adic property: a 0-adic property is an entity which does not need the help of any objects to become a state of affairs; in other words, a state of affairs is what you get when you take a state of affairs and remove no objects. At first, this might strike you as a pretty unhelpful, circular definition. I explained what an *n*-adic property is by saying that it is an entity which combines with *n* objects to make a state of affairs, and then when I asked what a state of affairs is, I turned back on myself and said that it is a o-adic property. And this definition would be unhelpfully circular if I had nothing more to say about what an *n*-adic property is. But I am a Fregean realist, and Fregean realists have a lot more to say.

According to Fregean realism, *n*-adic properties are the referents of *n*-adic predicates. And an *n*-adic predicate is an expression which combines with *n* terms to make a sentence.[1] The limiting case is a o-adic predicate: a o-adic predicate is an expression which does not need the help of any terms to become a sentence; in other words, a o-adic predicate is just a sentence.[2]

So for the Fregean realists, states of affairs (i.e., o-adic properties) are the referents of sentences (i.e., o-adic predicates). Or at least, that is how Fregean realists will put things when they are speaking loosely. Really, though, it is a bit misleading. It makes it sound like sentences refer to states of affairs in the same way that singular terms refer to objects. But we can see that this cannot be right, simply by appealing to the version of the Reference Principle that I argued for in Chapter 5:

(RP$_3$) If it makes sense to say that α refers$_\alpha$ to what β refers$_\beta$ to, then α and β are everywhere sense-intersubstitutable.

Terms and sentences have radically different kinds of sense: terms *pick out* objects; sentences *say that things are thus-and-so*. (That is why sentences are truth-evaluable, and singular terms are not.) As a result, they are not everywhere sense-intersubstitutable. And so, by (RP$_3$), it follows that terms and sentences cannot both refer in the same sense.[3]

Really, sentences refer in their own bespoke sense. In §6.1, I argued that what it is for a monadic predicate to refer to a property is just for it to have a *satisfaction condition*. Similarly, I would now like to suggest that what

---

[1] At this point, I should mention again that, in this book, I mean *declarative sentence* by 'sentence', unless I clearly indicate otherwise.

[2] Prior (1971, 33) attributes the insight that you can think of sentences as o-adic predicates to Peirce. Unfortunately, Prior does not provide any citations in support of this attribution.

[3] Fregean realists thus combine a belief that sentences refer to states of affairs with Strawson's (1950, 194) insight that a 'logically fundamental type-mistake' is involved in the idea that sentences are related to states of affairs in the way that terms are related to objects. The only difference between Strawson and the Fregean realists is that the Fregean realists see no reason to deny that sentences stand in a different *type* of relation to states of affairs.

it is for a sentence to refer to a state of affairs is just for it to have a *truth condition*. Or to put it a little more carefully, we should use something along the following lines to express the reference relation for sentences:

(T) x is true $\leftrightarrow$ P.

The x marks a gap for a term, and the P marks a gap for a sentence. So if we wanted to say what 'Socrates is wise' refers to, we should say:

(1) 'Socrates is wise' is true $\leftrightarrow$ Socrates is wise.

At first, it might not be clear that (1) attributes any kind of reference to 'Socrates is wise'. *Everyone* should accept (1), even people who do not believe in states of affairs! However, according to Fregean realism, the *only* way to refer to a state of affairs is with a whole sentence. So the *only* way of expressing a relation between a sentence and a state of affairs is with something like (1).

Now, so far, I have been a little bit cagey. I have said that we must use something *like* (T) to express sentence-reference. That's because, as it stands, (T) is a little bit crude. If we use (T) to express sentence-reference, we will end up saying that all true sentences co-refer, as do all false sentences. We will be left with just two states of affairs, the True and the False. As it happens, that was one of Frege's doctrines, but it is probably a little *too* Fregean for many people's tastes. Maybe (T) would do as our expression for sentence-reference if we only had to deal with extensional contexts, but we have to deal with intensional contexts too. So while it involves departing from the historical Frege, a Fregean realist should probably look for some way of making (T) more fine grained. As a start, we could swap (T) for:

(Modal-T) $\forall w$(x is true relative to w $\leftrightarrow$ P at w).

This would at least let us deal with modal contexts. It may be that we need to refine (T) even further to deal with hyper-intensional contexts, but I will not try to figure out how best to do that now. Instead, I will settle for (Modal-T), and trust that all of the arguments that follow would still run even if we decided to tweak (Modal-T) further.[4]

If we express sentence-reference with (Modal-T), or something like it, then we can say what states of affairs are: they are truth conditions. Again,

---

[4] I kept my discussion of properties simple by focussing on extensional contexts; as a result, I was able to pretend that (S) was the right way of expressing predicate-reference. However, I do not think that this strategy would work so well for states of affairs. Pretending that (T) is the right way of expressing sentence-reference, and thus that there are just two states of affairs, would probably be more of a distraction than a help.

though, this is loose talk. We need to introduce a new higher-level predicate, '$SOA(P)$', which we can use to characterise the referents of sentences. The best way to approach this predicate is by first asking how we should express *identity* between states of affairs. If we use (Modal-T) to express sentence-reference, then two sentences co-refer iff they are true relative to exactly the same worlds as each other. As a result, we should express identity between states of affairs with this:

(Modal-I) $\Box(P \leftrightarrow Q)$.

And if this is how we express identity between states of affairs, then we should take '$SOA(P)$' to be:

(SOA) $\exists Q\Box(P \leftrightarrow Q)$.

The quantifier in (SOA) binds a variable in sentence-position. There are obviously good questions to ask about how this kind of higher-order quantification works, and what exactly is being quantified over. Fortunately, however, it would be easy to extend our discussion of quantification into predicate-position from Chapter 7 to cover quantification into sentence-position. For now, it will suffice to say that for a Fregean realist, quantification into sentence-position is quantification over truth conditions – i.e., states of affairs.

Speaking somewhat loosely, then, (SOA) says *of* a state of affairs *that* it is (identical to) a state of affairs. So rather than saying '*Socrates is wise* is a state of affairs' or '*Socrates is wise* is a truth condition', we should say:

(2) $\exists Q\Box$(Socrates is wise $\leftrightarrow Q$).

This is the Fregean realist conception of states of affairs. I should admit, though, that it is not all that *Fregean*, in the sense that the real historical Frege did not endorse anything like it. That is not just because Frege thought that all true sentences co-refer. Even more significantly, in *Grundgesetze* (1893, §2), Frege took sentences to be singular terms; the only difference between 'Socrates' and 'Socrates is wise' is that 'Socrates' refers to a person, and 'Socrates is wise' refers to a truth-value. However, like almost every latter-day Fregean, I think that this was a terrible mistake. Terms and sentences clearly play fundamentally different roles: terms pick out objects, and sentences say that things are *thus-and-so*.[5] And when we eliminate that

---

[5] For arguments that it was a mistake to treat sentences as terms, see Wittgenstein 1922, 4.063 and 6.111; Dummett 1981a, 196 and 644–5; 1981b, 408–9; Sullivan 1994.

mistake, my picture of states of affairs flows naturally from the Fregean realist picture of properties. So, with due apologies to Frege himself, I will continue to call it 'Fregean realism'.

11.2   Negative and Disjunctive States of Affairs

Fregean realism is an abundant conception of states of affairs: all it means to say that a sentence refers to a state of affairs is that it has a truth condition, and every sentence has one of those. So not only do atomic, positive sentences like 'Socrates is wise' and 'Plato is a philosopher' stand for states of affairs; so do disjunctive sentences, like 'Socrates is wise or Plato is a philosopher', and negative sentences, like 'Plato is not foolish'. We can make the same point without the semantic ascent. According to Fregean realism, we should understand the claim that these states of affairs exist as higher-order generalisations:

(3a) $\exists Q \Box ((\text{Socrates is wise or Plato is foolish}) \leftrightarrow Q)$
(4a) $\exists Q \Box (\text{Plato is not foolish} \leftrightarrow Q)$.

Both of these generalisations are trivially true, since they follow straight-away from the following theorems of modal logic:

(3b) $\Box ((\text{Socrates is wise or Plato is foolish}) \leftrightarrow (\text{Socrates is wise or Plato is foolish}))$
(4b) $\Box (\text{Plato is not foolish} \leftrightarrow \text{Plato is not foolish})$.

So for the Fregean realists, negative and disjunctive states of affairs are just as real as the positive ones.

Now, plenty of philosophers have thought that there was something suspicious about negative and disjunctive states of affairs.[6] So is the fact that Fregean realism includes these states in its ontology any cause for concern? I do not think so. As far as I can tell, much of the intuitive distaste for these states of affairs has its roots in the gut feeling that they are somehow too insubstantial to be considered parts of reality.[7] Here is how Russell, himself an advocate of negative states of affairs, expressed this gut feeling:

---

[6] For a clear rejection of disjunctive and negative states of affairs, see Armstrong 1997, 134–5; 2004, 54–5.
[7] Compare Lewis' (1986c, 66–7) insistence that 'it is just absurd to think that a thing has ... non-spatiotemporal parts for *all* its countless abundant properties'. Lewis' point was not that there are no abundant properties, but that they cannot be *parts* of the objects which instantiate them.

One has a certain repugnance to negative facts, the same sort of feeling that makes you wish not to have a fact "*p* or *q*" going about the world. You have a feeling that there are only positive facts, and that negative propositions have somehow or other got to be expressions of positive facts. When I was lecturing on this subject at Harvard I argued that there were negative facts, and it nearly produced a riot: the class would not hear of there being negative facts at all. (Russell 1918, 211)

Importantly, however, the Fregean realists reject the idea that any state of affairs, including positive ones, is a *part* of reality, or the sort of thing that 'goes about the world'. States of affairs are truth conditions, which the world does or does not satisfy. Put slightly more picturesquely, states of affairs are *ways for the world to be*. This is not to say that states of affairs are monadic properties, instantiated or not by some object called THE WORLD. To repeat what I said in §11.1, states of affairs are *o-adic* properties. Really, 'the world' is functioning here as a dummy term, like the 'it' in 'It is raining'. It might be better, then, to say that states of affairs are ways for *it* to be.[8] When we think of states of affairs like that, the gut feeling that there is something wrong with negative and disjunctive states of affairs loses much of its force: *Plato is not foolish*, for example, is just how it is when Plato is not foolish.[9]

11.3 Facts as Obtaining States of Affairs

Fregean realists do not stop with negative and disjunctive states of affairs. They are happy to include *unobtaining* states of affairs in their (higher-order) ontology too. Consider the sentence 'Plato is foolish'. This sentence is false, but it still has a perfectly good truth condition:

(5a) $\forall w$('Plato is foolish' is true relative to $w \leftrightarrow$ Plato is foolish at w).

And since all it means to say that a sentence refers to a state of affairs is that it has a truth condition, 'Plato is foolish' refers to a state of affairs. Again, we can make this point without the semantic ascent. For Fregean realists, the claim that *Plato is foolish* exists becomes a trivial higher-order generalisation:

(5b) $\exists Q \Box$(Plato is foolish $\leftrightarrow Q$).

---

[8] This conception of states of affairs is very similar to the one proposed by Johnston (2013, 386), who suggests that we think of them as *ways things may be*.

[9] For the record, I am also not convinced that you should reject negative and disjunctive states even if you do think of states as 'parts of the world'. For some very interesting rehabilitations of negative states, see Barker and Jago 2012; Jago 2018, §5.5.

According to Fregean realism, the state of affairs *Plato is foolish* exists, in just the same sense that *Plato is a philosopher* does. Of course, we still have to recognise some difference between these states of affairs, since Plato is a philosopher, but he is not foolish. Following the standard philosophical terminology, we will say that *Plato is a philosopher* 'obtains', whereas *Plato is foolish* does not.

So for the Fregean realists, there are unobtaining states as well as obtaining ones. But what exactly does it mean to say that a state of affairs 'obtains'? What magical metaphysical halo surrounds *Plato is a philosopher*? And what is left of a state like *Plato is foolish* when that halo is taken away? In Russell's (1910a, 150–2) apt phrase, *Plato is foolish* would have to be some sort of 'objective falsehood'. But is it really plausible that the world contains objective falsehoods, mixing company with the objective truths?

Again, it is important to emphasise that for the Fregean realists, states of affairs are not 'parts' of the world. That goes for obtaining states as well as unobtaining ones. States of affairs are ways for the world to be. (Or, better: ways for *it* to be.) We can, then, think of the obtaining states of affairs as the ways that the world is. The unobtaining states are then just the ways that the world is not. Plato is a philosopher, that is how the world is, and so *Plato is a philosopher* obtains. Plato is not foolish, that is not how the world is, and so *Plato is foolish* does not obtain. Thought of like this, unobtaining states of affairs are no more mysterious than uninstantiated properties. Now, of course, there have been plenty of philosophers who would say that that this is still pretty mysterious, but no Fregean realist should be among them.

Take the following sentence:

(6a) The state of affairs *Plato is a philosopher* obtains.

In this sentence, we appear to refer to a state of affairs with a singular term, 'the state of affairs *Plato is a philosopher*', and then say of it that it obtains. But this cannot be the right way to read (6a) for a Fregean realist: according to Fregean realism, we cannot refer to states of affairs with singular terms; the *only* way of referring to them is with whole sentences. Instead, the Fregean realists should take (6a) to be nothing more than a fancy periphrasis of:

(6b) Plato is a philosopher.

Similarly, they should take the sentence,

(7a) The state of affairs *Plato is foolish* does not obtain, to just be a very long way of writing:

(7b) Plato is not foolish.

As a general rule, then, to say that the state P obtains is just to say that P. In the final analysis, all talk of 'obtaining' simply vanishes. It is needed only when we are speaking loosely and pretending that states of affairs are objects we can refer to with singular terms.

Still, it can be very useful to speak in this way, and so it will be helpful to introduce a little more loose talk. When it is convenient, I will call obtaining states of affairs *facts*. So *Plato is a philosopher* is a fact, but *Plato is foolish* is not. But it is important not to let this new way of speaking confuse us. Talk of facts should be analysed in just the same way as talk of obtaining states of affairs: so just like (6a), '*Plato is a philosopher* is a fact' is nothing but a wordy reformulation of (6b). Quantification over facts should be understood as restricted higher-order quantification: 'All facts are. . .' becomes '$\forall P(P \rightarrow \ldots P \ldots)$', and 'Some fact is. . .' becomes '$\exists P(P \wedge \ldots P \ldots)$'.

11.4 The Structure of States of Affairs

It seems natural to think of states of affairs as being *complex* entities, somehow composed out of properties and objects.[10] However, it can be difficult to see how to square this natural thought with the Fregean doctrine that states are truth conditions. At the very least, states cannot be *mereologically* composed out of properties and objects, since mereology deals with the composition of complex *objects*, and according to Fregean realism, states aren't objects.[11]

Fortunately, however, Fregean realists can think of the structure of states in other terms. Let's start with what it means to say that some object is a constituent of some state of affairs. What does it mean, for example, to say that Daniel is a constituent of state P? To a first approximation, it means that P is the result of combining Daniel with some property X; or, in other words, that there is some X such that P is identical to the state $X(Daniel)$. Now, this is rough, because we are still talking as if states of affairs were objects. But if we continue to use '$\Box(P \leftrightarrow Q)$' to express identity between states of affairs, we can explain precisely what it means to say that object x is a constituent of state P:

(Const) x is a constituent of $P \leftrightarrow_{df} \exists X \Box(Xx \leftrightarrow P)$.

---

[10]   See Russell 1903, §51; 1913, 79–81; 1918, Lecture II; Armstrong 1997, ch. 8 esp. §8.2; Fine 2000, 4–5.
[11]   Mind you, as Lewis (1986a, 94–7, 1986b) emphasised, it is not obvious that we could think of states in mereological terms even if they were objects.

We can give an analogous explanation of the sense in which properties are constituents of states of affairs, simply by pushing the variables x and X up one level: x should be replaced with a variable first-level predicate, and X should be replaced with a variable second-level predicate. The quantifier binding the second of these variables would be of *third-order*, and it would quantify over second-level properties – i.e., properties of first-level properties.[12] From here we could continue upwards as long as we liked, explaining the senses in which higher and higher level properties are constituents of states of affairs.

But for now, let's return to earth and focus on the original version of (Const), which defines what it means for an object to be a constituent of a state of affairs. It turns out that this definition has some peculiar results. Intuitively, I would have said that Daniel is a constituent of *Daniel loves Simon*, but Daniel's singleton set, {Daniel}, is not. However, the following is certainly true:

(8a) $\Box$(Daniel loves Simon $\leftrightarrow \exists y (y \in$ {Daniel} $\land y$ loves Simon)).

Given the Fregean realist's abundant conception of properties, (8a) implies:

(8b) $\exists X \Box$(Daniel loves Simon $\leftrightarrow X$\{Daniel\}).[13]

And when we combine (8b) with (Const), we reach the conclusion that {Daniel} is also a constituent of *Daniel loves Simon*, after all. Moreover, this style of argument is wholly general: if a cannot exist without b and *vice versa*, then (Const) implies that a and b are constituents of exactly the same facts. This result is particularly striking for anyone who accepts Williamson's (2013) *necessitism*, which states that necessarily, everything necessarily exists. Combine that necessitism with (Const), and you reach the conclusion that if *any* object is a constituent of a given state, then *every* object is a constituent of that state.[14]

As I said, these are peculiar results. We could try to to dodge them if we liked. The obvious strategy would be to find a more demanding identity condition for states of affairs than mere necessary equivalence. (See §14.5 for related discussion.) However, we could also just take the results and live with them. All they really show is that a single state of affairs can be decomposed in multiple ways. On one decomposition, *Daniel loves Simon*

---

12 Things actually get even more complicated, because we should really indicate how many argument places the variable first-level predicate has, and indicate that the variable second-level predicate can be combined with first-level predicates which have that many argument places.
13 I am here assuming that Fregean realists individuate properties at least as finely as (Modal-I) from §6.2.
14 Thanks to Jeremy Goodman for first introducing me to these points.

is composed of Daniel and *loves Simon*, and on another, it is composed of {Daniel} and *has a member who loves Simon*. This option should be attractive to anyone who has ever felt sceptical about the idea that there is just *one* right way to describe a given state of affairs.

This talk of multiple decompositions is obviously reminiscent of Frege's (1884, §64) famous discussion of *content re-carving*. Frege was considering the suggestion that we treat *Hume's Principle* as an implicit definition of 'the number of. . .':

(HP) The number of *F*s = the number of *G*s iff *F* and *G* are equinumerous.

The idea was that by laying down (HP) as a definition, we manage to re-carve the content of an equinumerosity claim into the content of an identity claim. However, I want to be clear that nothing I have said is meant to vindicate this use of (HP). I am happy to accept that there is a sense in which the two sides of (HP) have the same content, namely that they stand for the same state of affairs. For me, that is just the claim that they have the same truth-value at every world, and anyone who believes in numbers should accept that. But that is not to accept that we can *make* the left-hand side have the same content as the right *by* stipulating (HP). My own view is that if we read the left-hand side in the way that its surface form suggests – i.e., as expressing an identity between numbers – then no stipulation can guarantee that it stands for the same state of affairs as the right-hand side (see Trueman 2014).

This is not the only Fregean theme which my talk of multiple decompositions brings to mind. The other is Frege's (1891, 137–9; 1891–5, 174) mature doctrine that properties (or, as he called them, *concepts*) are functions. Frege meant this in the most straightforward sense. He thought that a sentence was just a singular term referring to one of two special objects, called the *True* and the *False*. So for Frege, the property *wise* was a function which mapped wise objects to the True, and every other object to the False. Now, for my Fregean realist, properties cannot be functions in this straightforward sense: unlike Frege, the Fregean realists do not think that states are objects, and so a property cannot be a function from objects to objects. However, as Dummett (1981b, ch. 8) rightly emphasised, it can still be useful to think of properties on the model of functions: not as functions from objects to objects, but from objects to states of affairs. Certainly, if we think of the composition of states of affairs on a functional model, then the idea that states of affairs can be decomposed into properties and objects in multiple ways will no longer seem mysterious: just as the number 3 is the result of applying the successor function to 2 *and also* the result of applying the predecessor function to 4, *Daniel loves Simon* is the result of applying *x loves Simon* to Daniel *and also* the result of applying *a member of x loves Simon* to {Daniel}.

Having said that, however, it is important not to let this functional model bully us into conclusions we might otherwise want to resist. In modern mathematics, it is usually assumed that *any* mapping between two collections of objects counts as a function, no matter how arbitrary. But we might not want to grant that every arbitrary mapping between objects and states of affairs is a property. For example, we might baulk at the idea that there is a property X such that $X(Socrates)$ is *Queen Anne is dead*, $X(Plato)$ is *Einstein is a great man*, and so on, arbitrarily mapping objects to states.[15]

So while it may be helpful to think of the structure of states in broadly functional terms, it is important not to assume that rules which apply to functions from objects to objects also automatically apply to properties. States are composed in their own bespoke sense, designed to fit states of affairs and nothing else.

---

[15]   I took this example from Ramsey's 'The Foundations of Mathematics' (1924, 52). Ramsey's ambition in that paper was to combine the Principian doctrine that all mathematical truths are logical truths with the Tractarian doctrine that all logical truths are tautologies. In his attempt to fulfil this ambition, Ramsey was forced to introduce *propositional functions in extension*, which were meant to be arbitrary mappings between individuals and propositions. For critical discussion of this new breed of propositional function, see Wittgenstein 1974, 315–17; 1975, 141–3; Sullivan 1995; Trueman 2011.

CHAPTER 12

The Prenective View of Propositional Content

In the last chapter, I sketched the picture of states of affairs which drops out of Fregean realism. On this picture, states of affairs are the truth conditions of sentences, just as properties are the satisfaction conditions of predicates. Over the next two chapters, I want to argue that we should have exactly the same picture of propositions: they are the truth conditions of sentences too.

Importantly, this picture of propositions does not just drop out of Fregean realism in the way that the picture of states of affairs did. This may be obscured by the fact that philosophers often gloss quantification into sentence-position as quantification over propositions, so that '$\exists P(P \vee \neg P)$' becomes 'Some proposition is either true or false'. If you combine that with the Fregean doctrine that quantification into sentence-position is quantification over truth conditions, you reach the conclusion that propositions are truth conditions. But to content ourselves with this quick argument would be to place far too much weight on the rough and ready translations that philosophers sometimes give of higher-order generalisations.

My main aim in this chapter is to explain what we really need to add to Fregean realism to reach the conclusion that propositions are truth conditions. But to be clear, I do not intend to offer much by way of argument for these additions here; that is a task that I will save for Chapter 13. For now, all I want to do is get clear on what it is that I need to argue for.

12.1 Propositional Content

The first thing we need to do is get clearer on what we mean by 'proposition'. One good way of doing that is by asking ourselves what roles we want our propositions to play. There are a number of different roles that we might suggest. We might characterise propositions as the the fundamental bearers of truth and falsity, or as the premises and conclusions of arguments.[1] However, as I understand it, the concept of a proposition gets its life in connection with the concept of *propositional content*.[2]

The best way to explain what I mean by 'propositional content' is to give a few examples. Beliefs have propositional content, in the sense that a belief is always a belief *that so-and-so*: a belief *that grass is green*, or a belief *that snow is white*, or whatever. And other things have propositional content too. The most obvious examples are sentences: 'Grass is green' *says that grass is green*. But, of course, this list can be carried on much further.

Propositions enter the scene when we try to give a general characterisation of what it is to have propositional content. What it is for someone to believe something is for them to stand in the *believing* relation to a proposition; for example, what it is for Simon to believe that Sharon is funny is for Simon to stand in the *believing* relation to the proposition that Sharon is funny. Similarly, what it is for a sentence to say something is for it to stand in the *saying* relation to a proposition, what it is for someone to assert something is for them to stand in the *asserting* relation to a proposition, and so on. Speaking in the most general terms possible: to have propositional content is to stand in an appropriate relation to a proposition.

I certainly do not mean to suggest that this is the *only* way of thinking about propositions. But it is a common way of thinking about them, and it is the way that I will be thinking about them in this book. So when I say that propositions are truth conditions, what I mean is this: to have a propositional content is *not* to stand in any relation to an object; it is to stand in a relation to a truth condition, a higher-order entity which we can refer to only with whole sentences, not with singular terms.

12.2 Two Views of Propositional Content

At this point, you may still find my claim that propositions are truth conditions a little opaque. What exactly does it mean to say that to have a propositional content is to stand in a relation to a truth condition, not an object? Well, it is helpful to contrast my view of propositions with the *Standard View* amongst philosophers. Take the sentence 'Simon believes

---

[1] Both of these characterisations play important roles in Merricks 2015. As I will explain in §13.4, in my view it would be misleading at best to describe propositions as the fundamental bearers of truth and falsehood.

[2] Everything I have to say about propositions and propositional content has been deeply influenced by Ramsey's unfinished manuscript *On Truth* (first published in 1991). Ramsey himself talked about 'propositional reference', but he meant the same thing I mean by 'propositional content'.

that Sharon is funny'. On the Standard View, this sentence is parsed as follows:

[Simon] believes [that Sharon is funny].

Here we are supposed to have two singular terms, 'Simon' and 'that Sharon is funny', and a two-place predicate joining them together, 'x believes y'; the idea is that 'Simon' refers to a thinking subject, 'that Sharon is funny' refers to the proposition that Sharon is funny, and 'x believes y' expresses the *believing* relation that holds between them. The same goes for other sentences that ascribe propositional content, for example:

['Grass is green'] says [that grass is green].[3]

In its most general form, the Standard View tells us that the form of propositional content ascriptions is '$R(x, y)$'. This is precisely the view of propositional content that I am anxious to reject. By reading content ascriptions in this way, and categorising expressions like 'that Sharon is funny' as singular terms, the Standard View reifies propositions, which, I want to insist, is a terrible mistake.

I think it would be better to take our lead from Prior (1971, ch. 2), who parsed 'Simon believes that Sharon is funny' as follows:

[Simon] believes that [Sharon is funny].

Now we have a singular term, 'Simon'; a sentence, 'Sharon is funny'; and what is sometimes called a *prenective* joining them together, 'x believes that P'. ('x believes that P' is called a 'prenective' because it behaves like a predicate at one end, and a sentential connective on the other: the x marks an argument place for a singular term, whereas the P marks an argument place for a sentence.[4]) And, of course, the same goes for other sentences that ascribe propositional content, for example:

['Grass is green'] says that [grass is green].

Put in the most general terms, the *Prenective View* tells us that the form of propositional content ascriptions is '$R(x, P)$'. When we read content ascriptions in this way, we neatly avoid the reification of propositions. There is

---

3 We could also imagine a *paratactic* version of the Standard View. On this version of the view, 'Simon believes that Sharon is funny' is really of the form 'Simon believes that: Sharon is funny', where the 'that' is a demonstrative referring to the proposition expressed by the sentence displayed after the colon. (See Dodd 2000, 34.) As far as I can tell, the argument I develop against the Standard View in Chapter 13 could easily be redirected at this paratactic spin-off.

4 It was Künne (2003, 68) who first coined the word 'prenective'.

no term referring to a proposition in 'Simon believes that Sharon is funny'. Instead of getting at the content of Simon's belief by using a term to refer to a proposition, we simply use the sentence 'Sharon is funny' to express that content for ourselves.[5]

If we combine the Prenective View with Fregean realism, we reach the following conclusion: 'Simon believes that Sharon is funny' does not express a (first-level) relation between Simon and a special object; it expresses a (mixed-level) relation between Simon and the truth condition of 'Sharon is funny'.[6] So what it is for Simon to believe that Sharon is funny is for him to bear the *believing* relation to the appropriate truth condition.[7] Given the way that I characterised propositions in §12.1, it follows that propositions are truth conditions.[8]

So that is what I need to add to Fregean realism to extend it to cover propositions: the Prenective View of propositional content. I present my argument for the Prenective View in the next chapter. But before that, I want to spend the rest of this chapter developing the view in a little more detail. I should also mention now that this chapter marks an important point of departure from Frege. Frege was most definitely an advocate of the Standard View. In fact, Frege (1918) was one of the philosophers who helped to establish the Standard View as the standard view in the first place![9] From this point on, then, I will not be drawing on the ideas of Frege, but on the ideas of Prior, Ramsey and the early Wittgenstein instead.

12.3   Formalising Inferences

It is often noted that the Standard View has an easy time handling certain inferences that we are all happy to make. Here is an example:

(1) Simon believes that Sharon is funny

---

[5] This approach to belief ascriptions also seems to be fairly close to the one recommended by McKinsey (1999).

[6] Jones (2019) presents a similar metaphysics of cognitive relations.

[7] When people are first introduced to the Prenective View, they sometimes mistake it for the view that to believe that Sharon is funny is to stand in a relation to the sentence 'Sharon is funny'. But on the Prenective View, the sentence 'Sharon is funny' is *used*, not *mentioned*, in 'Simon believes that Sharon is funny'. Prior (1963, 116–17; 1971, 17–18) was very clear on this point.

[8] Prior was sometimes hostile to all talk of facts and propositions (e.g., 1971, 18 and 38–9). However, in 'Correspondence Theory of Truth' (1967, 229), Prior was happy to agree that there are facts and propositions in the sense I intend here.

[9] The early Russell (1903) was, of course, one of the others. For two recent books developing various versions of the Standard View, see King, Soames and Speaks (2014) *New Thinking about Propositions*, and Hanks (2015) *Propositional Content*.

(2) Daniel believes that Sharon is funny

∴ (3) There is something that Simon and Daniel both believe

If we read (1) and (2) in accordance with the Standard View, we can formalise (3) using nothing but the familiar resources of first-order logic:

(3$_S$) $\exists x$(Simon believes x and Daniel believes x).

But if we want to read (1) and (2) in accordance with the Prenective View, then we will not be able to give this first-order formalisation of (3). Instead, we will have to help ourselves to some higher-order resources:

(3$_P$) $\exists P$(Simon believes that P and Daniel believes that P).

Here the quantifier binds the variable P, which appears in sentence-position, not term-position. Defenders of the Standard View tend to take this as a serious point in their favour.[10] However, I want to convince Fregean realists to adopt the Prenective View, and Fregean realists do not share this prejudice against higher-order logic.[11] We can translate (3$_P$) back into natural language as 'There is some way for things to be such that Simon believes that things are that way, and Daniel believes that things are that way'. In doing so, we are taking advantage of Wittgenstein's (1953, §134) observation that phrases like 'this is how things are' and 'that is the way it is' can be used as *prosentences*, the natural language analogues of variables in sentence-position.[12]

Let's grant, then, that there is nothing per se problematic with quantification into sentence-position. That is still not quite enough to show that there is nothing problematic with the quantification involved in (3$_P$). In (3$_P$), we are not only dealing with higher-order quantification; we are

---

[10] See Künne 2003, 69; King 2007, 1; King et al. 2014, 7; Speaks (King et al. 2014, 9–16).

[11] This marks an important difference between the Prenective View and a related suggestion made by Quine (1960, 216). According to Quine, we should read 'x believes that P' as an operator which turns a sentence – e.g., 'Sharon is funny' – into a monadic predicate, 'x believes that Sharon is funny'. So far, this sounds exactly like the Prenective View, and in fact, Prior (1971, 20) explicitly claimed that there was no difference between the two. But this was a misleading thing to claim, given the wider context of Quine's beliefs. According to Quine (1970, 66–8), the higher-order quantification involved in (3$_P$) is illegitimate: all quantification is first-order quantification. However, a key component of the Prenective View as I understand it, and as Prior (1971, ch. 3) himself laid it out, is the idea that there is nothing wrong with quantifying into sentence-position. Without this kind of higher-order quantification, it would be very difficult to know how to formalise arguments like (1)–(3).

[12] We can translate the universal generalisation '$\forall P$(Simon believes that $P \rightarrow$ Daniel believes that P)' as 'However Simon believes things are, Daniel believes that they are that way too'. For more on these natural language prosentences, see Prior 1967, 228–9; Grover 1992a, 138–40; Künne 2003, 364–5; Rumfitt 2014, 27.

dealing with higher-order quantification into a *hyper-intensional* context. To say that 'belief'-contexts are hyper-intensional is to say that '*a* believes that *P*' and '*a* believes that *Q*' may have different truth-values, even if '*P*' and '*Q*' have the same truth-value relative to every world. Here is an example of such a pair:

(4a) Daniel believes that Hesperus is Hesperus
(4b) Daniel believes that Hesperus is Phosphorus.

It may be that (4a) is true and (4b) is false – just imagine that Daniel is good at logic but terrible at astronomy – even though '□(Hesperus is Hesperus ↔ Hesperus is Phosphorus)' is true. So far, I have said nothing about how to understand quantification into hyper-intensional contexts like these. And in all honesty, I have nothing much to say. The one thing that seems clear is that we will need to individuate propositions much more finely than we have been individuating states of affairs. In §11.1, I used '□(P ↔ Q)' to express identity between states of affairs. We will obviously have to set a more demanding standard for identity between propositions,[13] but I have no very helpful suggestions about what that standard should be.

One natural suggestion would be that propositions are identical iff they are indistinguishable. And we could then use higher-order logic to formalise the claim that *P* and *Q* are indistinguishable as follows: $\forall \eta (\eta P \leftrightarrow \eta Q)$. The η here is a variable in the position of a one-place sentential operator, like ¬. This is certainly an unusual kind of variable, but I cannot see why a Fregean realist would object to its use. However, absent a worked-out theory of the range of this new kind of variable, it is still not all that informative to say that *P* and *Q* are indistinguishable in this sense.

We might hope to make some progress on this problem by deploying the functional model of properties. In §11.4, I said that we can think of first-level properties as functions from objects to states of affairs. Now we might suggest that the values of η are functions from propositions to propositions.[14] But that only gets us so far; we still need an account of how these functions behave. And at this point, it does not help much to say that they are simply arbitrary mappings from propositions to propositions. That cannot tell us anything substantial about the totality of these functions, unless

---

[13] That much *seems* obvious, but some philosophers have disagreed. See Stalnaker 1984; 1999, esp. pt. II; Rayo 2013, 99–118.
[14] Thanks to Michael Rieppel for pushing me to consider this suggestion.

we say more about what propositions there are and how finely they are individuated.

This is all very disappointing. But it is not at all surprising. As far as I know, *no one* has a fully satisfying, worked-out semantics for hyper-intensional contexts. There have, of course, been plenty of proposals,[15] but it would take us too far off course to review them here. All that really matters is that no reason has yet been given to think that the problems posed by hyper-intensionality are any more challenging on the Prenective View than they are on the Standard View. So, since my ultimate aim is just to argue that the Prenective View should be preferred to the Standard View, I will largely set questions about hyper-intensionality to one side in what follows.[16]

12.4   The Prenective View versus Natural Language

Consider the following two sentences:

(5a) Simon believes that Sharon is funny
(5b) That Sharon is funny is what Simon believes.

According to the Prenective View as Prior originally presented it, 'that Sharon is funny' is not a syntactic unit in (5a); on his parsing, the 'that' is attached to 'believes', not to 'Sharon is funny'. But as Künne (2003, 68–9) points out, when we move from (5a) to (5b), the 'that' follows 'Sharon is funny'; it does not stick where it is, on the other side of 'believes'. This strongly suggests that 'that Sharon is funny' does appear as a syntactic unit in these sentences.[17] What is more, this suggestion has been taken up by empirical linguists. They standardly represent (5a) with the following phrase structure tree:[18]

---

[15] For some of Frege's attempts to offer a criteria of individuation for propositions, see Frege 1906a and his letter to Husserl dated 9 December 1906 (reprinted in Beaney 1997, 305–7). For an attempt to refine Frege's criteria, and to expose their limitations, see Rumfitt 2016. And for two recent attempts to tackle hyper-intensionality from a higher-order perspective, see Dorr 2016; Bacon 2019.

[16] I will, however, briefly return to questions surrounding higher-order quantification into 'that'-clauses in §13.2, and to questions surrounding the individuation of propositions in §14.5.

[17] This observation also tells against the paratactic theory. On that theory, the mystery isn't why 'that' moves to the front of the sentence in (5b); it is why 'Sharon is funny' does. What it seems you should expect on the paratactic theory is, 'That is what Simon believes: Sharon is funny'.

[18] For an excellent introduction to phrase structure trees, see Heim and Kratzer 1998.

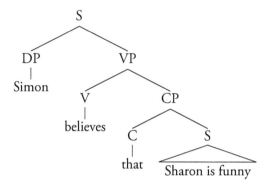

In this tree, the sentence 'Sharon is funny' is first combined with the complementiser 'that', and then the whole complement phrase 'that Sharon is funny' is combined with the verb 'believes'. It is then easy to transform this into a tree for the relative clause 'what Simon believes':

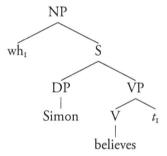

In this tree, 'wh$_1$' binds the trace 't_1', and importantly, that trace replaces the *entire* complement phrase 'that Sharon is funny'.

It seems, then, that the Prenective View does not fit the linguistic evidence at all well.[19] By contrast, the Standard View fits it perfectly so far: on the Standard View, 'that Sharon is funny' does appear in (5a) and (5b) as a syntactic unit; it is a singular term referring to a proposition.

This is certainly a serious problem for Prior's version of the Prenective View, but I do not think it requires rejecting it entirely. We just need to tweak it slightly. I want to propose a new version of the view, which concedes to the Standard View that 'that Sharon is funny' *is* a syntactic unit, but denies that it functions as a singular term; instead, my version of the Prenective View has it that 'that Sharon is funny' functions as a *sentence* in

---

[19] This is a point to which I was insufficiently sensitive in Trueman 2018a. The rest of this section should be seen as a correction to that paper.

(5a).[20] In other words, this use of the complementiser 'that' is semantically vacuous, and 'that Sharon is funny' has exactly the same sense as 'Sharon is funny'. Just like Prior's original version of the Prenective View, this way of parsing (5a) breaks it down into a term, a sentence and a prenective; the only difference is that Prior took the prenective to be 'x believes that P', whereas I take it to be 'x believes P'.[21]

There is no obvious contradiction between this new version of the Prenective View and empirical linguistics. It is certainly not a given that if 'that Sharon is funny' is a syntactic unit, then it functions as a singular term. It is philosophers, not linguists, who make that jump. Of course, what is true is that linguists standardly assign entities they call 'propositions' (which are normally just functions from indices to truth-values) to 'that'-clauses as their semantic values. But as Rosefeldt (2008, 318 and 325) and Hofweber (2016b, 210–14) rightly emphasise, it is a big leap from there to the conclusion that 'that'-clauses are singular terms which refer to those semantic values. Indeed, it is also common to assign the very same semantic values to sentences themselves, but no one would take that as proof that sentences are a kind of singular term.

But if 'that'-clauses are not singular terms which *refer* to their semantic values, then what relationship *do* they have to those values? Well, the semantic value of an expression is meant to encode the *semantic role* of that expression – i.e., the contribution which that expression makes to the truth-values of the sentences in which it appears. So when we say that the semantic value of a 'that'-clause is a certain function from indices to truth-values, we are saying that the semantic role of that 'that'-clause can somehow be extracted from the fact that it has that function as its value. When we then deny that 'that'-clauses *refer* to their values, we are denying that a sentence which *uses* a 'that'-clause thereby *says something about* the semantic value of that 'that'-clause.[22] (5a), for example, does not express a relation between Simon and the semantic value of 'that Sharon is funny'. What it expresses

---

[20] I should mention that 'that'-clauses are used in many different contexts, including ones which have absolutely nothing to do with propositional content. Every claim I make about 'that'-clauses in this chapter should be taken as a claim about how they function in sentences which attribute propositional content.

[21] Hofweber (2016a; 2016b, ch. 8) recommends a very similar view of 'that'-clauses. The only major difference between my position and Hofweber's concerns quantification. We both think that there is an important difference between quantification over propositions and quantification over ordinary objects, but we disagree about what the difference is: I think the difference is that quantification over objects is *first*-order, and quantification over propositions is *higher*-order; Hofweber thinks that quantification over objects is (at least sometimes) bona fide quantification over a domain, whereas quantification over propositions is just a device for expressing infinite truthfunctions. This is an important difference, which I discuss in: Trueman in press.

[22] For similar remarks, see Grover 1992a, 140–3.

is a relation between Simon and the truth condition of 'Sharon is funny', where truth conditions are conceived of in the Fregean realist's distinctively higher-order way.[23]

At this point, you may wonder why we bother turning sentences into 'that'-clauses if I am right, and 'that' is semantically vacuous. But it may be that 'that' has a useful *non-semantic* role to play. If nothing else, 'that' certainly plays a useful *syntactic* role. By attaching 'that' to 'Sharon is funny' in (5a), we indicate that 'Sharon is funny' appears as the complement to 'believes', rather than as a free standing sentence. Now, this may not seem all that helpful when we focus on sentences like (5a), since the word order also makes it clear that is how 'Sharon is funny' appears. But its utility quickly becomes evident when we consider sentences like (5b), where word order is not such a helpful guide.[24]

Clearly, this is not the place to offer a full account of the syntactic role played by 'that'. That is a job for real empirical linguistics. All that matters for now is that when we modify the Prenective View in the way that I have suggested, it seems to fit the empirical evidence at least as well as the Standard View.

12.5   The Standard View versus Natural Language

So far, we have seen no reason to think that the Prenective View fits the empirical data any worse than the Standard View. Can we press the advantage, and argue that the Prenective View actually fits the data *better* than the Standard View? According to the Standard View, 'that'-clauses are singular terms which refer to propositions. However, a number of philosophers have observed that substituting 'the proposition that *P*' for 'that *P*' does not always preserve grammaticality. Take this sentence, for example:

(6a) Sharon hopes that the train will be on time.

If we substitute 'the proposition that the train will be on time' for 'that the train will be on time', we end up with something ungrammatical:

(6b) # Sharon hopes the proposition that the train will be on time.

---

[23]   For discussion of the intentionality of reference, see Chapter 4. It may be useful to compare what I have said here with my discussion of the relation between a predicate and its extension in §7.4.
[24]   It may be helpful to compare this with my discussion of the difference between 'I' and 'me' in §8.3.1.

If we combine this observation with the Reference Principle,

> (RP) Co-referring expressions are everywhere intersubstitutable *salva congruitate*,

we reach the conclusion that these two expressions do not co-refer. Thus 'that'-clauses are not singular terms referring to propositions, and the Standard View is false.[25]

So far, this is only an argument *against* the Standard View, but if it stands, we might hope to convert it into an argument *for* the Prenective View. Compare (6b) with (6c):

> (6c) Sharon hopes the train will be on time.

(6c) may not be *strictly* grammatical, but it seems good enough for colloquial, everyday purposes. This would be easily explained on my view of 'that'-clauses: (6c) is readily intelligible because 'the train will be on time' has exactly the same sense as 'that the train will be on time'; the 'that' in 'that the train will be on time' merely indicates that 'the train will be on time' is the complement of 'hopes', and that is already made clear enough in (6c) by the word order.

This argument for the Prenective View is pleasingly straightforward. Unfortunately, however, I do not think that it is all that forceful. The trouble is that it focusses on failures of *simple-substitution*, and so relies on the following version of (RP):

> (RP$_1$) Co-referring expressions are everywhere simple-intersubstitutable *salva congruitate*.

I have already argued in Chapter 1 that it is a mistake to draw substantial philosophical conclusions from simple-substitution failures. If we want to draw substantial conclusions from substitution failures, we have to work with *sense-substitution*. This, then, is the version of (RP) that we should use:

> (RP$_3$) If it makes sense to say that α refers$_\alpha$ to what β refers$_\beta$ to, then α and β are everywhere sense-intersubstitutable.

And the sad fact is, no reason has yet been given to think that 'that the train will be on time' and 'the proposition that the train will be on time'

---

[25] This objection, or something like it, has been urged by Bach (1997, 224–5), McKinsey (1999, 530), Moltmann (2003, §2.1; 2013, ch. 4 §3.1), Rosefeldt (2008, §3) and Hofweber (2016a, 68–70). Advocates of the Standard View are also well aware of this kind of objection: King (2002; 2007, 137–63) discusses versions of it, it is a recurring theme in *New Thinking about Propositions* (King et al. 2014, 87–8, 178–9, 201–4), and it has recently been tackled by Nebel (2019).

are not everywhere sense-intersubstitutable. They certainly have different grammatical profiles, but so do 'I' and 'me'. It would clearly be a mistake to jump from this grammatical difference to the conclusion that 'I' and 'me' refer to different things. But if that jump is unwarranted for 'I' and 'me', then it is just as unwarranted for 'that P' and 'the proposition that P'.

It should also be acknowledged that the Prenective View faces its own failures of simple-substitution. Here are two examples:

(7a) That Simon is in a good mood is surprising.
(7b) # Simon is in a good mood is surprising.

(8a) 'Socrates is wise' is true iff Socrates is wise.
(8b) # 'Socrates is wise' is true iff that Socrates is wise.

If we accepted (RP_1), we would have to say that 'that'-clauses and bare sentences stand for different things. To make this problem go away, we need to swap simple-substitution for sense-substitution. If I am right, and 'that' is semantically vacuous, then (7a) is *itself* a result of sense-substituting 'Simon is in a good mood' for 'that Simon is a good mood' in (7a); likewise, (8a) is itself a result of sense-substituting 'that Socrates is wise' for 'Socrates is wise' in (8a). We can then explain away the ungrammaticality of (7b) and (8b) in purely syntactic terms. When we turn a sentence into a 'that'-clause, we syntactically mark that sentence as a complement clause. That syntactic marking is required in (7a), since word order alone does not make it clear that 'Simon is in a good mood' appears as the complement of 'is surprising'. By contrast, 'Socrates is wise' does not appear as a complement in (8a), and so we are not grammatically permitted to mark it as such.

There is, then, no quick argument for the Prenective View from a principle like (RP): the Standard View and the Prenective View both face simple-substitution failures, but for all we have so far seen, they can both survive them. I will present an alternative, and hopefully more robust, argument for the Prenective View in the next chapter. My strategy will be to cause trouble by asking about the contents of *propositions* themselves. I will argue that advocates of the Standard View owe us an account of those contents, but the attempt to supply one will drive them toward the Prenective View.

CHAPTER 13

On Content and Object

In this chapter, I will present my argument for the Prenective View. I will start in §13.1 by presenting a simple, and I think fatal, objection to a completely general version of the Standard View: the Standard View requires that propositions themselves have propositional contents, but it would be incoherent to apply the Standard View to the contents of propositions. This initial objection will not pack too much of a punch all by itself, since no one I can think of has ever actually wanted to apply the Standard View to propositions. However, in §§13.2–13.3, I will consider two ways of thinking about the contents of propositions and argue that they both drive us to the Prenective View. I will end in §13.4, by explaining how the Prenective View dodges the objection that kicked things off in §13.1.

I should be clear about the extent of my ambitions in this chapter. I am not going to try to argue for the Prenective View from a standing start. All I really hope to do is convert those philosophers who, up until now, have subscribed to the Standard View. My aim is to show that pressures *internal to* the Standard View force us toward the Prenective alternative. So for the duration of this argument, I will speak as if the Standard View were correct, and propositions were objects. This pretence will eventually be dropped, but not until §13.4.

13.1   The Limits of the Standard View

Do propositions have propositional contents? My own answer to this question is an emphatic *no*: propositions do not *have* propositional contents; they *are* propositional contents! However, it is not *my* answer that I am interested in right now. (That can wait until §13.4.) I want to think through how an advocate of the Standard View should answer the question.

I think that they should answer *yes*: propositions have propositional contents. According to the Standard View, propositions are a kind of object.

But if propositions are objects, then they must be *truth-apt* objects. After all, to believe one of these objects must surely be to believe it *to be true*. Otherwise, it would be mysterious how standing in the *believing* relation to one of these objects could amount to taking a stand on how things are.[1] So on the Standard View, propositions must be truth-apt. But there is a platitudinous relationship between propositional content and truth-aptitude: *x* is true just in case things are as *x says* that they are.[2] So on the Standard View, propositions must have propositional contents.

Here is another way of putting the same point. Suppose that Simon believes that Sharon is funny. Simon is right about Sharon if she is funny, and he is wrong about her if she is not. Now suppose that the Standard View is correct, and for Simon to believe that Sharon is funny is for Simon to stand in the *believing* relation to some object. Why should standing in this relation to this object make Simon right about Sharon if she is funny, and wrong otherwise? The only intelligible answer is that this object is representational: it *says that* Sharon is funny, and so is true iff Sharon is funny.

These arguments are short and simple, but they seem enough to establish that on the Standard View, propositions have propositional contents. Maybe they were *more* than enough, and we never really needed any arguments to establish this conclusion. Certainly, there do not seem to be many advocates of the Standard View who would want to resist it. For the most part, they seem to be happy to agree that propositions have propositional contents. In fact, many claim that what makes propositions special is the fact that they not only have propositional contents, but have them *essentially*. Much of the recent work on propositions has been dedicated to offering satisfactory accounts of how propositions could be essentially representational in this way.[3]

[1] Thanks to Dan Brigham for first introducing me to this point.
[2] We might take this to be the import of Aristotle's famous definition of truth: 'Thus we define what the true and the false are. To say of what is that it is not, or of what is not that it is, is false, while to say of what is that it is, and of what is not that it is not, is true' (*Metaphysics* 1011^b, 25–8, reprinted in McKeon 1941, 1697). Strawson (1969, 180) emphasises this platitude, and Künne (2003, 334) and Rumfitt (2014, 29) both quote Strawson approvingly on this point. Merricks (2008, 343; 2015, 20 and 192) has also placed great importance on this platitude in his recent work on truth and propositions.
[3] For examples, see King 2007; Soames 2010; King et al. 2014; Hanks 2015. Speaks (King et al. 2014, ch. 5) is a recent counterexample. He identifies the proposition that *P* with the property of being such that *P*, which he takes to be a kind of object. He is happy to say that propositions are truth-apt, and offers a reductive definition of what it is for a proposition to be true: it is true iff it is instantiated. Nonetheless, Speaks (King et al. 2014, 147–8) denies that his propositions are representational. He does so on the grounds that, as a general rule, properties are not representational. However, that general rule does not prevent Speaks' property-cum-propositions from being representational, as a special case. I would suggest that the moment Speaks said that certain properties are truth-apt, he committed himself to the claim that those properties have propositional contents.

But now a difficult question: how should we think about the propositional contents of propositions? How, for example, should we understand the following?

(1a) The proposition that Sharon is funny says that Sharon is funny.

We are currently trying to see things from the Standard View, and on that view, (1a) should be parsed as follows:

(1b) [The proposition that Sharon is funny] says [that Sharon is funny],

where 'that Sharon is funny' is a term referring to the proposition that Sharon is funny. So (1b) expresses a relationship between the proposition that Sharon is funny and *itself*. But isn't that absurd? How could a proposition possibly say something about Sharon simply by standing in a relation to itself? Surely it needs to stand in a relation to *Sharon* to do that!

The Standard View has got itself into a tangle. It pictures propositions as truth-apt objects, and thus the sorts of thing that have propositional content; but when we apply the Standard View to the contents of propositions, we end up with the absurd result that propositions have their contents merely by standing in relations to themselves. The link between representation and reality has been severed, and the propositions have turned in on themselves in a closed circle.

Now, you may not yet be convinced that things are quite as bad for the Standard View as I am making out. You might try to defend it by pointing out that nothing in the Standard View requires that the proposition that Sharon is funny be a featureless point. We are free to add all sorts of internal relations between this proposition and Sharon, or funniness, or anything else we like. With these relations in place, it does not seem so bad to think that the proposition says what it does by virtue of standing in a relation to itself: standing in a relation to the proposition that Sharon is funny is a way of standing in an indirect relation to Sharon herself. But really, this is no defence. Clearly, it is not the relation between the proposition that Sharon is funny and *itself* which accounts for its saying that Sharon is funny, but the additional internal relations between this proposition, Sharon and whatever else. To claim otherwise would be as bizarre as claiming that what it is for Simon to be a sibling of Daniel is for Simon to stand in a relation to himself, and then defending this claim by pointing out that being related to Simon is a way of being indirectly related to his siblings.

Is this enough to refute the Standard View? Only a completely general version of the view, which applies to absolutely everything that has a propositional content. It is not yet enough to undermine a restricted version of the Standard View which applies to beliefs, sentences and so on, but not to propositions. However, if we do restrict the Standard View in this way, then we will be confronted with the question of how we *should* think about the contents of propositions. And we cannot dodge this question by saying that propositions have their contents intrinsically or primitively. That move may excuse us from explaining *how* or *why* propositions have the contents that they do: if I were to ask you why the proposition that *P* says that *P*, you might reasonably reply that that is just what that proposition does (see Merricks 2015, ch. 6). But we still need an explanation of *what it is* for a proposition to have a content. The Standard View tells us what it is for everything but a proposition to have a propositional content: it is to stand in an appropriate relation to a proposition. But that account doesn't work for propositions. So if a proposition's saying that *P* does not amount to its standing in a relation to a proposition, then what *does* it amount to?

My aim in this chapter is to make a case for the following claim: any acceptable account of the contents of propositions will be a version of my Prenective View, and once we accept the Prenective View for propositions, we should accept it across the board for everything that has a propositional content. Of course, it would be quite impossible to make a definitive case for such a claim. There will always be more options to dream up. But we can make a compelling start.

13.2   A Truth Conditional Approach

What view should we take of the contents of propositions, if not the Standard one? Well, earlier I emphasised the platitudinous relation between having a propositional content and having a truth condition. It would be natural, then, to suggest that *what it is* for a proposition to have the content it has is simply for it to have the truth condition it has. So, for example, when we say,

(1a) The proposition that Sharon is funny says that Sharon is funny,

all we really mean is:

(1c) Necessarily, the proposition that Sharon is funny is true iff Sharon is funny.

This is certainly a tempting way to think about the propositional contents of propositions. (It fits particularly well with a conception of propositions as sets of possible worlds.) But crucially, it is just a version of the Prenective View, applied to propositions. Recall that in its most general form, the Prenective View tells us that the form of propositional content ascriptions is '$R(x, P)$'. We can display the relevant parsing of (1c) as follows:

> (1d) Necessarily, [the proposition that Sharon is funny] is true iff [Sharon is funny].

Here we have a term referring to a proposition, 'the proposition that Sharon is funny', a sentence expressing the content of that proposition, 'Sharon is funny', and a prenective connecting the two, 'Necessarily, x is true iff P'.

So if we think of the contents of propositions in this truth conditional way, we will be subscribing to a Prenective View of the contents of propositions. And now I would like to ask, pointedly: once we have accepted the Prenective View for propositions, why wouldn't we want to accept it across the board? We can bring out the force of this question with the following two considerations.

The first point is the obvious one. On the face of it, propositional content appears to be a unified phenomenon. That propositions have propositional content is something they have in common with sentences, beliefs, etc. Of course, there are some differences between these cases. For example, propositions have their contents essentially and sentences do not, and this difference will certainly force us to complicate the story when we deal with sentences. But still, it seems like the story for sentences should just be a complicated version of the story for propositions. Otherwise, we are merely punning when we say that a sentence and proposition both have 'propositional content'.

Of course, this sort of consideration is hardly conclusive, and so we come to the second, and I would say much more important, point. If we tried combining a Prenective View of the contents of propositions with a Standard View of the contents of (say) sentences, then propositions would become an idle wheel in this story. 'Sharon is funny' gets its content by standing in a relation to the proposition that Sharon is funny. But standing in this relation to this proposition only bestows 'Sharon is funny' with content because the proposition has its *own* content, and its having that content is properly understood on the Prenective model. Why bother, then, having the proposition that Sharon is funny act as an intermediary for the content of 'Sharon is funny'? Why do we need this middleman proposition to pass its Prenective content on to the sentence? It seems far simpler to apply the Prenective View directly to the sentence 'Sharon is funny' (and to the belief that Sharon is funny, and so on).

Now, philosophers have given reasons for thinking that we *have to* apply the Standard View to beliefs, sentences, etc., and thus that propositions are not idle wheels here. One of the most commonly cited reasons concerns the formalisation of arguments like this one:

(2) Simon believes that Sharon is funny
(3) Daniel believes that Sharon is funny
∴ (4) There is something that Simon and Daniel both believe

Advocates of the Standard View take it to be a serious point in their favour that they can formalise (4) in first-order logic:

(4_S) $\exists x$(Simon believes x and Daniel believes x).

By contrast, if we read (2) and (3) in accordance with the Prenective View, we have no choice but to use a higher-order quantifier to formalise (4):

(4_P) $\exists P$(Simon believes that P and Daniel believes that P).

I explained in §12.3 why I am not much impressed by this supposed advantage of the Standard View. But now we can go further. Consider the following criterion of identity for propositions:

(5) Proposition a = proposition b iff a and b say the same thing.

I imagine that most advocates of the Standard View would say that (5) is true. And even the dissenters would agree that (5) is an interesting criterion, worth taking seriously. However, if the advocates of the Standard View decide to endorse a version of the Prenective View for the special case of propositions, they will be unable to give (5) a first-order formalisation. Instead, they will also have to use a higher-order logic:

(5_P) Proposition a = proposition b iff $\exists P$(a says that P and b says that P).

But if that is how they end up formalising (5), then they cannot complain when the thoroughgoing advocate of the Prenective View, who applies the view to everything with a propositional content, likewise formalises (4) as (4_P).

I think that all of this is enough to uncover just how unnatural it would be to maintain the Prenective View for propositions but the Standard View for everything else. (This intermediate conclusion will be appealed to again at the end of the next section.) So, if we were to offer the sort of truth conditional account of the contents of propositions that was outlined at the beginning of this section, which is an instance of the Prenective View, then we should endorse the Prenective View in its fully general form.

13.3 The Constituents of Propositions

Many philosophers today think that propositions are *structured* entities – that propositions are in some sense 'built' out of their *constituents*. This immediately suggests an alternative way of accounting for the propositional contents of propositions: what it is for a proposition to have the content it has is for it to be built out of its constituents in the way that it is. Call this approach *constituentism*.

The first thing to ask here is: what exactly are the constituents of propositions? As everybody knows, there are two broad answers to this question: the *Russellian* and the *Fregean*. According to Russellians, the constituents of a proposition are the things that the proposition is about; for example, the constituents of the proposition that Sharon is funny are Sharon and funniness. According to Fregeans, on the other hand, propositions are not built out of the things that they are about, but out of entities which somehow go proxy for those things. For Frege himself (1893, §32; 1923, 390), these proxies were his senses, and thus he held that the proposition that Sharon is funny is built out of the sense of 'Sharon' and the sense of 'x is funny'.

In what follows, I will focus on the Russellian brand of constituentism and leave the Fregean alternative to one side. Propositions make claims about things in the world, and so it seems to me that any account of the content of a proposition must somehow relate that proposition to the things it is about. Of course, a Fregean could try to secure this relation by accounting for the content of a proposition in terms of the things that its constituents *stand for*; but this would just be to incorporate a Russellian account of the proposition's *content* into a Fregean account of its *constituents*. It would, then, be a fairly simple matter to rework everything I say about Russellianism so that it applies to this kind of Fregeanism.

The second thing to ask is: how exactly are propositions 'built' out of their constituents? That is a difficult question, but happily, we do not need to give it a full answer here. All of the leading versions of constituentism are built on the fundamental idea that propositions are united via predication: the proposition that Sharon is funny *predicates* funniness of Sharon; that gives us the sense in which funniness and Sharon are the constituents of that proposition. Of course, there are lots of different ways to develop this fundamental idea, and I lay out some of the options in the appendix to this chapter (§13.A). But for now, we can set the details to one side and just use '*Pred*' to express the relation between a proposition and its constituents. So according to constituentism, what it is for *a* to say that Sharon is funny is for it to predicate funniness of Sharon:

(6) *Pred*(*a*, Sharon, funniness).

Importantly, constituentists tend to assume that properties are objects (see §13.A for evidence). So for most constituentists, 'funniness' functions as a bona fide singular term in (6). But if Fregean realism is right, then these constituentists are making a big mistake: predication is not the ascription of one object to another; when we say of Sharon that she is funny, we are ascribing her a Fregean property, not an object.

I have two aims for the rest of this section. First, in §13.3.1, I will try to make clear why it is such a big mistake to treat 'funniness' as a term in (6). (We could just say that it's a mistake because it contradicts Fregean realism, but I would rather show exactly how it causes trouble for constituentism.) And second, in §13.3.2, I will argue that when we correct this mistake, constituentism is transformed into a version of the Prenective View.

13.3.1   The Problem of Nonsensical Propositions

Assume that 'funniness' appears as a term in (6). In that case, we should be able to substitute any other term we like for it, for example:

(7) *Pred*(*a*, Sharon, Daniel).[4]

But (7) attributes a nonsensical content to proposition *a*: according to (7), *a* says that Sharon Daniels. And no theory should permit us to attribute nonsensical contents to propositions. (Early analytic fans will immediately spot this as nothing more than a reapplication of Wittgenstein's (1922, 5.5422) objection to Russell's multiple-relation theory of judgment. For further discussion, see Trueman 2018a.)

I just announced an adequacy constraint on theories of propositions: any theory which allows us to ascribe nonsensical contents to propositions is automatically inadequate. Why should we accept that adequacy constraint? Maybe we can all agree that no theory should imply that there really are propositions with nonsensical contents. But importantly, nothing has been

---

[4]   It probably does not need to be mentioned, but to be clear: the relevant notion of substitution to use here is sense-substitution.

said to suggest that (7) might actually be true. All I have pointed out is that if 'funniness' appears as a term in (6), then (7) must be meaningful. But *meaningful* doesn't imply *true*, or even *possibly true*. We are, then, free to insist that Daniel just isn't the right sort of thing to be predicated of Sharon. That would not stop (7) from making sense, but it would stop it from being true. Why isn't that enough?

The trouble with this response is that, really, it just does not make sense to ascribe nonsensical contents to propositions. Earlier I said: 'According to (7), *a* says that Sharon Daniels'. But, of course, that sentence itself does not mean anything. It could not mean anything, because 'Sharon Daniels' is nonsense. It is as if I had said: 'According to (7), *a* says that fribble frabble dibble dabble'.[5] The point of ascribing a propositional content to a proposition is to articulate how the world would have to be for the proposition to be true. In fact, this 'how the world would have to be' *is* the propositional content being ascribed. But now consider the following conditionals:

$Pred(a, \text{Sharon}, \text{funniness}) \rightarrow a$ is true iff Sharon is funny
$Pred(a, \text{Daniel}, \text{silliness}) \rightarrow a$ is true iff Daniel is silly
$Pred(a, \text{Sharon}, \text{Daniel}) \rightarrow a$ is true iff . . .

There is no intelligible way of filling the dots in the third conditional. If we try, then the best we can suggest is some nonsense like 'Sharon Daniels'. And at this point, the fact that (7) might not be true should not offer us any comfort. According to consitutentism, propositions get their contents by predicating one thing of another. Now, it might be impossible to predicate Daniel of Sharon, and so (7) might be necessarily false. But if (7) so much as makes sense, then it should still ascribe a content to *a*: (7) still *says* that *a* predicates one thing of another. And if (7) ascribes a propositional content to *a*, then there should be some way of filling in the dots; (7) should make a claim about how things would have to be for *a* to be true. But it makes no such claim, and so it cannot really ascribe a content to *a*.

To be clear, I do not think that this problem is a devastating objection to constituentism. What I think it shows is that 'funniness' cannot really function as a term in (6). I will discuss an alternative way of reading (6) in §13.3.2. But before that, I want to consider a different line of response that a constituentist might offer.

---

[5] I am greatly indebted here to Potter's (2009, ch. 13) discussion of Wittgenstein's objection to Russell's multiple-relation theory of judgment.

I asserted that there is no way of filling the dots in the above conditional. But a constituentist might disagree and suggest that we can fill them like this:

Pred(*a*, Sharon, Daniel) → *a* is true iff Sharon instantiates Daniel.

Of course, Sharon cannot instantiate Daniel, because he is not the sort of thing which can be instantiated. But it still makes sense to *say* that she does,[6] and so this conditional is perfectly intelligible. According to this reply, then, (7) does not really ascribe a nonsensical content to *a*; (7) tells us that *a* says that Sharon instantiates Daniel.

But if this is how we read (7), then we should likewise read (6) as telling us that *a* says that Sharon instantiates funniness. There is, then, a missing element in (6). *a* does not really predicate funniness of Sharon. It predicates *instantiation* of Sharon and funniness:

(6′) *Pred*(*a*, Sharon, funniness, instantiation).

But if 'instantiation' is treated as just another singular term, then we should be able to substitute any other term for it:

(7′) *Pred*(*a*, Sharon, funniness, Daniel).

And now (7′) ascribes a nonsensical content to *a*. There is no good way of filling the dots in the last of these conditionals:

Pred(*a*, Sharon, funniness, instantiation) → *a* is true iff Sharon insantiates funniness
Pred(*a*, Daniel, silliness, instantiation) → *a* is true iff Daniel instantiates silliness
Pred(*a*, Sharon, funniness, Daniel) → *a* is true iff . . .

Of course, a constituentist could suggest filling these dots with 'Sharon and funniness instantiate Daniel'. But this would obviously set them off down a regress. It would be better if they replied that 'instantiation' does not really appear as a term in (6′), and so we were not free to substitute 'Daniel' in its place. But then, they could also have replied that 'funniness' is not really a term in (6). It seems, then, that the move from (6) to (6′) yielded no gain.

---

[6] The notion of 'instantiation' at play here cannot be the mixed-level relation discussed in §10.2. But that's fine. If you believe in universals as well as Fregean properties, then you need two instantiation relations: one mixed-level relation to connect objects to their properties and one first-level relation to connect individuals to their universals. (For further discussion, see Chapter 10, fn.22.)

13.3.2   *From Constituentism to the Prenective View*

If what I have just argued is correct, then constituentists should deny that 'funniness' functions as a term in (6).[7] Rather than reading '*Pred*' as a first-level predicate, '*Pred*(x, y, z)', they should read it as a mixed-level predicate, '*Pred*(x, y, **Z**)'. Now the final gap, marked **Z**, is a gap for predicates, not terms. So 'funniness' would have to be a predicate, not the term it initially appears to be, in (6). We could make this clearer by rewriting (6) as:

(6)   *Pred*(*a*, Sharon, is funny).

If this is how we understand '*Pred*', then (7) can be written off as the nonsensical attempt to substitute a term for a predicate. More generally, constituentism will no longer allow us to ascribe nonsensical contents to propositions: if an instance of '*Pred*(*a*, *b*, *F*)' is well formed, then so is the corresponding instance of '*Fb*'.

But how exactly are we now meant to read (6)? If 'is funny' genuinely appears as a predicate, then it must play the role of a predicate: its job must be to say of an object that it is funny. So how exactly does it play that role in (6)? The only sensible suggestion is that it says of Sharon that she is funny. After all, that is the content which (6) is meant to ascribe to *a*. However, if that is how we read (6), then we must admit that its formulation is a bit misleading. On the face of it, 'Sharon' and 'x is funny' appear to be two separate arguments to '*Pred*'. But in reality, 'x is funny' is being used to say something of the referent of 'Sharon'. It would be more perspicuous, then, to make this act of predication explicit by writing 'Sharon' into the argument place of 'x is funny', like this:

(6)   *Pred*(*a*, Sharon is funny).

In (8), we express what *a* predicates of Sharon by actually predicating it of her. But crucially, this is a version of the Prenective View, applied to the contents of propositions: (8) breaks down into the name '*a*', the sentence 'Sharon is funny', and what has now been revealed to be a prenective joining the two together, '*Pred*(x, P)'.

To be clear, this is not yet an objection to constituentism. The conclusion is just that the most defensible version of constituentism turns out to be a version of the Prenective View. However, as we saw in §13.2, if you give the Prenective View an inch, it takes a mile. Once we accept the Prenective

---

7   Alternatively, they might deny that 'instantiation' functions as a term in (6′). However, to keep things simple, I will focus on (6).

View for the contents of propositions, we are naturally compelled to accept it across the board.

13.4 Propositions Are Propositional Contents

What all of the foregoing shows is that there is a considerable force driving us away from the Standard View and towards the Prenective View. As we saw in §13.1, the Standard View must be restricted so as not to apply to propositions. But when we restrict the view in this way, we must offer an alternative account of the propositional contents of propositions. The two most obvious ways of trying to develop such an account turn out to be instances of the Prenective View for propositions. And the Prenective View cannot be contained: once we accept it for propositions, there is good reason to accept it in a fully general form. Now, I cannot pretend that any of this establishes, once and for all, that we should adopt the Prenective View, but I do think that this is more than enough to show that we should take the view seriously. In this section, I would like to say a little more about what the Prenective View amounts to.

If we combine the Prenective View with Fregean realism, we reach the following conclusion: to have a propositional content is *not* to stand in a relation to a special kind of object; it is to stand in a relation to a truth condition. Let's return to one of our old examples:

(9) Simon believes that Sharon is funny.

If the Standard View is a mistake, then it is a mistake to say that (9) expresses a relation between Simon and a special object referred to by 'that Sharon is funny'. Really, it expresses a relation between Simon and the *truth condition* of the sentence 'Sharon is funny'. This truth condition is not any kind of object. It is not the sort of thing that you can refer to with a singular term, or quantify over with a first-order quantifier. If you want to refer to it, you have to use a whole sentence, and if you want to quantify over it, you have to use a special kind of higher-order quantifier.

In §12.1, I explained that, as I understand it, the concept of a *proposition* is defined by its connection to *propositional content*: to have a propositional content is to stand in a certain relationship to a proposition, and that is all I mean by 'proposition'. So on this understanding, the Prenective View tells us that propositions are truth conditions, not objects. Importantly, this is not because the Standard View's reified 'propositions' do not exist. These reified 'propositions' are usually thought of as abstract objects which not only have propositional contents but have them essentially. I do not want to take any stand on whether there are any such reified 'propositions'. The point is that even if they do exist, they are not propositions in the sense that I am concerned with. They are not propositions because they do not play the proposition-role that I just described earlier. Believing that *P* is not a matter of bearing a relation to one of these objects. Nor is saying that *P*, hoping that *P*, fearing that *P*, or whatever. These are all relations to truth conditions, conceived of in the Fregean realist's distinctively higher-order way.

That completes my argument for the Prenective View. I would now like to conclude this chapter by considering two objections. The first begins by noting that as well as saying things like (9), we also say things like this:

(10) Bertrand believes logicism.

Here 'logicism' does appear to be a term, and so 'believes' does appear to be functioning as an ordinary first-level predicate, 'x believes y'. So despite what I have said, *believing* is at least sometimes a relation between a thinker and an object.[8] There are two ways of replying to this objection. We could try denying appearances and insisting that 'logicism' is not really a referring term.[9] Or, alternatively, we could distinguish between senses of 'believes'.[10] In its primary sense, the sense it has in (9), 'believes' would still express a mixed-level relation between a thinker and a truth condition. But 'believes' would also have a derivative sense in which it expressed a relation to a reified 'proposition'. This sense would count as derivative because it could be defined in terms of the primary sense: *a* derivatively believes *b* iff $\exists P(a$ believes that *P*, and *b* says that *P*). (This is the same derivative sense of 'believe' in which you can believe a sentence.) The important point would remain, though, that belief *in the primary sense* is a relation to a truth condition.

We turn now to the second objection, which is, I think, a bit more substantial. In §13.1, I made trouble for the Standard View by asking about the propositional contents of propositions. If the advocate of the Standard View tries to think of those contents on their Standard model, they end up with the absurd idea that a proposition has its content by virtue of standing in a relation to itself. Doesn't the Prenective View run into *exactly the same* trouble? Propositions may have moved up a level in the logical hierarchy,

---

[8] Künne pushes this sort objection throughout Künne (2003, ch. 2).
[9] See Hofweber 2016b, ch. 8.
[10] King (2002) distinguishes between senses of 'believes' in this sort of way, but to very different ends. See also Rosefeldt 2008, 305–6 and 315–16.

but it is hard to see why that should matter. We are still owed an account of the contents of these higher-order propositions. And if we try to think of those contents on the Prenective model, we still end up with the absurd idea that a proposition has its content by virtue of standing in a relation to itself.

The mistake in this challenge is the background assumption that propositions have propositional contents. We saw in §13.1 that this was something the Standard View was committed to. If propositions are objects, then they must be truth-apt objects, and there is a platitudinous relationship between propositional content and truth-aptitude: x is true just in case things are as x says that they are. But the Prenective View is very different. Consider the following claim:

(11a) The proposition that Sharon is funny is true.

(11a) appears to refer to a proposition with a singular term, 'the proposition that Sharon is funny', and then predicate truth of it. But this cannot be the right way to read (11a) on the Prenective View: propositions are now thought of as higher-order entities, which can only be referred to with whole sentences, not singular terms. So the apparent singular reference to a proposition needs to be eliminated. And it is easy to see how we should eliminate it. We should read (11a) as a mere periphrasis of:

(11b) Sharon is funny.

So on the Prenective View, (11a) does not ascribe the property of truth to the propositional content that Sharon is funny; rather, it just says that Sharon is funny, in a few extra words. The Prenective View thus incorporates an extreme form of the redundancy theory of truth for propositions. (We will talk about the truth of things other than propositions in §14.2.) I call it an *extreme* form because we are not merely saying that adding a truth-predicate to our discourse about propositions does not introduce any extra expressive power. We are saying that the truth-predicate *only* appears when we are speaking loosely, and pretending that propositions are objects that we can refer to with singular terms. When we speak strictly, the truth-predicate simply vanishes.[11]

---

[11] It might be helpful here to contrast this extreme brand of redundancy theory with Frege's less extreme brand. Frege (1918) would have said that (11a) has the same sense as (11b). However, he would also have said that 'x is true' appears in (11a) as a genuine, first-level predicate. In that minimal sense, then, Frege was committed to a first-level property of propositional truth. By contrast, I deny that there is any first-level truth-predicate that can be applied to propositions.

On the Prenective View, then, propositions are not really the sort of thing that can be true or false. There is no external property of truth that can be applied to a proposition. And that is what saves the view from the objection that I presented in §13.1. If propositions are not truth-apt, then we are not forced to say that propositions *have* propositional contents. We can instead rest easy with the idea that propositions *are* propositional contents. (9) does not express a relationship between Simon and something which has *Sharon is funny* as its truth condition; it expresses a relationship between Simon and the truth condition itself.

13.A Appendix: Contemporary Approaches to Structured Propositions

In §13.3, I spoke about structured propositions in deliberately abstract terms. Some readers may be perfectly happy with that level of abstraction, and they are welcome to skip this appendix and head straight to Chapter 14. However, other readers may suspect that by speaking abstractly, I some-how made my argument seem more compelling than it really is. To soothe any such suspicions, I will quickly outline some contemporary approaches to structured propositions; in each case, it will be immediately clear that they yield a version of the constituentism and are thus vulnerable to the argument from §13.3.

But before we get going, I would like to say a word about the scope of what I am trying to show. First, I am absolutely not trying to show that any of the structured entities that philosophers have identified with propositions do not exist. Nor am I trying to deny that these structured entities might be put to useful linguistic work. We might take them to be useful models of what propositions really are, and thought of in that way, we might even use them as the semantic values of 'that'-clauses (see §12.4). All I want to show is that if we try suggesting that these structured entities have propositional contents by virtue of being built out of their constituents in the way that they are, then we leave ourselves open to the argument of §13.3.

13.A.1 King's Propositions

We begin with King's influential account of propositions (King 2007, ch. 2; King et al. 2014, 49–59). According to King, the proposition that Sharon is funny with a certain complex fact, namely the fact that: *there is a context c and there are lexical items* α *and* β *of some language L such that* α *has Sharon as it semantic value in c,* β *has funniness as its semantic value in c, and* α *and* β *are related by some syntactic relation that encodes ascription in L.* This way of describing the fact is a bit of a mouthful, but it can be neatly summarised diagramatically. We start with the familiar use of a tree to represent the syntactic structure of 'Sharon is funny':[12]

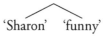

We then add some semantic information to this tree:

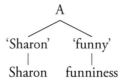

This tree expands on the first one by adding the ideas that 'Sharon' stands for Sharon and 'funny' stands for funniness (relative to some context *c*), and that the syntactic relation between 'Sharon' and 'funny' encodes ascription. (Importantly, this syntactic relation does not *stand for* ascription, as 'Sharon' stands for Sharon; rather, it 'encodes' ascription, in the sense that any fluent English speaker ascribes funniness to Sharon when they read 'Sharon is funny'. See King 2007, 34–8.) Finally, we existentially generalise away the lexical items 'Sharon' and 'is funny', yielding the fact that King identifies with the proposition that Sharon is funny:

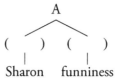

Call the relation that holds between Sharon and funniness in this fact $R(y, z)$: *there is a context c and there are lexical items* α *and* β *of some language L such that* α *has y as it semantic value in c,* β *has z as its semantic relation in c, and* α *and* β *are related by some syntactic relation that encodes*

---

[12] It is not standard practice to put quotation marks around expressions on a phrase structure tree. However, in a moment we will expand the tree by adding elements drawn from the realm of reference, and so it will be helpful to explicitly mark the use/mention distinction.

ascription in L. According to King (2007, 59–64; 2009, 265–73; King et al. 2014, 52–5), the proposition that Sharon is funny has its content by virtue of two factors coming together: the first is that this proposition is identical to the fact that R(Sharon, funniness); the second is that we interpret the R relation as also encoding ascription.[13] Putting these two factors together, we have a version of constituentism, according to which the proposition that Sharon is funny has its content by virtue of a fact of the following form:

(1) $Pred$(a, Sharon, funniness).

$Pred$(x, y, z) is here short for: x is the fact that $R(y, z)$, and R is interpreted as encoding ascription. From here, §13.3 can proceed exactly as it did.

However, there is one potential point of confusion that I need to clear up. King (2009, 274–6) claims that there could be a proposition that has Sharon and Daniel as its only constituents. But King is certainly not suggesting that there could be a nonsensical proposition that ascribes Daniel to Sharon. Rather, King's point is just that a relation between Sharon and Daniel could be interpreted as encoding *something* propositional; for example, it could be interpreted as ascribing the *is older than* relation. The important thing for our purposes is that King thinks it would be incoherent to imagine that any relation which holds between Sharon and Daniel could be interpreted as encoding *ascription*, at least in the sense in which he thinks that R encodes ascription. Thus, King would agree that the following must be ruled out somehow:

(2) $Pred$(a, Sharon, Daniel).

However, King does not seem to appreciate that (2) must be ruled out as nonsensical, and not merely false. To rule (2) out in this stronger way, King would need to swap the term 'funniness' for the predicate 'x is funny':

---

[13] In some places, King (e.g., 2007, 61; 2013, 77) says that the proposition that Sharon is funny is *really* the fact that *R(Sharon, funniness) and R encodes ascription*. He does this in an effort to ensure that propositions have their contents essentially. However, I do not think that this is the right way for him to secure that result. King initially introduces the idea that R encodes ascription to explain why the fact that R(Sharon, funniness) has a propositional content when most facts don't: the fact that R(Sharon, funniness) has a content because we interpret R in a certain way. But what we have here is an explanation of why the fact that R(Sharon, funniness) has a propositional content, not why the 'bigger' fact that *R(Sharon, funniness) and R encodes ascription* does. It seems crucial to King's explanation, then, that the proposition that Sharon is funny not be identified with this bigger fact but with the smaller fact that R(Sharon, funniness).

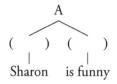

The expression 'is funny' is meant to appear at the bottom of this diagram as an actual, used predicate. This will require that we rethink what it means to say that the syntactic relation in this diagram 'encodes ascription' since, in ordinary English, it is ungrammatical to say 'is funny is ascribed to Sharon'. Fortunately, this is not too much of a problem. Presumably, this talk of 'encoding ascription' now just means that when we make a sentence by combining an expression which refers to Sharon with an expression that says of an object that it is funny, we end up with a sentence which says that Sharon is funny. And clearly, the 'says that P' here must be read in accordance with the Prenective View, not the Standard View; otherwise, we would be back to the absurd picture from §13.1, where we try to apply the Standard View to propositions. But now we have a version of the Prenective View, and (1) would be more perspicuously written as:

(3) *Pred*(*a*, Sharon is funny).

13.A.2   Soames' Propositions

Next we have Soames' (2010, ch. 6) theory that propositions are types of events.[14] According to Soames, when we entertain the thought that Sharon is funny, we predicate funniness of Sharon. He then suggests that we identify the proposition that Sharon is funny with the minimal event-type of predicating funniness of Sharon: this is the type under which an event falls iff it involves an agent predicating funniness of Sharon.

On Soames' (2010, 106–7; King et al. 2014, 96, 234–5 and 239–41) picture, particular, token acts of predication are inherently representational, and the events that Soames identifies with propositions somehow inherit their propositional contents from their tokens. The details of this aspect of Soames' theory are subtle and have changed over time. But for our purposes, these details do not matter. What is clear is that on Soames' view, the proposition that Sharon is funny says that Sharon is funny *because* it is the minimal event-type of predicating funniness of Sharon. Thus, he endorses a

---

[14] More recently, Soames (King et al. 2014, 240–1, esp. fn. 16) has become attracted to the idea that propositions are types of act, but this is not a difference that makes any real difference for us.

version of constituentism, according to which the proposition that Sharon is funny has its content by virtue of a fact of the form:

(1) *Pred*(*a*, Sharon, funniness).

But now, *Pred*(*x*, *y*, *z*) abbreviates: *x is the minimal event-type of predicating z of y*. The argument from §13.3 will therefore straightforwardly engage with Soames' account of propositions. Soames will need to find a way of ruling out the following as nonsensical:

(2) *Pred*(*a*, Sharon, Daniel).

This would require reading 'funniness' in (1) as a monadic predicate, and thus thinking of it as saying of objects that they are funny. The obvious suggestion is that 'funniness' discharges that function in (2) by saying of Sharon in particular that she is funny. But in that case, (2) can be perspicuously rewritten as:

(3) *Pred*(*a*, Sharon is funny).

Of course, this change from (1) to (3) would in turn require a new gloss on what relation *Pred* is. As best as I can tell, it should be thought of as *Pred*(*x*, *P*): *x is the minimal type-event of saying that P*. And again, the 'saying that *P*' here must be given the Prenective parsing, not the Standard parsing; otherwise, we would be back to the absurd picture from §13.1.

13.A.3 Hanks' Propositions

Finally, we come to Hanks' (2011; 2015) view, according to which propositions are types of act: roughly, the proposition that Sharon is funny is the act-type of predicating funniness of Sharon. So far, this sounds very similar to Soames' theory,[15] but there are two noteworthy differences. The first, which is not all that important for our purposes, is that Hanks insists that predication is inherently assertive: according to Hanks, to predicate funniness of Sharon is not to merely entertain the thought that Sharon is funny but to assert it.[16] Second, and much more to our point, Hanks does not think that Sharon and funniness are constituents of the proposition that Sharon is funny. He represents this proposition as follows:

---

[15] Especially given Soames' recent sympathy for the idea that propositions are *act*-types rather than *event*-types.

[16] In fact, Hanks (2015, 36–9) even accuses Soames' use of a non-assertive predication of being incoherent.

$$\vdash \langle \textbf{Sharon}, \textsc{funniness} \rangle$$

$\vdash$ is the act-type of predication, but **Sharon** is not the person Sharon, and FUNNINESS is not the property funniness. Instead, **Sharon** is the act-type of referring to Sharon, and FUNNINESS is the act-type of expressing funniness.[17] (Importantly, 'expressing' a property is simply a matter of singling the property out, and does not involve applying it to anything; it is $\vdash$ which does the applying. Equally importantly, Hanks is not using angle brackets to represent an ordered sequence, but simply to indicate the order in which one thing is predicated of another.) Hanks' theory is, then, more Fregean than Russellian: the constituents of a proposition are not the things that the proposition is about, but other entities which somehow go proxy for those things.

Nonetheless, Hanks ends up offering us a version of constituentism. Like Soames, Hanks (2015, ch. 3) thinks that his propositions – i.e., act-types of predication – inherit their propositional contents from their tokens. In particular, then, the proposition that Sharon is funny says that Sharon is funny because tokening it is a matter of predicating funniness (which we express by tokening FUNNINESS) of Sharon (whom we refer to by tokening **Sharon**). Thus, Hanks' view is that the proposition that Sharon is funny has its content by virtue of a fact of the following form:

(1′) $Pred(a, \textbf{Sharon}, \textsc{funniness})$.

Here $Pred(x, y, z)$ abbreviates: *x is the act-type of referring to an object by tokening y, expressing a property by tokening z, and (assertively) predicating that property of that object*. The problem for Hanks' theory would then be that it does not appropriately rule out:

(2′) $Pred(a, \textbf{Sharon}, \textbf{Daniel})$.

Although (1′) will be necessarily false on Hanks' view, since tokening **Daniel** is not a way of expressing a property, it will still be perfectly well formed: as Hanks explains it, 'FUNNINESS' and '**Daniel**' are both just singular terms referring to act-types of picking out entities.

Of course, Hanks could try installing a type distinction between 'FUNNINESS' and '**Daniel**', but it is important to be clear on what this would have to involve. It would not do just to say that 'FUNNINESS' and '**Daniel**' stand for different types of act. That might be enough to make (2′) false, but it should be nonsense. Instead, Hanks would need to introduce

---

[17] This is a little bit of a simplification. For very interesting discussions about which particular act-types **Sharon** and FUNNINESS are, see Hanks 2011, §§4–6; 2015, chs. 5 and 7.

some difference in the way that these expressions themselves function. My suggestion is that Hanks should treat 'FUNNINESS' as a functional expression (not a predicate). The idea is that 'FUNNINESS' stands for a function which maps **Sharon** to the act-type of referring to Sharon by tokening **Sharon** and asserting of her that she is funny; or, more simply put, it maps **Sharon** to the act-type of asserting that Sharon is funny. Of course, if that is how we think of 'FUNNINESS', then we should rewrite (1') as:

(3') *Pred*(a, FUNNINESS(**Sharon**)).

Again, this would require giving a new reading of '*Pred*'. The only suggestion that seems appropriate here is that (3') says that *a* is the act-type FUNNINESS(**Sharon**) – i.e., the act-type of asserting that Sharon is funny. And once more, 'asserting that *P*' must here be given the Prenective parsing, not the Standard parsing; otherwise, we will back to the absurd picture from §13.1. (3') is, then, just a heavily disguised version of the Prenective View for propositions.

CHAPTER 14

The Identity Theory of Truth

In Chapter 11, I presented the Fregean realist's picture of facts and states of affairs: a state of affairs is the truth condition of a sentence, and a fact is an obtaining state of affairs – i.e., a truth condition which is satisfied. Then, in Chapters 12–13, I argued that we should accept exactly the same picture of propositions: a proposition is the truth condition of a sentence, and a true proposition is a truth condition which is satisfied. Put these two pictures together, and you end up making the following two identifications: propositions *are* states of affairs, and true propositions *are* facts.

These results might at first seem a little strange. We are used to thinking of facts and propositions on the model of the *correspondence theory*: true propositions *correspond* to facts. But what we have been led to instead is a version of the *identity theory of truth*: true propositions do not merely correspond to facts; they *are* facts. Now, I suppose that you might just think of the identity theory as the limiting case of the correspondence theory. After all, there is no closer correspondence than identity! But that would be an unhelpful way of thinking about things. Correspondence theorists always assume that there is some sort of gap between a proposition and its corresponding fact.[1] The correspondence relation is meant to somehow bridge that gap. By contrast, the identity theorist sees no gap between facts and propositions. Where the correspondence theorist sees one thing corresponding to another, the identity theorist sees just the one thing.

The identity theory has been around for a long time. It was defended in one version or another by Frege (1918, 342), Bradley (1907), the early Moore (1901–2), the early Russell (1904) and the early Wittgenstein (1922).[2] However, despite having roots which go back all the way to the beginning of analytic philosophy, the identity theory has been largely neglected by the majority of philosophers. The theory does have a few contemporary

---

[1] This point was emphasised by Frege (1918, 327) and by Moore (1901–2, 20–1).
[2] For interesting work on the historical roots of the identity theory, see Cartwright 1987a; Candlish 1989, 1995; Baldwin 1991; Dodd 2000, 114–23; Sullivan 2005; MacBride 2018, 37–9.

advocates: McDowell (1994, 27–9; 2005), Hornsby (1997, 1999), Dodd (2000), Johnston (2013) and Methven (2018b) have all argued for versions of the identity theory.[3] But there is no denying that the identity theory is still a minority pursuit.

My aim in this chapter is not to offer new arguments for the identity theory. I have already given the only argument I have to give: the identity theory is what you get when you combine my picture of facts with my picture of propositions. Instead, my initial aim is just to explain what my version of the identity theory really amounts to (§§14.1–14.2). After that, I will consider a range of objections to the identity theory, and show how my version of the theory manages to avoid them (§§14.3–14.5). I will then end by using my identity theory to explain what I think is wrong with the idea that true propositions are *made true* by, or are *grounded* in, the facts (§§14.6–14.7).

14.1   An Immodest Identity Theory

If you extend Fregean realism to cover facts and propositions in the way that I have recommended, then you reach the conclusion that facts are true propositions. Taken out of context, this may just sound like a Fregean realist being orthodoxly Fregean. Frege (1918, 342) asked himself 'What is a fact?', and he answered, 'A fact is a thought [i.e., a proposition] that is true'. However, as I emphasised in §12.2, when I extended Fregean realism, I did so against Frege's wishes. My conception of propositions is thus very different from Frege's, and so I mean something very different when I say that facts are true propositions.

According to Frege (1918), propositions are objects in the realm of sense. By this, I mean more than that propositions are the senses of sentences. Talk of a 'realm of sense' is meant to capture Frege's belief that propositions are at an ontological distance from ordinary things like you and me and tables and chairs. On Frege's view, propositions are structured entities, but they are not built out of the entities that they are about. Sharon, for example, is not a constituent of the proposition that Sharon is funny. The constituents of propositions are senses, which somehow present the things that the propositions are about.[4]

---

[3]   Candlish (1999a, 1999b) also seems to be sympathetic to the identity theory although it is not clear to me whether he would count himself as an identity theorist.
[4]   Frege presents this view of propositions very clearly in a letter to Russell, dated 13 November 1904 and reprinted in McGuinness (1980, 160–6).

Frege's propositions are, then, objects wholly outside of the world of ordinary things.[5] And when Frege said that facts were true propositions, he was not trying to bring propositions back down to earth. Instead, he was evacuating facts from the ordinary world and rehoming them in the realm of sense. Dodd (1995, 161–2; 2000, 111–12) calls Frege's version of the identity theory *modest*, which he contrasts with *robust* identity theories:

> A robust identity theorist … takes facts to be states of affairs: things with objects and properties as constituents. Such an identity theory is appropriately labelled 'robust' because it preserves the idea, present in correspondence theories, that true propositions – in addition to their parts – have worldly relata. A robust identity theorist agrees with the correspondence theorist that each true proposition stands in a relation to a state of affairs; she departs from correspondence theories by taking the relation in question to be that of identity. If the robust identity theorist is correct, a true proposition *is* a chunk of reality. (Dodd 2000, 112)

> A robust identity theory, in identifying true propositions with such worldly items, eradicates the gap between content and reality. … [If] the robust identity theorist is correct, the facts which make up reality are literally thinkable: the world is composed of true propositions. (Dodd 1995, 161)[6]

I want to be absolutely clear: the version of the identity theory which I have argued for is *definitely not* modest. When I say that facts are true propositions, I do not mean to rip the facts out of the world. Facts are not *only* true propositions; they are *also* obtaining states of affairs. In short, I share the robust identity theorist's impulse to put propositions in immediate contact with the world.

However, having said that, I am not at all sure that this is enough to make my identity theory robust. The trouble is that Dodd's modest/robust distinction seems to presuppose that propositions and states of affairs are objects. That is certainly what is suggested by Dodd's claim that on the robust theory, a true proposition is a 'chunk of reality'. But that is precisely the conception of propositions and states of affairs that I have been arguing against. When I say that a true proposition is an obtaining state of affairs, what I mean is that (1a) and (1b),

(1a) The proposition that Sharon is funny is true
(1b) The state *Sharon is funny* obtains,

---

[5] It can be tempting to say that Frege's propositions are objects outside of the realm of *reference*. That is fine, so long as we do not let ourselves get confused. After all, Frege did think that it was possible to refer to propositions; in fact, he thought that we could refer to them with *singular terms*.

[6] Historical examples of robust identity theorists include the early Moore (1901–2) and the early Russell (1904).

are *both* periphrastic variants of plain old (1c):

(1c) Sharon is funny.

(1c) is not the name of some chunk of reality. (1c) expresses a truth condition, a way for the world to be. That way for the world to be is a state of affairs, but it is also a proposition; that proposition is true, and that state of affairs obtains, if the world is that way. This version of the identity theory is certainly immodest, but it also does not seem to be robust.

14.2 The Core of the Identity Theory

Facts are true propositions. That is the identity theory in slogan form. However, I do not think that this slogan gets to the heart of the theory. As I explained in §13.4, when we conceive of propositions as truth conditions, we commit ourselves to a radical version of the redundancy theory of truth for propositions. We only ever talk about the 'truth' of a proposition when we are speaking loosely, and pretending that propositions are objects. When we speak strictly, all mention of truth simply vanishes, as it does in the move from (1a) to (1c). (The same goes for all talk about the 'obtaining' of a state of affairs.)

We might sensibly worry that this extreme form of the redundancy theory will rob the identity theory of its substance. Fortunately, however, it does not. In fact, the full (immodest) impact of the identity theory is only felt when we turn away from propositions, and consider the real bearers of truth and falsehood.

Ever since §13.1, I have repeatedly emphasised that there is a platitudinous relationship between *truth* and *propositional content*: x is true iff things are as x says that they are. So the real bearers of truth and falsehood are things that have propositional contents – e.g., beliefs, sentences, assertions and even the Standard View's reified 'propositions', if they exist.[7] Ramsey provided us with the natural way of defining truth for these things in his unfinished manuscript *On Truth* (1991, 9):

(R) x is true $\leftrightarrow_{df} \exists P(P \land x$ says that $P)$,

---

[7] Recall that a reified 'proposition' is meant to be a special object which not only has a propositional content, but which has it essentially. I have taken no stand on whether these reified 'propositions' exist. My only complaint against them is that even if they do exist, they do not play the proposition-role that I identified in §12.1.

where 'x says that P' is used to express the generic relation between any object and its propositional content.[8] (R) should be acceptable to everyone, since it is nothing but a formal expression of the platitudinous relationship between *truth* and *propositional content*. However, exactly how you should *understand* (R) will depend on whether you subscribe to the Standard View or the Prenective View.[9]

Consider the following two questions we might ask about someone's belief:

(i) What does x believe?
(ii) How must the world be for x's belief to be true?

If we read (R) in accordance with the Standard View, then we will give these questions different answers: we will answer (i) by referring to a proposition with a singular term, 'that P'; we will answer (ii) by expressing a way for the world to be with a whole a sentence, 'P'. This is the difference between referring to the proposition that Sharon is funny, and actually saying that Sharon is funny.

But if we read (R) in accordance with the Prenective View, then we will give (i) and (ii) exactly the same answer. On the Prenective View, 'that P' is not a term referring to a proposition. There is no semantic difference between 'that P' and 'P': they both simply express ways for the world to be (see §12.4). So setting aside a purely syntactic distinction, P is both what x believes, and how the world has to be for that belief to be true. Put another way: saying what x believes is itself a matter of saying how the world must be for x's belief to be true. This is the central core of an immodest identity theory:

> there is no ontological gap between the sort of thing one can mean, or generally the sort of thing one can think, and the sort of thing that can be the case. When one thinks truly, what one thinks is what *is* the case. So since the world is everything that is the case [...], there is no gap between thought, as such, and the world. (McDowell 1994, 27)

---

[8] Ramsey's definition of truth only covered beliefs, but (R) is the obvious generalisation of that definition. I have sometimes heard (R) referred to as the *prosentential theory of truth*. However, that is misleading at best. (R) is the definition of a truth-predicate, but as originally presented by Grover, Camp and Belnap (1975), the prosentential theory denied that 'true' ever functions as a predicate, even when applied to sentences, beliefs, etc. Nonetheless, someone who defined truth with (R) might find it helpful to use the idea that 'is true' *sometimes* acts as a prosentence-forming operator, since that would provide us with one way of translating (R) into natural English. For more on the prosentential theory of truth, see Grover 1992b.

[9] Künne (2003, §6.2) advocates a similar definition of truth, precisely on the grounds that it is just a formalised platitude. However, Künne reads (R) in accordance with the Standard View. Rumfitt also defends this definition of truth in Rumfitt (2014), although in that paper he takes no stance on whether we should read it in accordance with the Standard View or the Prenective View; however, his remarks in Rumfitt 2016 suggest that he may prefer the latter.

14.3   The Identity Theory as a Form of Direct Realism

Over the next three sections, I plan to consider a range of objections to the identity theory. All of these objections can be answered, and answering them will shed further light on the nature of the theory.

When people are first introduced to the identity theory, they often accuse it of being a version of idealism. The argument runs as follows:

> On one very influential conception, the world is all that is the case.[10] In other words, the world is nothing over and above all the ways that the world is. But on the identity theory, a *way the world is* is the type of thing that can be thought. In that sense, these *ways* are thoughts. So the world is a totality of thoughts. What clearer statement of idealism could there be?

There is absolutely nothing wrong with this train of thought, *except* the suggestion that it leads us to a version of idealism. The first thing to emphasise is that there is an important difference between *acts* of thinking and the things which *can be thought*. Here is Hornsby on this distinction:

> Someone who objects to [the identity theory] supposes that, by denying any gap between thought and the world, one commits oneself to a sort of idealism. But such an objector confuses people's thinkings of things with the contents of their thoughts. If one says that there is no ontological gap between thoughts and what is the case, meaning by 'thoughts' cognitive activity on the part of beings such as ourselves, then one is indeed committed to a sort of idealism: one has to allow that nothing would be the case unless there were cognitive activity – that there could not be a mindless world. But someone who means by 'thoughts' the contents of such activity, and who denies a gap between thoughts and what is the case, suggests only that what someone thinks can be the case. (Hornsby 1997, 1–2)

A *way the world is* is a 'thought' only in the sense that it is the type of thing which can be thought. Following McDowell (1994, 28), we might call it a *thinkable*. But even this label needs to be treated with care. There is nothing incoherent in the suggestion that there are ways for the world to be which humans simply cannot think. Maybe we can grant that, with enough idealisation, each way for the world to be could be thought by some possible agent or other. But that is not part and parcel of the Prenective View. We could endorse that view, and the identity theory which flows out of it, and still insist that some ways for the world to be simply could not be thought by anyone at all. Ways for the world to be are 'thinkables' only in the sense that they are the *type* of thing which can be thought, and by 'type', I mean

---

10   This is, of course, the Tractarian conception of the world (Wittgenstein 1922, 1).

logical type: we express ways for the world to be with whole sentences, and we also use whole sentences to express what people believe.

Very well, according to the identity theory, the world is a totality of thinkables. How is *that* not a statement of idealism? At this point, I think it is helpful to draw a comparison between the Prenective View and *direct realism* about perception. I have in mind the kind of direct realism which opposes the sense-data theory. According to the sense-data theory, we perceive objects in our environment only indirectly; the direct objects of perception are sense-data, which somehow represent the worldly objects. Direct realism is a rejection of this picture of perception. According to direct realism, perception is a direct relation between a perceiver and the objects in their environment, without any representational intermediaries.[11]

The Standard View is a lot like the sense-data theory. To have a belief is to take a stand on how the world is. If Simon believes that Sharon is funny, he takes a stand on whether Sharon is funny; his belief is true iff the world is a certain way – in this case, iff Sharon is funny. But on the Standard View, belief is not a direct relation between Simon and this way for the world to be. It is a direct relation between Simon and a special object, called a 'proposition'. Standing in the *believing* relation to this reified proposition amounts to taking a stand on whether Sharon is funny, but only because that proposition *represents* Sharon as being funny.

By contrast, on the Prenective View, belief is not a relation to a special representational object. '*x* believes that *P*' has two arguments. The '*x*' stands for a believer, and according to the Prenective View, 'that *P*' expresses a way for the world to be. '*x* believes that *P*' thus expresses a direct relationship between a believer and a way for the world to be. To have a true belief that Sharon is funny is not to stand in a relation to an object which represents how things are with Sharon; it is to stand in a *direct* relation to how things are with Sharon. So on the Prenective View, thinkables are not special representational objects which depict ways for the world to be. Thinkables *are* ways for the world to be.[12]

If we conceived of thinkables in the way that the Standard View told us to, as objects which represent ways for the world to be, then to assert

---

[11]   For careful discussion of different senses in which perception might be 'direct', see Foster 2000, ch. 2. On Foster's taxonomy, I have *weak direct realism* in mind. Modern naïve realism (Martin 1997; Campbell 2002, ch. 6; Fish 2009) and intentionalism (Tye 1995; Siegel 2010) both count as types of direct realism in this sense.

[12]   Of course, it may be that in order to have a belief, your brain has to be in a certain representational state. But the point here is that your belief is not a relation to that representational state, or to any other representation. It is a relation to a way for the world to be, the way represented by the brain state.

that the world is a totality of thinkables would be to subscribe to a form of idealism. This idealism would trade the external world for mere representations. However, my identity theory flows out of the Prenective View, and if we conceive of thinkables in the way that the Prenective View tells us to, then there is nothing idealistic in the claim that the world is a totality of thinkables. Thinkables are *themselves* worldly. They are ways for the world to be. The identity theorist is not, then, trading the external world for mere representations. The identity theorist is rejecting the idea that belief is a relation to mere representations. If you have a true belief, then you stand in a direct relation to how the world is, without any representational intermediaries. To steal a remark from Wittgenstein:

> When we say, and *mean*, that such-and-such is the case, we – and our meanings – do not stop anywhere short of the fact; but we mean: *this-is-so*. (Wittgenstein 1953, §95)

14.4 Falsehood and Unity

It is widely thought that (immodest) identity theories will be unable to offer a satisfying account of falsehood. It is all well and good identifying *true* propositions with facts. But what about the *false* propositions? We seem to have no choice but to identify them with unobtaining states of affairs. But the broad consensus amongst philosophers seems to be that unobtaining states of affairs are mysterious, shadowy entities which have no place in a respectable ontology. As Baldwin (1991, 46) puts it, unobtaining states of affairs 'need to have, so to speak, all the substance of actual states of affairs, but just to lack their actuality'.[13]

I agree that false propositions are unobtaining states of affairs, but I deny that there is anything wrong with that. We already saw in §11.3 that the Fregean realist is committed to there being unobtaining states of affairs alongside the obtaining ones. A state of affairs is just the truth condition of a sentence, and false sentences have truth conditions too; those truth conditions are the unobtaining states of affairs. We can make all of this easier to stomach by remembering that the Fregean realist's states of affairs

---

[13] Versions of this objection are presented by Russell (1910a, 153–6), Baldwin (1991, 46), Candlish (1999b, 207–9), Dodd (1995, 163–4) and Merricks (2007, 181). When Hornsby (1999, 243–4) considers the question of how to account for falsehood, her answer is just: 'a thinkable is false if and only if it is not a fact'. Hornsby acknowledges that many philosophers will find this answer unsatisfying.

are best thought of as ways for the world to be. Unobtaining states of affairs are then just the ways that the world is not.[14]

This is enough to answer the objection that identity theorists run into trouble merely because they are committed to unobtaining states of affairs. However, Dodd (2000, 164–6) insists that falsehood poses a deeper problem for immodest identity theories than that.[15] Consider the proposition that Simon is older than Daniel. Immodest identity theorists want to identify this proposition with the state *Simon is older than Daniel*. Dodd takes it for granted that this state would be composed out of Simon, Daniel and the *is older than* relation. But crucially, this state cannot just be a collection of these elements. It displays a certain kind of *unity*: it is a single unified thing, capable of obtaining as a whole. The challenge now facing the immodest identity theorists is to find some way of accounting for this unity. But according to Dodd, the only way available to them is the early Russell's way: the state *Simon is older than Daniel* is unified by the *is older than* relation's actually relating Simon to Daniel (Russell 1903, §54). However, to say that the *is older than* relation actually relates Simon to Daniel is just a fancy way of saying that Simon is older than Daniel. So if the state *Simon is older than Daniel* exists at all, then it must be an obtaining state. The same goes for all states of affairs, and so there are no unobtaining states of affairs out there to be identified with false propositions.

Dodd's argument may well tell against some versions of the identity theory, but it does not tell against mine. Dodd seems to be thinking of states of affairs as complex *objects*, which are built out of simpler *objects*. Dodd's request for an account of the unity of states is an account of the metaphysical glue which holds three objects – Simon, Daniel and *is older than* – together in a single state – *Simon is older than Daniel*. But that is precisely the picture of states of affairs that I have rejected. The state *Simon is older than Daniel* is not an object, and nor is the *is older than* relation. The only way of referring to a state is with a sentence, and the only way of referring to a relation is with a predicate. So if we want to express the relation which unites Simon, Daniel and *is older than* into a single state, we must say something of the following form:

(2a) U(Simon, Daniel, is older than, Simon is older than Daniel).

---

[14] Johnston (2013, 386) makes the similar suggestion that states of affairs are *ways things may be*. And he also argues (390) that thinking about states of affairs in this way allows the identity theorist to account for false propositions.

[15] It is important to emphasise that this is an objection for *immodest* identity theories only. Dodd's own modest identity theory is not touched by it.

Crucially, 'is older than' appears in (2a) as a dyadic predicate – if it did not, then it would not be capable of referring to the *is older than* relation. But if 'is older than' is a dyadic predicate, then it comes with two argument places which cannot just be left dangling. Something must be done with them, and the only sensible suggestion is that we should fill them with 'Simon' and 'Daniel':

> (2b) *U*(Simon is older than Daniel, Simon is older than Daniel).

The claim that Simon, Daniel and *is older than* compose *Simon is older than Daniel* has thus become the claim that *Simon is older than Daniel* bears a certain relation to itself. Presumably, the relation that matters here is identity: we are identifying the result of combining Simon, Daniel and *is older than* with the state *Simon is older than Daniel*. Back in §11.1, I suggested that we use '□(P ↔ Q)' to express the identity relation for states. If we accept that suggestion, we will finally transform (2b) into:

> (2c) □(Simon is older than Daniel ↔ Simon is older than Daniel).

At this point, the claim that Simon, Daniel and *is older* than compose the state *Simon is older than Daniel* has evaporated into something entirely trivial. Of course, when I suggested that we use '□(P ↔ Q)' to express identity for states, I was explicitly setting hyper-intensional contexts to one side. They have now come centre stage, and so we may feel forced to swap '□(P ↔ Q)' for something more demanding. (More on that in the next section.) But whatever we choose, the identity relation for states will have to be trivially reflexive, and so (2b) will still be trivialised. In short, the problem of the unity of states and propositions is another of the *pseudo-problems* which come up only because we mistake properties, states and propositions for kinds of object.

14.5 The Individuation Problem

In §11.1, I suggested that we use '□(P ↔ Q) to express the identity relation for states of affairs. If we accepted that suggestion, we would individuate states fairly coarsely: states are identical iff they are necessarily equivalent. Propositions cannot be individuated so coarsely. Amongst other things, propositions are what thinkers stand in the *believing* relation to. But a thinker can believe *P* without believing *Q*, even if *P* and *Q* are necessarily equivalent. For example, Daniel might believe that Hesperus is a planet

without believing that Phosphorus is a planet. We are thus confronted with
the *individuation problem*: propositions cannot be identified with states
of affairs, because propositions are individuated more finely than states of
affairs.[16]

There are two broad strategies for responding to this argument: we might
try individuating propositions more coarsely, or we might try individuating states of affairs more finely. I am going to focus on the second strategy.
There are certainly those who have defended a coarse-grained individuation of propositions,[17] but like many philosophers, I am convinced that
propositions should be individuated more finely. However, I want to be
clear that this is not something built into my immodest identity theory. If
you think that we can get away with individuating propositions coarsely,
then you should feel free to use that as your response to the individuation
problem.

Let us suppose, then, that we want to respond to the individuation problem by individuating states as finely as we individuate propositions. The
first question we might want to ask is: exactly how finely is that? Unfortunately, however, I do not have an answer to that question. As I said in
§12.3, no one yet has a fully worked out theory of hyper-intensionality,
and that definitely includes me.[18] But even without all of the details in
place, we can already see that this response to the individuation problem
has counter-intuitive consequences. 'Hesperus is a planet' expresses a different proposition from 'Phosphorus is a planet', but there is an intuitive
sense in which these two sentences make exactly the same demand on
reality: intuitively, the difference between *Hesperus is a planet* and *Phosphorus is a planet* is not a difference in the world, but a difference in
how we represent the world. It would be natural to want to put this by
saying that although 'Hesperus is a planet' and 'Phosphorus is a planet'
express different propositions, they still stand for the same state of affairs.
But by individuating states as finely as propositions, we have made that
impossible.[19]

---

[16] The individuation problem is presented by Künne (2003, 11–12). It is also closely related to Dodd's
(1995, 163; 1999b; 2000, 180–3) objection to McDowell and Hornsby. The reason I have chosen
not to tackle Dodd's objection directly is that it seems to presuppose that propositions are objects.
The simple argument presented here is, I think, what that objection becomes when you eliminate
that presupposition.

[17] The most famous defender of coarse-grained propositions is, of course, Stalnaker 1984; 1999,
esp. pt. II.

[18] The challenge is partly technical: if we individuate states/propositions too finely, then the Russell-
Myhill paradox beckons. For one recent discussion of that paradox, see Goodman 2017.

[19] For related discussion, see Sullivan 2005.

If you can't avoid counter-intuitive consequences, then the next best thing is to make them seem less counter-intuitive. Even if we say that 'Hesperus is a planet' and 'Phosphorus is a planet' stand for different states, we can still agree that they make the same demand on reality. It just turns out that making the same demand on reality is not a matter of standing for one and the same state of affairs. Rather, two sentences, s_1 and s_2, make the same demand on reality iff s_1 says that P, s_2 says that Q, and $\Box(P \leftrightarrow Q)$. s_1 and s_2 might express different ways for the world to be, but they still make the same demand on reality if it is impossible for the world to be one of these ways without being the other.

When we are speaking strictly, '$\Box(P \leftrightarrow Q)$' does not express the identity relation for states of affairs. States of affairs are identical to finely individuated propositions, and so the identity relation for states is really expressed by some hyper-intensional predicate, '$I(P, Q)$'. (As I said earlier, I currently have no concrete proposals about how to understand this hyper-intensional predicate.) But sometimes we speak loosely. When we only care about the demands we are placing on reality, we can harmlessly speak as if necessarily equivalent states are identical. In fact, if someone chooses to describe a state/proposition as a state, rather than as a proposition, we can take that as a (defeasible) sign that they are only interested in the demands it places on reality. So, if someone says that P is the same *state* as Q, rather than the same *proposition*, it would usually be uncharitable to interpret them strictly, as saying that $I(P, Q)$. It would probably be more charitable to interpret them loosely, as saying that $\Box(P \leftrightarrow Q)$. Take the claim that 'Hesperus is a planet' and 'Phosphorus is a planet' stand for the same state despite expressing different propositions. That claim is false on a strict interpretation, but that is an uncharitable interpretation. It is more charitable to interpret this claim as a loose way of saying something true: 'Hesperus is a planet' says that P, 'Phosphorus is a planet' says that Q, $\Box(P \leftrightarrow Q)$, but $\neg I(P, Q)$.

14.6 Truths Unmade and Ungrounded

As I said at the very start of this chapter, the identity theory can be thought of as an alternative to the correspondence theory: true propositions do not merely *correspond* to facts; true propositions *are* facts. But what do correspondence theorists mean when they say that true propositions 'correspond' to facts? Here is one answer that is often given: true propositions are *made true* by facts.[20] In this section, I want to explain exactly where my identity theory disagrees with this version of the correspondence theory.

The first thing we need to do is get clearer on what people mean when they talk about 'truthmaking'. As everyone is quick to point out, truthmaking is not meant to be any kind of causal relationship. Rather, to say that a fact is a truthmaker for a proposition is to say that the proposition is true *in virtue of* the fact.[21] The proposition that Socrates is wise, for example, is true in virtue of the fact that Socrates is wise.[22] What is more, it is usually assumed that the mere existence of this fact is what makes this proposition true. In other words:

> (5a) The proposition that Socrates is wise is true because the fact that Socrates is wise exists.

Importantly, the 'because' in (5a) is meant to express a metaphysically significant sort of explanation. In the now-standard terminology, (5a) says that the truth of the proposition that Socrates is wise is *grounded in* the existence of the fact that Socrates is wise. There is considerable disagreement about how best to understand the grounding relation, or whether there is any decent way of understanding it at all. Fortunately, however, we do not need to get bogged down in those kinds of issues here: I will make only one substantial claim about how grounding is meant to work, and that claim will be relatively uncontroversial.

When we think about truthmaking in the way I have described, we are quickly led to a principle known as *Necessitation*:

> (N) $\Box(T$ is a truthmaker for the proposition that $P \to \Box(T$ exists $\to$ it is true that $P)).$[23]

---

[20] The concept of truthmaking was first popularised by Armstrong (1997, 2004). After that, talk of truthmaking became ubiquitous in analytic metaphysics. For arguments in favour of the principle that truths have truthmakers, see Rodriguez-Pereyra 2005; Jago 2018. For sustained criticism of this truthmaking principle, see Merricks 2007. Not everyone agrees that truthmaker theory is a version of correspondence theory. For dissent, see Lewis 2001a, 277–9; Merricks 2007, 14–16; Horwich 2008, §3.

[21] See Armstrong 2004, 5; Rodriguez-Pereyra 2005, 18; Jago 2018, ch. 6.

[22] Most truthmaker theorists do not accept the fully general principle that if the proposition that P is true, then it is made true by the fact that P. They are, of course, happy to accept it whenever the fact that P exists, but truthmaker theorists typically work with sparse conceptions of facts. However, as I explained in Chapter 11, the Fregean realist theory of facts is thoroughly abundant: facts are just satisfied truth conditions, and so *every* true sentence expresses a fact. As a result, if you did want to try combining truthmaker theory with my Fregean account of facts, you should accept the fully general version of the principle.

[23] Armstrong argues for (N) in Armstrong 2004, 6–7. Merricks (2007, 5–11) criticises this and other arguments for (N). He replaces (N) with what he calls *Conditional Necessitation*: $\Box(T$ is a truthmaker for the proposition that $P \to \Box((T$ exists $\land$ the proposition that P exists) $\to$ it is true that $P)).$ For the purposes of my discussion, it would make no difference if we swapped Necessitation for Conditional Necessitation.

However, given (N), it is immediately clear that facts as I conceive of them cannot make propositions true. Imagine a world in which Socrates is not wise. In that world, the proposition that Socrates is wise is not true. However, the fact that Socrates is wise does exist in that world. Of course, it is not a *fact* in that world. But it still exists there as an *unobtaining* state of affairs.

If we want facts as I conceive of them to act as truthmakers, then we must reject (N). We were led to (N) by a particular conception of what it means to say that a fact makes a proposition true. On that conception, facts make propositions true *merely by existing*. But suppose we tweaked our conception and said instead: facts make propositions true *by obtaining*. On this conception of truthmaking, we swap (5a) for:

(5b) The proposition that Socrates is wise is true because the state *Socrates is wise* obtains.

There is no obvious path from here to (N). In fact, as far as I can tell, nothing I had to say about facts and states of affairs in Chapter 11 rules out (5b). All we can say is that (5b) is a little prolix. On the account I gave in §11.3, saying 'The state *Socrates is wise* obtains' is really just a pointlessly fancy way of saying 'Socrates is wise'. So when we eliminate this pointless fancy talk, (5b) becomes:

(5c) The proposition that Socrates is wise is true because Socrates is wise.[24]

Now, (5c) is not normally thought of as a claim about truthmaking. In fact, a number of philosophers have presented claims like (5c) as the sane and sensible alternative to truthmaking claims. The truth of the proposition that Socrates is wise is still grounded in Socrates' being wise, but there is no one *object* which makes that proposition true.[25] But whether or not it really deserves to be understood as a version of truthmaking, (5c) is the closest that my account of facts will let us come to the idea that facts make propositions true.[26]

---

[24] It is not easy to say exactly what sort of relation has to hold between 'Q' and 'R' to license the inference: P because Q ∴ P because R. However, I take it that this inference is licensed when 'Q' is just a periphrastic variant of 'R', or at least it is if the 'because' expresses some sort of metaphysical explanation.

[25] Fine (2012, §1.3) urges us to abandon truthmaking in favour of this kind of grounding. Hornsby (2005), Schnieder (2006) and Dodd (2007) all recommend non-metaphysical versions of this idea, according to which the truth of the proposition that Socrates is wise is *conceptually explained* by Socrates' being wise. For criticism of these conceptual explanations, see Liggins 2016.

[26] And not every truthmaker theorist would be disappointed with (5c). See Melia 2005, esp. §4; Tallant and Ingram 2017.

I said that nothing in my account of facts and states of affairs rules out (5b) or (5c). But things change when we include my account of propositions. As I explained in §13.4, that account forces us into a radical version of the redundancy theory of truth for propositions. To say 'The proposition that Socrates is wise is true' is also just a pointlessly fancy way of saying 'Socrates is wise'. So once we remove the final flourishes from (5c), we get:

(5d) Socrates is wise because Socrates is wise.[27]

But it is hard to see how (5d) could be true. For (5d) to be true, it would have to be possible to explain why Socrates is wise merely by repeating: Socrates is wise! This repetition does not seem like much of an explanation.

It might be helpful to recall here that the 'because' in (5d) is meant to express some sort of metaphysically significant grounding relation. And it is widely agreed that this grounding relation must be irreflexive:[28] it can never be that P is grounded in P; that is, we can never use P to metaphysically explain why P. Admittedly, there are some dissenting voices, who have suggested that some facts may be grounded in themselves.[29] But even these dissenters should be suspicious of (5d). We got to (5d) in our attempt to cash out the idea that the proposition that Socrates is wise is made true by the fact that Socrates is wise. But there was nothing special about this example. Whichever P we started with, the idea that the proposition that P is made true by the fact that P would be transformed into the idea that P is grounded in P. This is not at all how philosophers ordinarily think about grounding. And what is more, it is hard to believe that anyone would be happy to buy this trivialised form of grounding as a version of truthmaking.

So when we combine my account of facts with my account of propositions, there is no space left for the idea that facts make propositions true.[30] Now, strictly speaking, this is not quite enough to show that *nothing* makes propositions true. All I have argued is that *facts* do not make propositions true. But something else might. For example, following Mulligan, Simons and Smith (1984), you might suggest that *tropes* are the things which make

[27] Again, it is not easy to say exactly what sort of relation has to hold between 'P' and 'R' to license the inference: P because Q $\therefore$ R because Q. But again, I take it that if we are dealing with a metaphysical explanation, then this inference is licensed when 'P' is just a periphrastic variant of 'R'.
[28] Too many philosophers assert that grounding is irreflexive for me to list them all, but here are some examples: Schaffer 2009, 364; Audi 2012, 102; Fine 2012, 56; Raven 2013, §4; Bennett 2017, ch. 3.
[29] Jenkins (2011) argues that we should at least resist simply assuming that grounding is irreflexive. Rodriguez-Pereyra (2015) is less cautious, and outright asserts that grounding is not irreflexive. And Woods (2018) argues that grounding is irreflexive only in a restricted sense.
[30] Inspired by Lewis (2001b), we can still say that the class of true propositions supervenes on the class of facts. But that is a totally trivial type of supervenience: the class of true propositions *is* the class of facts!

propositions true. But that would be an odd move to make at this point.[31] The desire to find truthmakers for propositions is the desire to find some way of constraining the truths, of bringing true propositions into contact with the world. But the whole point of the identity theory is that it is a mistake to think of true propositions as standing over and above the world. True propositions are *facts*, and facts are worldly things. They are the ways that the world is. There is, then, no need to populate the world with anchors to hold the propositions down.

It would be better to say that there is no general explanation for why true propositions are true. In Russell's (1904, 523) words: 'some propositions are true and some false just as some roses are red and some white'. If this sounds unsettling, it is only because we are used to thinking of propositions as objects, and of truth as a property of those objects. (Unfortunately, this *was* how the early Russell thought of propositions.) If we reified propositions in this way, it would indeed be bizarre to think that the truth property magnetically attaches to some propositions but not others, for absolutely no discernible reason. But things are different when we refuse to reify propositions in this way. To say that the proposition that P is true is just to say that P. Little wonder, then, that we cannot give a general, one-size-fits-all explanation for why true propositions are true; that would require giving a general explanation for why all the facts are as they are.

14.7   Believing the Facts

Things have got a bit heady. The reason is that we have been focussing on propositional truth. Things become much more straightforward again when we focus on the *real* truth-bearers, the things that have propositional contents, like beliefs and sentences. Take the following, for example:

(6a) Sharon has a true belief that Socrates is wise, in part because Socrates is wise.

We could read the 'because' in (6a) in a number of different ways. We could, for example, read it as expressing some sort of *causal* explanation: Sharon was caused to believe that Socrates is wise by Socrates' being wise. But we could also read it as expressing the kind of *metaphysical* explanation that we were dealing with in the last section: Sharon's having a true belief that

---

[31]   And at any rate, the trope-theoretic approach to truthmaking is independently problematic. The tropes have to be *non-transferrable*, meaning that a's F-trope could not be b's F-trope. It is not at all clear why that should be so.

Socrates is wise is partly *grounded* in Socrates' being wise. And crucially, nothing that I have said shows that (6a) could not be true, so understood. After all, the fact that Sharon has a true belief that Socrates is wise is very different from the fact that Socrates is wise, and so there is no risk that (6a) will be reduced to explaining one fact in terms of itself.

So while it is a definite mistake to say that true propositions are grounded in the facts, there is a sense in which it is perfectly fine to say that true beliefs are grounded in facts. (The same would go for true sentences, true assertions, and so on.) However, it is important to realise how different these two claims are.

Let's return for a moment to the rarefied air of propositional truth, and compare these two sentences:

> (5c) The proposition that Socrates is wise is true because Socrates is wise.
>
> (5e) Socrates is wise because the proposition that Socrates is wise is true.

Philosophers who reify propositions (i.e., most philosophers) tend to think that (5c) is true and (5e) is false. However, everyone who believes in propositions also agrees on the following: necessarily, the proposition that Socrates is wise is true iff Socrates is wise. So the kind of explanation involved in (5c) will have to be of an exotic, hyper-intensional variety.

Maybe we will all have to make use of these kinds of explanations at some point or other. But the identity theorist is not forced to just in order to understand the way in which truth is grounded in the facts. As I explained in §14.6, the identity theorist should reject (5c) as a pseudo-explanation, equivalent to the claim that Socrates is wise because Socrates is wise. She should instead focus on the likes of (6a). And accounting for (6a) does not compel us to work with any exotic hyper-intensional variety of grounding. Consider the following generalised conditional:

> (6b) $\forall P(\exists x(x \text{ has a true belief that } P) \rightarrow P)$.

(6b) is true. More than that, it is *necessarily* true. More than *that*, it is *analytically* true. To see that, just apply (R), our Ramseyian definition of truth:

> (6c) $\forall P(\exists x(P \wedge x \text{ has a belief that } P) \rightarrow P)$.

We can say, then, that true beliefs *modally* and even *analytically* depend on the facts. This is enough to articulate what is right about (6a). It also explains what is wrong with (7a):

> (7a) Socrates is wise in part because Sharon has a true belief that Socrates is wise.

(7a) is false since facts do not in general depend modally or analytically on true beliefs. Consider the following generalised conditional:

(7b) $\forall P(P \rightarrow \exists x(x$ has a true belief that $P))$.

(7b) is not necessarily true, and it certainly is not *analytically* true.[32]

So that is the first important difference between the claim that true beliefs are grounded in the facts and the claim that true propositions are so grounded: we can make sense of the former, but not the latter, claim without helping ourselves to any exotic varieties of explanation. I would like to end this chapter (and the book!) by considering a second.

When we say that true beliefs are grounded in the facts, it is crucial to remember that we are talking about belief-states (or events, or acts, or whatever you prefer). We are *not* talking about the contents of those beliefs. Those are propositions, and we have already seen what is wrong with thinking of them as grounded in the facts. True beliefs *themselves* are grounded in the facts.

This is important to emphasise, because it helps to dispel a mistaken picture of how thinking agents come into cognitive contact with the world. On this mistaken picture, there are *two* gaps which have to be bridged. First, there is the gap between unthinking matter and conscious people. Somehow, but goodness knows how, configurations of mere stuff manage to have thoughts. The second gap is between thoughts and the world. Somehow, the thoughts that we have manage to answer to how the world is.

If you subscribed to this picture, you would imagine that you were confronted with two philosophical projects, one to fill each gap. So you would have your theory of what it takes for mere systems of stuff to have thoughts, and a separate theory of how these thoughts answer to the world. And crucially, because these would be two separate theories, you could work on them one at a time. You could first figure out what it takes for someone to believe that Socrates is wise (maybe it's being in a certain functional state?) and *then* work out what it takes for that belief to be true (maybe it has to correspond to the facts, or maybe it just has to be part of a coherent web of beliefs?).

---

[32] Having said that, some instances of (7b) may well be necessarily true, for example:

$\forall Q(Q \rightarrow \exists y(y$ believes that $Q)) \rightarrow$
$\exists x(x$ has a true belief that $\forall Q(Q \rightarrow \exists y(y$ believes that $Q)))$.

Roughly put: if every truth is believed by someone, then someone has a true belief that every truth is believed by someone. But the point remains that the fully general (7b) is not necessarily true, and so facts do not *in general* modally depend on true beliefs.

But this picture is all wrong. There is only *one* gap which needs to be bridged, not two. The deep philosophical questions all concern what it takes for a mere system of stuff to have thoughts. There is no second mystery about how beliefs manage to answer to the world: belief is a *direct* relation between a thinker and ways for the world to be. So once we have identified what it takes for someone to believe that Socrates is wise, there is no further question about what it would take for their belief to be true. To believe that Socrates is wise is to stand in a direct relation to a way for the world to be, and that belief is true iff the world is that way.[33]

This point is originally due to Ramsey. Ramsey is widely thought of as an early redundancy theorist, and it is certainly true that he held a redundancy theory of truth *for propositions* (Ramsey 1927, 142). But this is what he had to say when it came to the truth of judgments:

> It is, perhaps, also immediately obvious that if we have analysed judgment we have solved the problem of truth; for taking the mental factor in judgment (which is often itself called judgment), the truth or falsity of this depends only on what proposition it is that is judged, and what we have to explain is the meaning of saying that the judgment is a judgment that *a* has R to *b*, i.e. is true if *aRb*, false if not. We can, if we like, say that it is true if there exists a corresponding fact that *a* has R to *b*, but that is essentially not an analysis but a periphrasis, for 'The fact that *a* has R to *b* exists' is no different from '*a* has R to *b*'. (Ramsey 1927, 143)

Ramsey is not here denying that there are any substantial problems about truth. He is saying only that 'there is really no *separate* problem of truth' (1927, 142 – emphasis added) – i.e., that there are no problems of truth other than problems about how it is that some things come to be imbued with propositional content.[34] I think that Ramsey was absolutely right.

[33] Johnston (2013, 384) makes exactly this point. Horwich is an example of a philosopher who makes the mistake of thinking that there is a separate question about truth. This might sound like an absurd thing to say, since Horwich (1998b) is famously a deflationist about truth. However, Horwich attempts to combine his deflationism, according to which truth is not naturalistically reducible (Horwich 1998b, 38; 1998a, ch. 4; 2005, 74–5; 2010, 103–4), with a reductionist theory of meaning (Horwich 1998a; 2005, 63; 2010, 107–8). If I am right that there are not two questions, one about meaning and one about truth, then this combination should be impossible: a reductive theory of meaning yields a reductive theory of truth. For further discussion, see Trueman 2013b.

[34] See also Ramsey 1991, 13–14.

References

Anscombe, Elizabeth. 1959. *An Introduction to Wittgenstein's Tractatus*. London: Hutchinson.

Armstrong, David. 1978a. *Nominalism and Realism*. Universals & Scientific Realism, vol. 1. Cambridge: Cambridge University Press.

1978b. *A Theory of Universals*. Universals & Scientific Realism, vol. 2. Cambridge: Cambridge University Press.

1989. *Universals: An Opinionated Introduction*. Boulder, CO: Westview Press.

1997. *A World of States of Affairs*. Cambridge: Cambridge University Press.

2004. *Truth and Truthmakers*. Cambridge: Cambridge University Press.

Audi, Paul. 2012. A clarification and defense of the notion of grounding. Pages 101–21 of: Correia and Schnieder 2012.

Bach, Kent. 1997. Do belief reports report beliefs? *Pacific Philosophical Quarterly*, **78**, 215–41.

Bacon, Andrew. 2019. Substitution structures. *Journal of Philosophical Logic*, **48**, 1017–75.

Baldwin, Thomas. 1991. The identity theory of truth. *Mind*, **100**, 35–52.

(ed). 1993. *G.E. Moore: Selected Writings*. London: Routledge.

Barker, Chris, and Jacobson, Pauline (eds). 2007. *Direct Compositionality*. Oxford: Oxford University Press.

Barker, Stephen, and Jago, Mark. 2012. Being positive about negative facts. *Philosophy and Phenomenological Research*, **85**, 117–38.

Baxter, Donald. 2001. Instantiation as partial identity. *Australasian Journal of Philosophy*, **79**, 449–64.

Beaney, Michael (ed). 1997. *The Frege Reader*. Oxford: Blackwell.

2013. *The Oxford Handbook of the History of Analytic Philosophy*. Oxford: Oxford University Press.

Beebee, Helen, and Dodd, Julian (eds). 2005. *Truthmakers: The Contemporary Debate*. Oxford: Oxford University Press.

Benacerraf, Paul. 1973. Mathematical truth. *Journal of Philosophy*, **70**, 661–79.

Bennett, Karen. 2017. *Making Things Up*. Oxford: Oxford University Press.

Bergmann, Gustav. 1960. Ineffability, ontology, and method. *Philosophical Review*, **69**, 18–40.

Blanchette, Patricia. 2012. *Frege's Conception of Logic*. Oxford: Oxford University Press.

Boolos, George. 1975. On second-order logic. *The Journal of Philosophy*, **72**, 509–27.

1984. To be is to be the value of a variable (or to be some values of some variables). *The Journal of Philosophy*, **81**, 430–49.

1985. Nominalist platonism. *The Philosophical Review*, **94**, 327–44.

Bradley, Francis Herbert. 1893. *Appearance and Reality*. Oxford: Clarendon Press.

1907. On truth and copying. *Mind*, **16**, 165–80.

Braithwaite, Richard. (ed). 1931. *The Foundations of Mathematics and Other Logical Essays*. London: Routledge.

Brentano, Franz. 1874. *Psychologie vom Empirischen Standpunkt*. Leipzig: Duncker & Humblot.

Button, Tim. 2017. Exclusion problems and the cardinality of logical space. *Journal of Philosophical Logic*, **46**, 611–23.

Button, Tim, and Walsh, Sean. 2018. *Philosophy and Model Theory*. Oxford: Oxford University Press.

Campbell, John. 2002. *Reference and Consciousness*. Oxford: Oxford University Press.

Candlish, Stewart. 1989. The truth about F. H. Bradley. *Mind*, **98**, 331–48.

1995. Resurrecting the identity theory of truth. *Bradley Studies*, **1**, 116–24.

1999a. Identifying the identity theory of truth. *Proceedings of the Aristotelian Society*, **99**, 233–40.

1999b. A prolegomenon to an identity theory of truth. *Philosophy*, **74**, 199–220.

Cartwright, Richard. 1987a. A neglected theory of truth. Pages 71–93 of: Cartwright 1987b.

1987b. *Philosophical Essays*. Cambridge, MA: MIT Press.

Chalmers, David, Manley, David, and Wasserman, Ryan (eds). 2009. *Metametaphysics*. Oxford: Oxford University Press.

Chierchia, Gennaro, and Turner, Raymond. 1988. Semantics and property theory. *Linguistics and Philosophy*, **11**, 261–302.

Correia, Fabrice, and Schnieder, Benjamin (eds). 2012. *Metaphysical Grounding: Understanding the Structure of Reality*. Cambridge: Cambridge University Press.

Crary, Alice, and Read, Rupert (eds). 2000. *The New Wittgenstein*. London and New York: Routledge.

Davidson, Donald. 2005. *Truth & Predication*. Cambridge, MA: Harvard University Press.

Devitt, Michael. 1980. 'Ostrich nominalism' or 'mirage realism'? Pages 93–100 of: Mellor and Oliver 1997.

Diamond, Cora. 1991. *The Realistic Spirit*. Cambridge, MA: MIT Press.

Dodd, Julian. 1995. McDowell and identity theories of truth. *Analysis*, **55**, 160–5.

1999a. Farewell to states of affairs. *Australasian Journal of Philosophy*, **77**, 146–60.

1999b. Hornsby on the identity theory of truth. *Proceedings of the Aristotelian Society*, **99**, 225–32.

2000. *An Identity Theory of Truth*. Great Britain: Macmillan Press.

2007. Negative truths and truthmaker principles. *Synthese*, **156**, 383–401.

Dolby, David. 2009. The Reference Principle: a defence. *Analysis*, **69**, 286–96.

Dorr, Cian. 2016. To be F is to be G. *Philosophical Perspectives*, **30**, 39–134.

Dudman, Victor. 1976. *Bedeutung* for predicates. Pages 71–84 of: Schirn 1976.

Dummett, Michael. 1981a. *Frege: Philosophy of Language*. 2nd ed. Londond: Duckworth.

1981b. *The Interpretation of Frege's Philosophy*. London: Duckworth.

Edwards, Paul (ed). 1967. *The Encyclopedia of Philosophy*, vol. 2. New York: Macmillan Press.

Evans, Gareth. 1977. Pronouns, quantifiers, and relative clauses (I). *Canadian Journal of Philosophy*, **7**, 467–536.

Fine, Kit. 2000. Neutral relations. *The Philosophical Review*, **109**, 1–33.

2012. Guide to ground. Pages 37–80 of: Correia and Schnieder 2012.

Fish, William. 2009. *Perception, Hallucination, and Illusion*. Oxford: Oxford University Press.

Foster, John. 2000. *The Nature of Perception*. Oxford: Oxford University Press.

Frege, Gottlob. 1879. *Begriffsschrift, eine der arithmetischen nachgebildete Formelsprache des reinen Denkens*. Halle: Nerbert.

1884. *Die Grundlagen der Arithmetik*. Breslau: Koebner.

1891. Function and concept. Pages 130–48 of: Beaney 1997.

1891–5. Comments on sense and reference. Pages 172–80 of: Beaney 1997.

1892a. On concept and object. Pages 181–93 of: Beaney 1997.

1892b. On sense and reference. Pages 151–71 of: Beaney 1997.

1893. *Die Grundgesetze der Arithmetik*, vol. I. Jena: Pohle.

1906a. A brief survey of my logical doctrines. Pages 299–300 of: Beaney 1997.

1906b. Foundations of geometry: second series. Pages 293–340 of: McGuinness 1984.

1906c. Introduction to logic. Pages 293–8 of: Beaney 1997.

1918. Thought. Pages 325–45 of: Beaney 1997.

1923. Compound thoughts. Pages 390–406 of: McGuinness 1984.

Furth, Montgomery. 1968. Two types of denotation. Pages 9–45 of: Rescher 1968.

Gaskin, Richard. 1995. Bradley's Regress, the copula and the unity of the proposition. *The Philosophical Quarterly*, **45**, 161–80.

2008. *The Unity of the Proposition*. Oxford: Oxford University Press.

Geach, Peter. 1975. Names and identity. Pages 139–58 of: Guttenplan 1975.

1976. Saying and showing in Frege and Wittgenstein. *Acta Philosophica Fennica*, **28**, 54–70.

Geurts, Bart. 2006. Take 'five': the meaning and use of a number a word. Pages 311–29 of: Vogeleer and Tasmowski 2006.

Goodman, Jeremy. 2017. Reality is not structured. *Analysis*, **77**, 43–53.

Gray, Aidan. 2017. Names in strange places. *Linguistics and Philosophy*, **40**, 429–72.

Groenendijk, Jeroen, and Stokhof, Martin. 1989. Type-shifting rules and the semantics of interrogatives. Pages 421–56 of: Portner and Partee 2002.

Grover, Dorothy. 1992a. Prosentences and propositional quantification: a response to Zimmerman. Pages 137–45 of: Grover 1992b.

1992b. *A Prosentential Theory of Truth*. Princeton, NJ: Princeton University Press.

Grover, Dorothy, Camp, Joseph, and Belnap, Nuel. 1975. A prosentential theory of truth. Pages 70–120 of: Grover 1992b.

Guttenplan, Samuel (ed). 1975. *Mind and Language*. Oxford: Clarendon Press.

Hacker, Peter. 1972. *Insight and Illusion*. Oxford: Oxford University Press.

Hale, Bob. 1994. Singular terms (2). Pages 48–71 of: Hale and Wright 2001.

1996. Singular terms (1). Pages 31–47 of: Hale and Wright 2001.

2010. The bearable lightness of being. *Axiomathes*, **20**, 399–422.

2013. *Necessary Beings*. Oxford: Oxford University Press.

2020. *Essays on Essence and Existence*. Oxford: Oxford University Press.

Hale, Bob, and Linnebo, Øystein. 2020. Ontological categories and the problem of expressibility. Pages 73–103 of: Hale 2020.

Hale, Bob, and Wright, Crispin. 2001. *The Reason's Proper Study*. Oxford: Oxford University Press.

2002. Benacerraf's dilemma revisited. *European Journal of Philosophy*, **10**, 101–29.

2012. Horse sense. *The Journal of Philosophy*, **109**, 85–131.

Hanks, Peter. 2011. Structured propositions as types. *Mind*, **120**, 11–52.

2015. *Propositional Content*. Oxford: Oxford University Press.

Heck, Richard, and May, Robert. 2006. Frege's contribution to philosophy of language. Pages 3–39 of: Lepore and Smith 2006.

2013. The function is unsaturated. Pages 825–50 of: Beaney 2013.

Heim, Irene, and Kratzer, Angelika. 1998. *Semantics in Generative Grammar*. Oxford: Blackwell.

Hirsch, Eli. 2011. *Quantifier Variance and Realism*. Oxford: Oxford University Press.

Hofweber, Thomas. 2007. Innocent statements and their metaphysically loaded counterparts. *Philosophers' Imprint*, **7**, 1–33.

2016a. From *Remnants* to *Things*, and back again. Pages 54–72 of: Ostertag 2016.

2016b. *Ontology and the Ambitions of Metaphysics*. Oxford: Oxford University Press.

Hornsby, Jennifer. 1997. Truth: the identity theory. *Proceedings of the Aristotelian Society*, **97**, 1–24.

Hornsby, Jennifer. 1999. The facts in question: a response to Dodd and to Candlish. *Proceedings of the Aristotelian Society*, **99**, 241–5.

2005. Truth without truthmaking entities. Pages 33–48 of: Beebee and Dodd 2005.

Horwich, Paul. 1998a. *Meaning*. Oxford: Oxford University Press.

1998b. *Truth*. 2nd ed. Oxford: Clarendon.

2005. *Reflections on Meaning*. Oxford: Oxford University Press.

2008. Truth and being. *Midwest Studies in Philosophy*, **22**, 258–73.

2010. *Truth-Meaning-Reality*. Oxford: Oxford University Press.

Jackson, Frank, and Priest, Graham (eds). 2004. *Lewisian Themes: The Philosophy of David K. Lewis*. Oxford: Clarendon Press.

Jago, Mark. 2018. *What Truth Is*. Oxford: Oxford University Press.

Jenkins, Carrie. 2011. Is metaphysical dependence irreflexive? *The Monist*, **94**, 267–76.

Johnston, Colin. 2013. Judgment and the identity theory of truth. *Philosophical Studies*, **166**, 381–97.

Jones, Nicholas. 2016. A higher-order solution to the problem of the concept *horse*. *Ergo*, **3**, 132–66.

  2018. Nominalist realism. *Noûs*, **52**, 808–35.

  2019. Propositions and cognitive relations. *Proceedings of the Aristotelian Society*, **119**, 157–78.

King, Jeffrey. 2002. Designating propositions. *Noûs*, **111**, 341–71.

  2007. *The Nature and Structure of Content*. Oxford: Oxford University Press.

  2009. Questions of unity. *Proceedings of the Aristotelian Society*, **109**, 257–77.

  2013. Propositional unity: what's the problem, who has it and who solves it? *Philosophical Studies*, **165**, 71–93.

King, Jeffrey, Soames, Scott, and Speaks, Jeff. 2014. *New Thinking about Propositions*. Oxford: Oxford University Press.

Klein, Udo, and Sternefeld, Wolfgang. 2017. Same same but different: an alphabetically innocent compositional predicate logic. *Journal of Philosophical Logic*, **46**, 65–95.

Krämer, Stephan. 2014a. *On What There Is for Things to Be*. Studies in Theoretical Philosophy, vol. 1. Frankfurt: Klostermann.

  2014b. Semantic values in higher-order semantics. *Philosophical Studies*, **168**, 709–24.

Kremer, Michael. 2001. The purpose of Tractarian nonsense. *Noûs*, **35**, 39–73.

Künne, Wolfgang. 2003. *Conceptions of Truth*. Oxford: Oxford University Press.

Langacker, Ronald. 2002. *Concept, Image, and Symbol*. 2nd ed. Berlin: Mouton de Gruyter.

Larson, Richard, and Segal, Gabriel. 1995. *Knowledge of Meaning*. Cambridge, MA: MIT Press.

Leng, Mary, Paseau, Alex, and Potter, Michael (eds). 2007. *Mathematical Knowledge*. Oxford: Oxford University Press.

Lepore, Ernest, and Smith, Barry (eds). 2006. *The Oxford Handbook of Philosophy of Language*. Oxford: Oxford University Press.

Levine, James. 2013. Logic and solipsism. Pages 170–238 of: Sullivan and Potter 2013.

Lewis, David. 1983. New work for a theory of universals. *Australasian Journal of Philosophy*, **61**, 343–77.

  1986a. Against structural universals. Pages 78–107 of: Lewis 1999.

  1986b. A comment on Armstrong and Forrest. Pages 108–10 of: Lewis 1999.

  1986c. *On the Plurality of Worlds*. Oxford: Blackwell.

  1999. *Papers in Metaphysics and Epistemology*. Cambridge: Cambridge University Press.

  2001a. Forget about the 'correspondence theory of truth'. *Analysis*, **61**, 275–80.

  2001b. Truthmaking and difference-making. *Noûs*, **35**, 602–15.

2002. Tensing the copula. *Mind*, **111**, 1–13.

Liebesman, David. 2015. Predication as ascription. *Mind*, **124**, 517–69.

Liggins, David. 2016. Deflationism, conceptual explanation and the truth asymmetry. *The Philosophical Quarterly*, **66**, 84–101.

Lillehammer, Hallvard, and Mellor, David Hugh (eds). 2005. *Ramsey's Legacy*. Oxford: Oxford University Press.

Linnebo, Øystein. 2006. Sets, properties, and unrestricted quantification. Pages 149–78 of: Rayo and Uzquiano 2006.

Linnebo, Øystein, and Rayo, Agustín. 2012. Hierarchies ontological and ideological. *Mind*, **121**, 269–308.

Long, Peter. 1969. Are predicates and relational expressions incomplete? *The Philosophical Review*, **78**, 90–8.

Lowe, Edward Jonathan. 2006. *The Four Category Ontology*. Oxford: Oxford University Press.

MacBride, Fraser. 1998. Where are particulars and universals? *Dialectica*, **52**, 203–27.

2005a. The particular-universal distinction: a dogma of metaphysics? *Mind*, **114**, 565–614.

2005b. Ramsey on universals. Pages 83–104 of: Lillehammer and Mellor 2005.

2006. Predicate reference. Pages 422–75 of: Lepore and Smith 2006.

2007. Neutral relations revisited. *Dialectica*, **61**, 25–56.

2011a. Impure reference: a way around the concept *horse* paradox. *Philosophical Perpectives*, **25**, 297–312.

2011b. Relations and truthmaking II. *Proceedings of the Aristotelain Society Supplementary Volume*, **111**, 161–79.

2014. How involved do you want to be in a non-symmetric relationship? *Australasian Journal of Philosophy*, **92**, 1–16.

2018. *On the Genealogy of Universals: The Metaphysical Origins of Analytic Philosophy*. Oxford: Oxford University Press.

Magidor, Ofra. 2009. The last dogma of type confusions. *Proceedings of the Aristotelian Society*, **109**, 1–29.

Martin, Michael. 1997. The reality of appearances. Pages 81–106 of: Sainsbury 1997.

Mates, Benson. 1972. *Elementary Logic*. 2nd ed. Oxford: Oxford University Press.

McDaniel, Kris. 2003. Against MaxCon Simples. *Australasian Journal of Philosophy*, **81**, 265–75.

2007. Extended simples. *Philosophical Studies*, **133**, 131–41.

2009a. Extended simples and qualitative heterogeneity. *The Philosophical Quarterly*, **59**, 325–31.

2009b. Ways of being. Pages 290–319 of: Chalmers, Manley and Wasserman 2009.

2017. *The Fragmentation of Being*. Oxford: Oxford University Press.

McDowell, John. 1977. On the sense and reference of a proper name. *Mind*, **86**, 159–85.

1994. *Mind and World*. Cambridge, MA: Harvard University Press.

2005. The true modesty of an identity conception of truth: a note in response to Pascal Engel (2001). *International Journal of Philosophical Studies*, **13**, 83–8.

McGuinness, Brian (ed). 1980. *Philosophical and Mathematical Correspondence*. Oxford: Blackwell.

1984. *Collected Papers on Mathematics, Logic and Philosophy*. Oxford: Blackwell.

McKeon, Richard (ed). 1941. *The Basic Works of Aristotle*. New York: Random House.

McKinsey, Michael. 1999. The semantics of belief ascriptions. *Noûs*, **33**, 519–57.

Melia, Joseph. 2005. Truthmaking without truthmakers. Pages 67–84 of: Beebee and Dodd 2005.

Mellor, David Hugh, and Oliver, Alex (eds). 1997. *Properties*. Oxford: Oxford University Press.

Mendelshon, Richard. 1981. Frege on predication. *Midwest Studies in Philosophy*, **6**, 69–82.

Merricks, Trenton. 2007. *Truth and Ontology*. Oxford: Oxford University Press.

2008. Replies to Cameron, Schaffer, and Soames. *Philosophical Books*, **49**, 328–43.

2015. *Propositions*. Oxford: Oxford University Press.

Methven, Steven. 2018a. Ramsey, 'universals' and atomic propositions. *British Journal for the History of Philosophy*, **27**, 134–54.

2018b. Sense and the identity conception of truth. *European Journal of Philosophy*, **26**, 1041–56.

Mill, John Stewart. 1843. *A System of Logic*, vol. I. London: Longmans.

Moltmann, Friederike. 2003. Propositional attitudes without propositions. *Synthese*, **135**, 77–118.

2013. *Abstract Objects and the Semantics of Natural Languages*. Oxford: Oxford University Press.

Montague, Richard. 1973. The proper treatment of quantification in ordinary English. In: Portner and Partee 2002.

Moore, Adrian. 1997. *Points of View*. Oxford: Clarendon Press.

2003. Ineffability and nonsense (I). *Proceedings of the Aristotelian Society Supplementary Volume*, **77**, 169–93.

Moore, George Edward. 1901–2. Truth and falsity. Pages 20–2 of: Baldwin 1993.

Morris, Michael, and Dodd, Julian. 2007. Mysticism and nonsense in the *Tractatus*. *European Journal of Philosophy*, **17**, 247–76.

Mulligan, Kevin, Simons, Peter, and Smith, Barry. 1984. Truth-makers. *Philosophy and Phenomenological Research*, **44**, 287–321.

Nebel, Jacob. 2019. Hopes, fears and other grammatical scarecrows. *Philosophical Review*, **128**, 63–105.

Noonan, Harold. 2006. The concept horse. Pages 155–76 of: Strawson and Chackrabarti 2006.

Oliver, Alex. 1996. The metaphysics of properties. *Mind*, **105**, 1–80.

2005. The Reference Principle. *Analysis*, **65**, 177–87.

2010. What is a predicate? Pages 118–48 of: Potter and Ricketts 2010.

Ostertag, Gary (ed). 2016. *Meanings and Other Things: Themes from the Work of Stephen Schiffer*. Oxford: Oxford University Press.

Parsons, Josh. 1999. There is no 'truthmaker' argument against nominalism. *Australasian Journal of Philosophy*, **77**, 325–34.

2004. Distributional properties. Pages 173–80 of: Jackson and Priest 2004.

Parsons, Terence. 1970. Criticism of 'are predicates and relational expressions incomplete?'. *The Philosophical Review*, **79**, 240–5.

1986. Why Frege should not have said 'the concept *horse* is not a concept'. *History of Philosophy Quarterly*, **3**, 449–65.

Partee, Barbara. 1986. Noun phrase interpretation and type-shifting principles. Pages 357–81 of: Portner and Partee 2002.

Partee, Barbara, and Rooth, Mats. 1983. Generalised conjunction and type ambiguity. Pages 334–56 of: Portner and Partee 2002.

Paul, Laurie. 2002. Logical parts. *Noûs*, **36**, 578–96.

Peacock, Howard. 2009. What's wrong with ostrich nominalism? *Philosophical Papers*, **38**, 183–217.

2012. Bradley's Regress, truthmaking and constitution. *Grazer Philosophische Studien*, **86**, 1–21.

Portner, Paul, and Partee, Barbara (eds). 2002. *Formal Semantics – The Essential Readings*. Oxford: Blackwell.

Potter, Michael. 2009. *Wittgenstein's Notes on Logic*. Oxford: Oxford University Press.

Potter, Michael, and Ricketts, Thomas (eds). 2010. *The Cambridge Companion to Frege*. Cambridge: Cambridge University Press.

Price, Michael. 2016. Naming the concept *horse*. *Philosophical Studies*, **173**, 2727–43.

Priest, Graham. 2014. *One: Being an Investigation into the Unity of Reality and of its Parts, Including the Singular Object Which Is Nothingness*. Oxford: Oxford University Press.

Prior, Arthur. 1963. Oratio obliqua (I). *Proceedings of the Aristotelain Society Supplementary Volume*, **37**, 115–26.

1967. Correspondence theory of truth. Pages 223–32 of: Edwards 1967.

1971. *Objects of Thought*. Oxford: Oxford University Press.

Quine, Willard Van Orman. 1939. Designation and existence. *Journal of Philosophy*, **36**, 701–9.

1948. On what there is. Pages 1–19 of: Quine 1980a.

1951a. Semantics and abstract objects. *Proceedings of the American Academy of Arts and Sciences*, **80**, 90–6.

1951b. Two dogmas of empiricism. Pages 20–46 of: Quine 1980a.

1953a. Logic and the reification of universals. Pages 102–29 of: Quine 1980a.

1953b. Reference and modality. Pages 139–59 of: Quine 1980a.

1960. *Word and Object*. USA: MIT Press.

1970. *Philosophy of Logic*. Englewood Cliffs, NJ: Prentice-Hall.

1980a. *From a Logical Point of View*. 2nd revised ed. Cambridge, MA: Harvard University Press.

1980b. The variable and its place in reference. Pages 164–73 of: van Straaten 1980.

Ramsey, Frank Plumpton. 1924. The foundations of mathematics. Pages 1–61 of: Braithwaite 1931.

1925. Universals. Pages 112–34 of: Braithwaite 1931.

1926. Universals and the 'method of analysis'. Pages 135–7 of: Braithwaite 1931.

1927. Facts and propositions. Pages 138–55 of: Braithwaite 1931.

1991. *On Truth*. Episteme, no. 16. Dordrecht: Kluwer Academic Publishers.

Raven, Michael. 2013. Is ground a strict partial order? *American Philosophical Quarterly*, **50**, 193–201.

Rayo, Agustín. 2006. Beyond plurals. Pages 220–54 of: Rayo and Uzquiano 2006.

2013. *The Construction of Logical Space*. Oxford: Oxford University Press.

Rayo, Agustín, and Uzquiano, Gabriel. 1999. Toward a theory of second-order consequence. *Notre Dame Journal of Formal Logic*, **40**, 315–25.

(eds). 2006. *Absolute Generality*. Oxford: Oxford University Press.

Rayo, Agustín, and Yablo, Stephen. 2001. Nominalism through denominalization. *Noûs*, **35**, 74–92.

Rescher, Nicholas (ed). 1968. *Studies in Logical Theory*. American Philosophical Quarterly Monograph Series, vol. 2. Oxford: Blackwell.

Rieppel, Michael. 2016. Being something: properties and predicative quantification. *Mind*, **125**, 643–89.

2018. Denoting and disquoting. *Australasian Journal of Philosophy*, **96**, 548–61.

Rodriguez-Pereyra, Gonzalo. 2000. What is the problem of universals? *Mind*, **109**, 255–74.

2002. *Resemblance Nominalism*. Oxford: Oxford University Press.

2005. Why truthmakers. Pages 17–32 of: Beebee and Dodd 2005.

2015. Grounding is not a strict order. *Journal of the American Philosophical Association*, **1**, 517–34.

Rosefeldt, Tobias. 2008. 'That'-clauses and non-nominal quantification. *Philosophical Studies*, **137**, 301–33.

Rumfitt, Ian. 2003. Singular terms and arithmetical logicism. *Philosophical Books*, **44**, 193–219.

2014. Truth and Meaning. *Proceedings of the Aristotelian Society Supplementary Volume*, **88**, 21–55.

2016. Objects of thought. Pages 73–94 of: Ostertag 2016.

Russell, Bertrand. 1903. *The Principles of Mathematics*. London: Allen and Unwin.

1904. Meinong's theory of complexes and assumptions III. *Mind*, **13**, 509–24.

1910a. On the nature of truth and falsehood. Pages 147–59 of: Russell 1910b.

1910b. *Philosophical Essays*. London: Allen and Unwin.

1913. *Theory of Knowledge*. The Collected Papers of Bertrand Russell, vol. 7. London: Routledge.

1918. The philosophy of logical atomism. Pages 175–281 of: Russell 2007.

2007. *Logic and Knowledge*. 2nd ed. Nottingham: Spokesman.

Russinoff, Susan. 1992. Frege and Dummett on the problem with the concept horse. *Noûs*, **26**(1), 63–78.

Ryle, Gilbert. 1945–6. Knowing how and knowing that. *Proceedings of the Aristotelian Society*, **46**, 1–16.

1949. *The Concept of Mind*. Chicago: The Chicago University Press.

Sainsbury, Mark (ed). 1997. *Thought and Ontology*. Milan: F. Angeli.

2018. *Thinking about Things*. Oxford: Oxford University Press.

Schaffer, Jonathan. 2009. On what grounds what. Pages 347–83 of: Chalmers, Manley and Wasserman 2009.

Schiffer, Stephen. 2003. *The Things We Mean*. Oxford: Oxford University Press.

Schirn, Matthias (ed). 1976. *Studien zu Frege*, vol. 3. Stuttgart: Frommann Holzboog.

Schnieder, Benjamin. 2006. Truth-making without truth-makers. *Synthese*, **152**, 21–46.

Seargent, David. 1985. *Plurality and Continuity: An Essay in G.F. Stout's Theory of Universals*. Dordrecht: Martinus Nijhoff Publishers.

Sider, Theodore. 2006. 'Bare Particulars'. *Philosophical Perspectives*, **20**, 388–97.

2011. *Writing the Book of the World*. Oxford: Clarendon Press.

Siegel, Susanna. 2010. *The Contents Visual of Experience*. New York: Oxford University Press.

Simons, Peter. 1991. Ramsey, particulars, and universals. *Theoria*, **57**, 150–61.

Soames, Scott. 2010. *What Is Meaning?* Princeton: Princeton University Press.

Stalnaker, Robert. 1984. *Inquiry*. Cambridge, MA: MIT Press.

1999. *Context and Content: Essays on Intentionality in Speech and Thought*. Oxford Cognitive Science. Oxford: Oxford University Press.

Stanley, Jason, and Williamson, Timothy. 2001. Knowing how. *The Journal of Philosophy*, **98**, 411–44.

Strawson, Peter Frederick. 1950. Truth. Pages 190–213 of: Strawson 1971.

1959. *Individuals*. London: Methuen & Co.

1969. Meaning and truth. Pages 170–89 of: Strawson 1971.

1971. *Logico-Linguistic Papers*. London: Methuen & Co.

1974. *Subject and Predicate in Logic and Grammar*. London: Methuen & Co.

1987. Concepts and properties or predication and copulation. *The Philosophical Quarterly*, **37**, 402–6.

Strawson, Peter Frederick, and Chakrabarti, Arindam (eds). 2006. *Universals, Concepts and Qualities*. Aldershot: Ashgate.

Sullivan, Peter. 1994. The sense of 'a name of a truth-value'. *The Philosophical Quarterly*, **44**, 476–81.

1995. Wittgenstein on *The Foundations of Mathematics*, June 1927. *Theoria*, **61**, 105–42.

2002. On trying to be resolute: a response to Kremer on the *Tractatus*. *European Journal of Philosophy*, **10**, 42–78.

2003. Ineffability and nonsense (II). *Proceedings of the Aristotelian Society Supplementary Volume*, **77**, 195–223.

2005. Identity theories of truth and the *Tractatus*. *Philosophical Investigations*, **28**, 43–62.

2010. Dummett's Frege. Pages 86–117 of: Potter and Ricketts 2010.

Sullivan, Peter, and Potter, Michael (eds). 2013. *Wittgenstein's* Tractatus. Oxford: Oxford University Press.

Tallant, Jonathan, and Ingram, David. 2017. Truth and dependence. *Ergo*, **4**, 955–80.

Trueman, Robert. 2011. Propositional functions in extension. *Theoria*, **77**, 292–311.

2013a. Neutralism within the semantic tradition. *Thought*, **1**, 246–51.

2013b. Reducing truth through meaning. *Erkenntnis*, **78**, 823–32.

2014. A dilemma for neo-Fregeanism. *Philosophia Mathematica*, **22**, 361–79.

2015. The concept *horse* with no name. *Philosophical Studies*, **172**, 1889–906.

2018a. The prenective view of propositional content. *Synthese*, **195**, 1799–825.

2018b. Substitution in a sense. *Philosophical Studies*, **175**, 3069–98.

In press. Idealism and the identity theory of truth. *Mind*.

Turner, Jason. 2010. Ontological pluralism. *Journal of Philosophy*, **107**, 5–34.

2012. Logic and ontological pluralism. *Journal of Philosophical Logic*, **41**, 419–48.

Tye, Michael. 1995. *Ten Problems of Consciousness*. Cambridge, MA: MIT Press.

Vallicella, William. 2000. Three conceptions of states of affairs. *Noûs*, **34**, 237–59.

2002. Relations, monism and the vindication of Bradley's Regress. *Dialectica*, **56**, 3–35.

van Cleve, James. 1994. Predication without universals? A fling with ostrich nominalism. *Philosophy and Phenomenological Research*, **54**, 577–90.

van Inwagen, Peter. 2004. A theory of properties. Pages 153–82 of: van Inwagen 2014.

2014. *Existence: Essays in Ontology*. Cambridge: Cambridge University Press.

van Straaten, Zak (ed). 1980. *Philosophical Subjects: Essays Presented to PF Strawson*. Oxford: Clarendon Press.

Vogeleer, Svetlana, and Tasmowski, Liliane (eds). 2006. *Non-definiteness and Plurality*. Amsterdam: John Benjamins Publishing Company.

Whitehead, Alfred, and Russell, Bertrand. 1927. *Principia Mathematica*. 2nd ed., vol. 1. Cambridge: Cambridge University Press.

Whorf, Benjamin. 1956. *Language, Thought and Reality: Selected Writings by Benjamin Lee Whorf*. Cambridge, MA: MIT Press.

Wiggins, David. 1984. The sense and reference of predicates: a running repair to Frege's doctrine and a plea for the copula. *The Philosophical Quarterly*, **34**(136), 311–28.

Williamson, Timothy. 1985. Converse relations. *The Philosophical Review*, **94**, 249–62.

2003. Everything. *Philosophical Perspectives*, **17**, 415–65.

2013. *Modal Logic as Metaphysics*. Oxford: Oxford University Press.

Winter, Yoad. 2007. Type-shifting with semantic features. Pages 164–87 of: Barker and Jacobson 2007.

Wittgenstein, Ludwig. 1922. *Tractatus Logico-Philosophicus*. London: Kegan Paul and Trubner.

1953. *Philosophical Investigations*. Oxford: Blackwell.

1974. *Philosophical Grammar*. Oxford: Blackwell.

1975. *Philosophical Remarks*. Oxford: Blackwell.

Woods, Jack. 2018. Emptying a paradox of ground. *Journal of Philosophical Logic*, **47**, 631–48.

Wright, Crispin. 1983. *Frege's Conception of Numbers as Objects*. Scots Philosophical Monographs, no. 2. Great Britain: Aberdeen University Press.

   1998. Why Frege does not deserve his grain of salt. Pages 72–90 of: Hale and Wright 2001.

   2007. On quantifying into predicate position: steps towards a new(tralist) perspective. Pages 150–74 of: Leng, Paseau et al. 2007.

Index

For EU product safety concerns, contact us at Calle de José Abascal, 56–1°,
28003 Madrid, Spain or eugpsr@cambridge.org.

www.ingramcontent.com/pod-product-compliance
Ingram Content Group UK Ltd.
Pitfield, Milton Keynes, MK11 3LW, UK
UKHW020353140625
459647UK00020B/2440